A Traveler's Guide

THROUGH SUFFERING AND JOY

Changed by Theology that Feeds and Leads

A 12-Week Bible Journey

Karen Thomas Olsen

SILVERSMITH
PRESS

Published by Silversmith Press-Houston, Texas
www.silversmithpress.com

Copyright © 2024 Karen Thomas Olsen

All rights reserved.

This book, or parts thereof, may not be reproduced in any form or by any means without written permission from the author, except for brief passages for purposes of reviews. For more information, contact the publisher at office@publishandgo.com.

The views and opinions expressed herein belong to the author and do not necessarily represent those of the publisher.

Unless otherwise indicated, Scripture quotations are taken from the New American Standard Bible (NASB), The Lockman Foundation.

Cover Photo Credit and Cover Design: captis.camera

ISBN 978-1-961093-83-6 (Softcover Book)

BOOK ENDORSEMENTS

It is a special joy to give my commendation and endorsement to Karen's beautiful work which you hold in your hands. May our LORD bless all who read her labor of love. My prayers go with this book that our LORD may wonderfully use to repair many a broken heart.

Walter C. Kaiser, Jr., PhD
Colman M. Mockler distinguished Professor of Old Testament
President Emeritus of Gordon-Conwell Theological Seminary

My husband of 45 years went to be with Jesus on March 3, 2020 after battling heart failure for over fifteen years. Then Covid shut our world down and church and friends weren't able to meet together. Providentially, I had encouraged Karen, my long-time friend, to develop a Bible study based upon her dissertation. My small group started our study March 12, printing unpublished chapters of this book. It came at a time when I needed it so much! It really helped me and others to dig deeper into the Bible and our relationship with God and each other. I pray that this study will help others the way it has helped me.

Sandra Jacobs
Nurse Practitioner, Bible study leader, and fellow Pedestrian Theologian.

Karen Thomas Olsen is a wounded healer. The research that led to this book didn't come out of Karen's intellectual curiosity but from her travels down the rugged road of chronic emotional and physical pain. She communicates deep biblical and theological insights as she challenges readers to engage suffering actively with the resources God provides, rather than letting suffering control them. I highly recommend this soul-nurturing book.

David L. Turner, PhD
Scholar in Residence for New Testament Studies,
Puritan Reformed Theological Seminary
drdavidlturner.com

Karen's years of study and personal experience have enabled her with God's help to explain biblically the whys of various suffering in the world, and to understand and experience God's promises and provision of joy and peace through any of life's circumstances, step by step. I have known Karen for over 40 years and have witnessed her Pedestrian Theologian walk. She has been my personal, helpful guide many times, and this book can help you too.

Judi Lucarini
Bible student, teacher, and fellow Pedestrian Theologian

Travel with Dr. Karen Olsen through the biblical path to a practical application of how God can use suffering to increase our joy of living significant lives for God's glory. Ministry EquipNet video series on Suffering and Joy is based on Dr. Olsen's doctoral dissertation and the material of this book. Her insights, both theological and practical, are indeed a path to joy found in God-permitted suffering. Soli Deo Gloria.

Louis Mann
Academic Dean of Ministry EquipNet, the training program of CB Matrix

Dedicated to my loving husband, Paul Olsen,
who has faithfully and patiently supported me for forty-four years.
Without your encouragement, this project never would have happened.

Dedicated also to my children and grandchildren.
May this legacy direct your hearts and lives toward your Creator and Savior
through whom every breath of your challenging lives holds eternal significance.

―――――――――

"Beloved, do not be surprised at the fiery ordeal among you,
which comes upon you for your testing,
as though some strange thing were happening to you;
but to the degree that you share the sufferings of Christ, keep on rejoicing;
so that also at the revelation of His glory, you may rejoice with exultation."

1 Peter 4:12-13

CONTENTS

Introduction: Preparing to Travel xi

Part I
SAMPLING THE SOIL: THE GROUND UNDER OUR FEET

Chapter 1   *Where Are We?* 3
                The Three Cosmos

Chapter 2   *Which Comes First: Suffering or Joy?* 21
                Discovery One

Chapter 3   *How Do I Make Sense of the Senseless?* 37
                Discovery Two

Chapter 4   *Will I Ever Be the Same?* 57
                Discovery Three

Part II
EXPLORING NEW TERRITORY: THE WINDING WAY UP

Chapter 5   *What Good Is My Suffering?* 75
                Discovery Four

Chapter 6   *"Father, Where Is the Lamb?" "Lord, What Is My Sacrifice?"* 91
                Discovery Five

Chapter 7   *What Is the Message of My Witness?* 113
                Discovery Six

Part III
BEHOLDING THE DEPTHS AND PEAKS: THE UNEXPECTED VIEWS

Chapter 8   *If I'm Never Alone, How Do I Live that Way?* **135**
    Discovery Seven

Chapter 9   *How Does My Tomorrow Change My Today?* **146**
    Discovery Eight

Chapter 10   *How Can My Messy Life Glorify God?* **166**
    Discovery Nine

Chapter 11   *O Joy, Why Do You Seek Me through Pain?* **183**
    Traveler's Tales: Tracing Rainbows

Appendix
    1. Vocab Café **197**
    2. Charts **206**
    3. Travel Guidelines:
        A. Directions and Options **213**
        B. What Kind of Pedestrian Theologian Am I? **217**

Recommended Tours:
    Tour 1: Additional Resources for Personal Study **225**
    Tour 2: Additional Resources for Extended Study **229**

My SoJournal **235**

ACKNOWLEDGEMENTS

I would like to honor the following people who have impacted this work:

Dr. Braxton Hunter, my dissertation chair from Trinity College of the Bible and Theological Seminary. He chose to advise me (from 2013 through 2016) even as he was adjusting to his new role as president of the schools. This book is based upon the research I did under his leadership. His trust in me greatly encouraged me.

Dr. Walter C. Kaiser Jr., whose writings informed and inspired me. His book, *A Biblical Approach to Personal Suffering*, helped me organize a biblical taxonomy of suffering, directing much of the basic shape of this theology of suffering and joy. Moreover, some email correspondence with him strengthened me, while his humility and humor delighted me.

The librarians at Phoenix Seminary, especially Mitch Miller and Jim Santeford, who took interest in my work and provided assistance.

My dear high school friend, Sandra Jacobs, a nurse practitioner, who sees suffering daily and has experienced her own depths of grief. She pushed me to turn my research into a Bible study and told me in the fall of 2019 she wanted to start teaching it in the spring of 2020. I needed her fire, and she needed this study more than either of us knew. Her husband of nearly forty-five years passed away a month before her class was to begin. I thought she would not want to pursue teaching this study so soon after the home-going of Bill. "Oh, I'm doing it! I need it!" she insisted. Her group printed and copied chapters of the first, pre-publication version. Sandy continues to thank me for the strength the journey has especially imparted her.

Prayer partners: Paul Olsen, Judi Lucarini, Martin and Brenda Zuidervaart, Louis and Ruth Ann Mann, Shirley Tamplin, Beverly Buckingham Steele, Mary Wooten, and Luke

Kjergaard. Many people have been and are still praying for the fruit of this project. I thank God for you all!

My publisher, Joanna Hunt and her team at Silversmith Press. Joanna's direction, patience, and diligence have brought this work to print and to the market. Her joy and excitement motivate and bless so many people. I thank God for her and her team!

INTRODUCTION

PREPARING TO TRAVEL

We are born expecting life to be good. All should be well. Evil, as everything *not* good, feels like an intruder. We have suffered its timing, its unexpectedness, its audacity, its irregularity, and its wildness. Evil violates the good.[1] What to do; what to do! We can't demand good. We can't tame evil. We are not in control. We think we should be.

I remember when I first became aware of evil. That first blow happened when I was in second grade. I suppose everyone on this planet would like to have the kind of shock I had. My experience did not involve any personal abuse or tragedy. No hurt, offense, or harm came to me.

I recognized evil in a story in my second-grade reading book. It pierced through my soul. I never forgot it. I was in the lowest reading group and felt the pressure that I was behind everyone else, yet this story stole my attention and changed my developing perception of reality. Here is the story as I remember it.

Walking through the woods, a boy happens upon a leprechaun. The little creature shows the child a chest full of gold and offers it to him. Excited, the boy thinks about all the ways this treasure will help his poor family!

---

1. *Evil* and *good* are defined and described in the Vocab Café in the appendix, along with many other terms. For further exploration, I recommend D.A. Carson's book, *How Long O Lord*, subtitled *Reflections on Suffering and Evil*. He writes, "When we suffer, there will sometimes be mystery. Will there also be faith?" (159). His text is eye-opening and comforting.

The only problem is the boy cannot carry the treasure and has no cart to transport it. So he buries it under a tree while the leprechaun watches. Then the boy ties a red ribbon around the tree trunk to identify the tree while insisting the leprechaun promise not to remove the ribbon.

Promising, the little creature crosses his heart. He will never remove the ribbon. Away the boy scurries to fetch the cart and to tell his family their woes are over. The boy returns to the woods, traveling deep within it, looking for his ribbon. Suddenly, he discovers he is surrounded by trees with ribbons. And all the ribbons are exactly the same color, size, and shape as his ribbon!

Just as he promised, the little creature did not remove the ribbon. Instead, he duplicated identical ribbons on the other trees! Keeping his word, the leprechaun had lied. He had tricked the boy. The story lets the reader suppose the boy will never find the treasure.

Such is the way of leprechauns. They trick and deceive. The moral of the story was clear to me. Even as an eight-year-old, I connected this tale to real life and saw a message I'd never seen before.

Telling the truth can be a way of lying. I recognized twisted thinking for the first time. Leprechauns, people, leprechauns, people. Is the way of these little creatures one way of people? A darkness presented itself previously unknown to me. I was stunned.

That this darkness, called sin, lived within me too was a realization I would not clearly face until later. For now, I was alerted to the presence of some real evil.

This story of my childhood experience may seem cute. It is a mild way to be initiated into the brokenness of this world. I am totally grateful. I was reared in a loving and godly home. Suffering, a result of evil, opened its door for me at the age of twelve, though not through cruelty or dishonesty but through an accident that introduced me to physical pain. Physical pain was to become a lifetime partner.[2]

---

2. You will find some of my story occasionally referenced or described in a few of the chapters. Some have suggested I tell more of my story. This is not easy. I tell what I think is appropriate for this public publication.

While this book is not about me, it is as much for me as it is for you. It is for the Body of Christ of which I am a part.

What does the Bible say about good and evil, suffering and joy? What is the meaning? How do the Scriptures nourish and navigate us through life? How do we make sense of reality? How do we come to terms with brokenness? Nearly twelve years ago I began a focused exploration of biblical texts and Christian literature showcasing and addressing suffering.

Why would I do that? Why are you holding this book? Certainly, there are similarities between my answer to the first question and your answer to the second. Thus, we are drawn together. Pain rivets our attention. Obviously, pain was visiting me. Surely, suffering has pursued you. If you are not currently experiencing it directly, you feel, hear, and see it all around you. Once, you thought you could evade it. Now, you know better, and you want to be prepared. For those in the middle of distress, you want to know how to deal with it. Moreover, you want to know how to live a meaningful life, no matter the challenges.

In his classic, *The Problem of Pain,* C.S. Lewis famously explains that "pain insists upon being attended to. God whispers to us in our pleasures, speaks in our conscience, but shouts in our pain: it is His megaphone to rouse a deaf world."[3] World? Narrowing his focus to the individual, he states that pain "plants the flag of truth within the fortress of a rebel soul."[4] So I am the individual with the rebel soul, living in a deaf world of rebel souls. *"He who has ears, let him hear."* Megaphone? Sometimes, the loudest pain is delivered in the longest silence.[5] Pain has its purposes. What are they? Is it true as some claim that some pain can be purposeless? What are we to understand? How are we to navigate life?

---

3. C.S. Lewis, *The Problem of Pain* (New York: HarperCollins Publishers, 1940, 1996), 91.

4. *Ibid.*, 94.

5. 1 Kings 19 tells the story of Elijah and the prophets of Baal, Elijah's despair after dramatic victory, and his fear which energizes him to run. When he stops, he hears God not in the wind, earthquake, or fire, but in the whisper. While Lewis' megaphone insight is true, we need to recognize another reality. Trauma's noise includes resounding quiet, calling for acquiescent patience (an intolerable virtue to "rebel souls").

Ajith Fernando writes in his book, *The Call to Joy and Pain*, "I think one of the most serious theological blind spots in the Western church is a defective understanding of suffering.... We have a lot of teaching about escape from and therapy for suffering but there is inadequate teaching about the theology of suffering."[6]

Fernando's challenge grabbed my attention as I sought to determine the direction of my doctoral research for my dissertation in the early 2010s. I was in my fifties working on a theology degree. As a Christian school teacher who had moved into curriculum development, I regularly did graduate work over the years to maintain teacher certification. Initially, my interest was to earn a doctorate in curriculum development through a Christian higher-education institution. My attention was providentially diverted, and I pursued a degree in theology.[7]

This book is based upon the research I did for my dissertation. After one year of researching the theme of suffering in the Scriptures and various literature, I said to the Lord, "I can't do this anymore." I was exhausted and overwhelmed. Then the Lord encouraged me through portions of the very Scriptures that overwhelmed me. The data stacked up:

"Jesus ... for the joy set before Him endured the cross ..." (Hebrews 2:2).

"Beloved, do not be surprised at the fiery ordeal among you, which comes upon you for your testing as though some strange thing were happening to you; but to the degree that you share the sufferings of Christ, keep on rejoicing; so that also at the revelation of His glory, you may rejoice with exultation" (1 Peter 4:12-13).

"Consider it all joy ... when you encounter various trials ..." (James 1:2).

"For I consider that the sufferings of this present time are not worthy to be compared with the glory that is to be revealed to us" (Romans 8:18).

---

6. Ajith Fernando, *The Call to Joy and Pain*, (Wheaton, IL: Crossway Books, 2007), 51. He explains that a theology of suffering "must form the basis of all therapy for suffering", 11.

7. I graduated from Trinity Theological Seminary (Newburgh, Indiana) in 2016 with a Doctor of Religious Studies (DRS) degree in theology.

I could build a tower with the biblical bricks. I saw it clearly. As deficient as we are in a theology of suffering, a theology of suffering is insufficient without its counterpoint, joy. Did not Fernando's text make just such a case? For the following two years, I explored both themes and arranged them into a framework of categories that spoke to each other. This framework shapes this theology of suffering and joy.[8]

A TRAVELING THEOLOGY

What is a **theology**?[9] A theology, in part, is a framework for thinking, valuing, and living. Just as biology is the study of living organisms, theology is the study of God. Just as biology is then divided into many fields of study, so theology is divided into many fields that study God's nature, ways, and revelation of Himself to humans in creation and through Scripture. Each "ology" has many subdivisions making observations and learning possible for our finite minds and hearts.

This traveler's guide journeys through key locations in both testaments of Scripture seeking to discover a biblically grounded theology of suffering and joy. At first this may sound too academic. So let's use two realities from daily life as metaphors: nutrition and exercise. Our theology provides us with biblical nourishment for our lives and with direction for our movement. Good theology feeds us and leads us. It is practical. It is life-saving!

The Apostle Paul wrote to Timothy telling him that by teaching the local church the Word of God, he was being a "good servant of Christ Jesus, constantly nourished on the words of the faith and of the sound doctrine which [he has] been following" (1 Tim. 4:6). Timothy was nourished on Scripture and was following Christ so that the people he led would be properly fed and led.

---

8. I coined a title for this new theological category: **Pascharology** from the Greek *pascho*—suffering—and *chara*—joy. Pascharology is the study of suffering and joy and their interrelation. It is pronounced "pass-car-o'-logy." Note the Vocab Café for further explanation. We will use the term in this adventure, but do remember it is not a recognized term in the literature of systematic theology.

9. Each bolded term when first or early encountered is entered in a glossary in the back of this book entitled Vocab Café. It is an excellent source of study enabling you to gain more from this journey.

In this study we will employ John Frame's excellent definition of theology: "the application of God's Word by persons to all areas of life."[10] What a disarming definition. What does he assume? Yes, he assumes "persons" have a vibrant knowledge of the Word, which they imbibe in their hearts and implement in their own situations.

What does he mean by "persons?" He means Christians. All Christians. He implies professional theologians are not the only theologians. I have a term for these "persons," professional or not: **Pedestrian Theologians**. Professional and nonprofessional theologians are Pedestrian Theologians—walking with Christ, though imperfectly, through the Word and through life.

"As you therefore have received Christ Jesus the Lord, so walk in Him" (Colossians 2:6).

Jesus said, "I am the light of the world; he who follows Me shall not walk in the darkness, but shall have the light of life" (John 8:12).

These are Guidepost passages enlightening our entire study.[11] No matter what, in suffering and in joy, we walk in Christ and in His light.

"My sheep hear My voice, and I know them, and they follow Me" (John 10:27).

"For we walk by faith not by sight" (2 Corinthians 5:7).

Walkers are pedestrians, and more specifically, because we walk in and with Christ, we follow the Scriptures.

Again, "As you therefore have received Christ Jesus the Lord, so walk in Him" (Colossians 2:6). Have you received Christ Jesus as your Lord? Are you walking in Him and with Him?

Throughout the Bible, "walk" is employed as a metaphor speaking of relationship, lifestyle, and destiny or direction. Enoch walked with God, which means he was in close

---

10. John Frame, *The Doctrine of the Knowledge of God*, (Phillipsburg, NJ: P&R Pub. 1987), 76.
11. Each chapter will present a Guidepost passage or verse. You will find a chart listing all of them in the appendices in the back. This book's overarching Guideposts are Colossians 2:6 and 1 Peter 4:12-13.

relationship with God; therefore, he was heading in the right direction![12] Amazing! Note the direction his walk took him. His metaphorical walk turned into a literal flight! Enoch, whose name means *dedicated*, walked with God for 365 years, and then God took him straight to heaven without dying (Gen. 5:22-24). What a way to live! Abraham walked with God. Moses walked with God. Each walk is unique, yet each is *with* God. And so we too hear the call to walk with Him.

We walk with Christ. We are Pedestrian Theologians. I hope this encourages and inspires you to live up to who you are in the Lord!

NAMING THE PAIN AND THE JOY

In life we walk through many challenges. 1 Peter 1:6 and James 1:2 speak of "various trials" along with accompanying joy:

"In this you greatly rejoice, even though now for a little while, if necessary, you have been distressed by various trials" (I Peter 1:6).

"Consider it all joy, my brethren, when you encounter various trials..." (James 1:2). What could "various" mean in "various trials?" Could these trials be of various kinds?

In this theological Bible study, we will name and organize kinds or categories of suffering and joy. Why? Naming is essential to understanding. While our understanding is limited, there is much we can understand and name. Naming helps us come to terms with reality, stay sane, and walk with God. God's first assignment to Adam, His linguistically capable image bearer, was to name the animals, creating the first system of classification (a **taxonomy**).

The book of Lamentations presents a deeply human and personal naming of pain at the time of the horrifying destruction of Jerusalem in 586 BC. Written probably by Jeremiah,

---

12. Enoch was the father of Methuselah.

often called the weeping prophet, the poet organizes five acrostic poems or elegies. Into these he pours his heart-throbbing descriptions of disaster, which enables him truly to lament and mourn. Walter C. Kaiser Jr. explains that "the acrostic form contributes to the meaning and significance of all serious discomfort, each hurt, loss, disease, or tragedy. It patiently goes over each step in the process... Therefore, the acrostic will help to itemize, organize, and finalize grief."[13] This is naming the pain. (While itemizing and organizing hurt and grief may not "finalize" grief, the process does provide respectful space, nurturing healing.)

It is good and sane to name the pain and to name the joy. It is good to explain what can be explained, to pray over it all, and to trust in the name of the Lord our God with both the known and the unknown. This is wholesome theology.

A TRAVELER'S GUIDE

However, my research needed to be translated into a digestible, directional form. One of my closest friends, Sandra Jacobs, asked me when she could start teaching it to her Bible study group, so then I knew I needed to drop the work of fiction I was experimenting with and focus on creating a Bible study. What should it look like? Finally, I chose the "traveling" motif and named it *A Traveler's Guide through Suffering and Joy*.

I have wonderful memories of going on tours led by tour guides—through the Prado Museum in Madrid, the garden tomb in Jerusalem, the World Equestrian Center in Ocala, Florida—all these and so many other fascinating places and sites! Such tours are controlled adventures. The tour guides story-tell history. They point to things you would not notice. They stir your curiosity and answer your questions. No, they can't show and explain everything. Yet, their guidance gives you much more insight so that you can

---

13. Walter C. Kaiser Jr., *A Biblical Approach to Personal Suffering* (Eugene, Oregon: Wipf and Stock Publishers, 2003; previously published by Moody Press, 1982), 17. In Kaiser's last chapter, he names and organizes eight basic kinds of suffering presented in the Old Testament. His categories became the foundation and inspiration for my framework here of nine categories divided into three triads. I organized the triads into three ascending tiers, inspired by Bloom's taxonomy of educational goals, which build from the bottom up: rote learning precedes understanding which precedes analysis or "critical thinking." In the same way, suffering and joy can be viewed through a growth ladder building from the foundation upward. (Check out *taxonomy* in the Vocab Café as well as the charts in the appendices.)

further explore on your own. You even want to because they've opened your eyes and heart to see, understand, and appreciate so much more! I hope that's what this guide will do for you.

"Whoa!" you say. "Those are tours I'd want to take! Traveling through suffering is another story! Yet, I'm drawn to this study by the crazy challenges of my life and what I see around me!"

I agree. This study into suffering was no tour I wanted to join. It was the pain of my own life that seemed to first draw me to it. Ultimately, I realized that behind the alarm of evil, something beckoned me. The wooing winds of joy flirted with my soul. *"The wind blows where it wills."* Was this the nose of God's hovering Spirit nudging me to journey with Him? I believe so. Come with me. This is the path the Lord has put me on, so with the Shepherd's leading, this is a tour through Scripture and life I've been given to travel with you.

I began this chapter describing a childhood memory about a story I read in school. This leprechaun story impacted my understanding of the way the world works. My little mind followed the plot, finding the theme and moral of the story. Both hemispheres of my mind were at work: the global, right side, taking in the patterns of the story and the linear, left side, identifying and listing the lessons. My mind was informed and my conscience alerted. I learned and grew through this experience. This traveler's guide is a tour of Scripture, not children's literature. However, we will engage those two hemispheres of our divinely designed, maturing minds, observing and interpreting biblical narratives and directives. We'll also consider some other historical narratives offering more enlightening illustrations.

"In the world you will have tribulation," Jesus warned (John 16:33). Encouraging His followers, He also said, "My joy will be in you" (15:11). His words are for us today. Therefore, I know this tour is for you too!

You may want to invite a friend to travel with you through this study. You can be your own book club. Or use this book as a group Bible study guidebook. The journey will be enriched if a friend or others can journey with you because we belong not only to the

Lord but to each other as the Body of Christ! Whether you journey through this book with the Lord as your singular partner or also with another person or in a group—you will never be traveling alone.

GETTING ACQUAINTED WITH THE TRAVEL GUIDE LAYOUT

In preparing to begin, you will want to get acquainted with the book. Take a moment to read the table of contents. You are reading "Introduction: Preparing to Travel." I'm glad you did not skip this. After this important introduction, the book is divided into three parts. Note their titles.

"Part I: Sampling the Soil: The Ground Under Our Feet." In chapters 1-4, we will explore the three cosmos and then the foundational three categories or genres of suffering and joy. Note that we start with the broad, cosmic view and then zoom in to travel from the foundation up, as if we are trekking up a mountain, one tier at a time. (We'll encounter three tiers with three categories per tier.)

"Part II: Exploring New Territory: The Winding Way Up." In chapters 5-7, we will explore the three categories or genres of suffering and joy that build on or sprout from the foundational tier which we studied in Part I.

"Part III: Beholding the Depths and Peaks: The Unexpected Views." In chapters 8-10, we will explore the highest levels of suffering and joy that emerge from our travels through the first six categories. Now, we have traveled through all nine kinds, climbing our three upward tiers.

Chapter 11 concludes Part III and our travels. Here we will trace the story of a man who found joy through pain and wrote beautiful lyrics that feed and lead our souls nearly two centuries after he poured out his heart on paper. Then we look back upon our travels and review from whence we came and commit our future travels to our great Guide, Shepherd, King, and Bridegroom.

Introduction

Except for this and the last chapter, each chapter will be divided into five sections. The following are the five divisions per chapter:

1. Travel Scope

2. Viewing the Biblical Map

3. Adjusting the Focus

4. Trekking the Trail

5. Rest Stop

Moving to the rear of this book, you will discover an appendix with three parts and two bibliographies. I recommend you explore these before you begin part I. Refer back to them as needed.

1: Vocab Café: a glossary of terms and definitions.

2: Travel Charts: concise information showing relationships of ideas.

3: Travel Guidelines

    A. Travel Options: How might I approach this journey?

    B. My Profile: What shape am I in for this journey?

Recommended Tours: Two bibliographies, one short and one longer.

Finally, you will find a few blank pages in the back to use as the beginnings of a journal. On this journey, you are invited to **sojournal** in your ***My SoJournal***.[14] If you choose to participate in sojournaling, you will need a separate journal. Another option would be to use 3 x 5 cards to copy quotations (with page numbers) to collect and maybe place in strategic locations to keep you on track.

---

14. Travel to the Vocab Café and read an interesting explanation of *sojournaling*. Bolded terms as well as other important vocabulary are defined in the Vocab Café. You will also find some blank pages in the back as a start for your *My SoJournal*.

YOUR TRAVEL PLAN

You need to make your own adventure plan for traipsing through this book. You can treat this book as a textbook or a Bible study workbook; it is both. If you don't like to look up passages or answer questions (may the Lord change your heart) or you think you can't make such a time/energy investment, you can still gain much from reading this book, although your gains will not be as rich. I reduced the workbook interaction and typed out much Scripture, so there are some longer stretches of reading. You are given a meaningful variety. At least highlight main points in the text which will help you mark out bite sizes to digest. Any engagement you can invest will be profitable! In the appendices you will find Travel Guidelines providing various approaches for embarking upon this journey.

Here is my approach to most books. My first goal is to make friends with the book immediately by reading the front material, back material, and then scanning and skimming most chapters. During this stage, I use colored pencils to highlight what stands out as important in following the flow. I may pencil in some questions or comments, but not much of that at this point. After globally consuming what I can, then I'm ready to traverse it chapter by chapter.

For Bible studies, I look up most of the texts and write responses in the spaces and margins. I do not think I have to look up or research everything offered, although that would be better. I do not have to write an answer to every question. I continue to highlight with various colored pencils of lighter hues. With the Lord's help, I am in charge of my own learning. I do as much as is appropriate for me, given my time, need, and energy. Since I am making friends with the book, I know I can return to it and explore it more deeply at any time. Good readers reread good stuff!

If you are traversing this trail with the Lord on your own rather than with a group, of course you can devour and travel at your own speed. I do recommend you pace yourself. I suggest you travel one chapter a week. While the chapters contain five sections each, I am not recommending you do one section a day for five days, a common practice in many Bible studies. The five divisions are uneven in length, so some sections will need more time than others. Divide each chapter in a way that works best with your time and attention. To have a full week on which to traverse the region and meditate on the views will give you opportunity to savor what God is feeding you.

This is a challenging study but oh so worth the journey. I trust the Lord to walk with you through it. As you travel, please know the author of this travel guide is praying for you. Here is a prayer we can pray and sing together.

Gentle Shepherd[15]

Gentle Shepherd, come and lead us,
For we need You to help us find our way.
Gentle Shepherd, come and feed us,
For we need Your strength from day to day.
There's no other we can turn to
Who can help us face another day.
Gentle Shepherd, come and lead us,
For we need You to help us find our way.

Isaiah 40:11; John 10: 1-30

Music Playlist for A Traveler's Guide

---

15. Gloria Gaither and William J. Gaither. "Gentle Shepherd." *The Hymnal for Worship & Celebration* (Waco, Texas: Word Music, 1986), 458.

OVERARCHING GUIDEPOSTS

*As you therefore have received Christ Jesus the Lord,
so walk in Him. (Colossians 2:6)*

*Beloved, do not be surprised at the fiery ordeal among you,
which comes upon you for your testing, as though some strange thing
were happening to you; but to the degree that you share the sufferings of Christ,
keep on rejoicing; so that also at the revelation of His glory,
you may rejoice with exultation. (1 Peter 4:12-13)*

Part I

Sampling the Soil:
THE GROUND UNDER OUR FEET

CHAPTER 1

WHERE ARE WE? THE THREE COSMOS

We need to place our theology of suffering and joy in time, space, and eternity. Therefore, we will fly over broad vistas preparing us for the specific discoveries emerging in the following chapters. Let's take in the sweep of this chapter and grab the big ideas. Details can come later. We will refer back to foundations laid here in future chapters.

"Where are you?"
(Genesis 3:9).

"Where are you?" This is an interesting question for the omniscient Creator to ask His young, adult human whom He has placed in His meticulously designed, original garden.

"Where are you?!" you reply. "That's not where the story begins!" True. So let's go back to the beginning. In your own Bible, joyfully read Genesis chapters 1-2. You can't help but smile. Now, read chapter 3. Sigh.

Remember that John Frame defined theology as "the application of God's Word by persons to all areas of life." (I trust you have read the introduction before pursuing this chapter.) We think of "application" as the way in which we use something. I want to suggest that applying theology to life will mean we will practice interpreting life through our understanding of Scripture. In this way we come to terms with reality. This honors God, who thus renews and strengthens us to follow Christ.

CHAPTER 1

We are Pedestrian Theologians on our journeys of life. This chapter sets us up to trek the three winding legs of our journey in the three parts of this study. The trajectory is listed in the table of contents and more specifically in chart 1 on pages 206 and 207.

1.1 TRAVEL SCOPE

- We will learn to observe through two lenses.
- We will identify three **cosmos**[1] in which humans have lived, are living, and will live.
- We will observe changes (similarities and differences) in human nature through these eras.
- We will learn to trek the trail through spiritual disciplines.
- We will face the impact of these cosmic changes upon our personal lives.

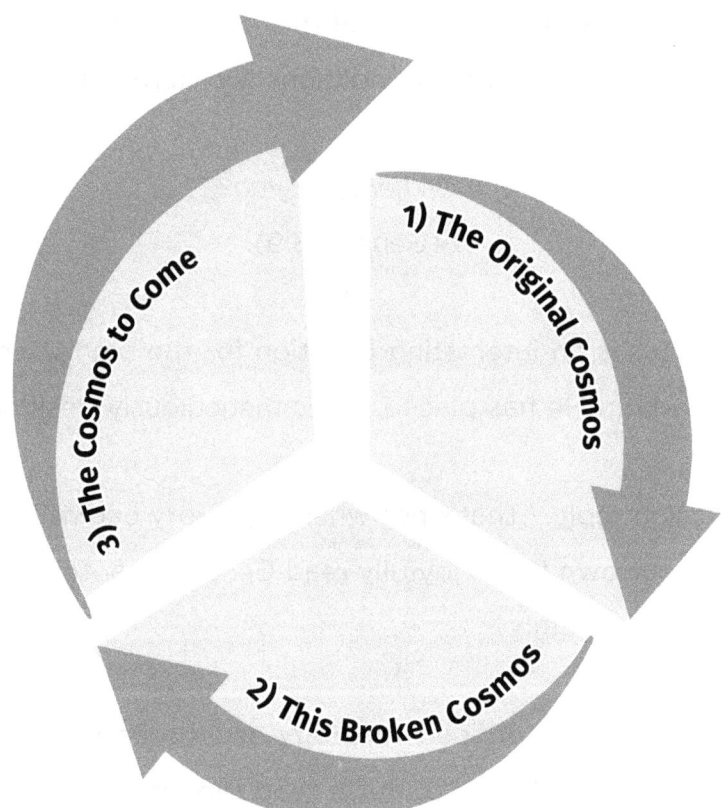

---

1. Cosmos: order or world; an order of operation; how something works or is governed. It is defined more fully in the Vocab Café in the appendices in the back.

GUIDEPOST

Train yourself to be godly. For physical training is of some value, but godliness has value for all things, holding promise for both the present life and the life to come. (1 Timothy 4:7b-8 NIV)

1.2 VIEWING THE BIBLICAL MAP THROUGH NARRATIVE AND DECLARATIVE BINOCULARS

Wearing Biblical Lenses

We have just read Genesis chapters 1-3, but what have we been reading? Let's consider the nature of this communication. Genesis is recorded as a narrative, a story. Is it historical or mythological? Much has been written debating this issue. Whether or not you've studied this, come to a conclusion or not, I recommend that you take the Genesis record very seriously. Jesus did.[2] The New Testament writers did. All of them utilized the books of Moses, the Psalms, and writings of the prophets (all of the Old Testament) from the perspective of historicity. I will proceed with their presupposition.

It is also important for you to pay attention to the kind (genre) of literature you are reading in the Bible. This entire travel guide pays attention to the main, biblical genre called narrative/story. Story becomes the nest for most of the biblical teaching. The *narratives* showcase or house the instructional statements which I call *declaratives* and *imperatives* (precepts, principles, and commands). Biblical authors also communicate through such literary genres as prophecy, poetry, and epistles (letters), but in these as well we find scenarios and instructional statements. Similarly, we note the fictional parables of Jesus are stories illustrating his declaratives and imperatives.

---

2. Jesus was clear on his stance and the consequence of taking another stance. Consider the following in their contexts: Matt. 22:29; Luke 24:25-27, 32, 44-47; John 5:39, 46-47.

CHAPTER 1

We "see" the text through binoculars containing the narrative lens and the declarative-imperative lens. Two eyes. Two ways of understanding. Two hemispheres of the brain observing and analyzing the biblical narrative and declarative-imperative Word of God. God, the author of Scripture (2 Tim. 3:16-17), is also the designer of your mind/heart (Ps. 139: 13-15). Beautifully, our minds and God's Word are orchestrated to resonate (Ps. 119:11; Heb. 4:12).

Defining "Cosmos"

Back to Genesis. Moving to the farthest distance, we take in a panoramic view and discover the three cosmos in the grand arch of biblical revelation. How do we define "cosmos?"

We are defining "cosmos" (plural is also "cosmos") as an order or arrangement (a world or era) in which we can observe how reality works, its orders of operation.[3] There is "order in the courtroom": protocols and procedures apply. A *cosmetologist* (from the Greek *kosmetos*, *kosmos*) brings order, thus beauty, by applying *cosmetics* to the face and an arrangement to the hair. Whatever the cosmos, it has its own order—the ways in which things work within it, or its own governing order.

Observing Three Cosmos through Descriptive Passages

Study the following charts and grasp the big picture showing the purpose and trajectory of our lives within God's good and grand design. Highlight key words or phrases.

---

3. *Kosmos*, Greek. Strong's #2889. *Kosmos* has multiple uses, and it could be argued that aion/eon (Strong's #165), meaning an age, a duration of time, would be a better term, but cosmos has been chosen first because it denotes "order"—how things are put together in order to work. We make sense of life by interpreting ourselves, others, and our environment through insight gained about the cosmos (order) in which we live.

The Original Cosmos	This Broken Cosmos	The Cosmos to Come
The Era of Exceeding Goodness Genesis chapters 1-2; ends in chapter 3	**The Era of Enmity and Grace** Genesis chapters 3 and on	**The Era of Eternal Goodness** Revelation chapters 21-22 Isaiah 65: 17-25 2 Peter 3:10-14
Focus Tree Tree of the Knowledge of Good and Evil Genesis 2:9, 16-17; 3:3 In the beginning, God created. Psalms 89:11-14: Creator is mighty, exalted, righteous, just, full of lovingkindness and truth Is. 43:7: Created for His glory Genesis 1: Seven days of creation: good and exceedingly good; mankind created on day 6; rest on day 7 Genesis 2: Expansion of Creation story with more details; describes the Garden of Eden with two special trees; God's directive to Adam; Adam's naming of animals, Creation of Eve **** Continuity of Creation extending beyond the original cosmos and throughout the following cosmologies: Psalm 148:5-6: He commanded and created; He established them forever and ever. Eccles. 12:1: Remember your Creator Mark 10:6: From the beginning of creation, God made them male and female. Colossians 1:16-17: He created, He sustains; by Him and for Him	**Focus Tree** Cross of Christ 1 Peter 2:24: On the tree Isaiah 53: A suffering Savior Genesis 3:15: Begins the era of enmity on earth: between Satan and Christ involving mankind 1 Samuel 19: Evil spirit on Saul from the Lord Romans 8: 19-22 Bonds of corruption; groaning of people and all creation John 1:29: the Lamb who takes away the sins of the world 1 Corinthians 9:24: A race with a coming prize Hebrews 2:14-15: Christ's death destroys the devil who holds the power of death 1 Corinthians 15:55 Death loses its victory and sting John 6:29-65: Son of Man come from heaven 2 Corinthians 5:6-8 At home in the body Ephesians 6:11- 18: Armor of God 1 Thessalonians 4: 11-18 Christian hope—caught up together, forever with the Lord Titus 2:11-15: This present age The Overlap Between Cosmos 2 and 3: "The best of life on earth is a glimpse of Heaven; the worst of life is a glimpse of Hell"[4] Is. 51:6: earth will wear out... heavens vanish, people die, His salvation to last forever. Is. 55:6 Seek the Lord while he may be found... while he is near Gospel's theme of the Kingdom of Heaven or God—near, within, and ultimately in the future. Example: "Thy kingdom come. Thy will be done, on earth as it is in heaven" Matthew 6:10. Purgation and Purification of This Present Cosmos to initiate the Coming Cosmos: Malachi 3:2-4; 1 Corinthians 3:12-15; Matthew 24:37-41; 2 Peter 3:3-13	**Focus Tree** Tree of Life Genesis 2:9; 3:22-24; Revelation 2:7; 22:2, 14, 19 A New Heaven and New Earth for restored people living with the Resurrected Lord [While the ultimate focus is on the eternal state, not the intermediate heaven, the current paradise where deceased believers dwell with Christ until the second coming, all these future events offer anticipatory instruction.] Jeremiah 31:31-34: God's rule written within God's peoples' hearts John 14: 2-3: A place Christ is preparing for believers 2 Corinthians 5:6-8 At home with the Lord Hebrews 11:16 A better country Jesus' talk about Hell: Matthew 8; 10:28; 13:40-42; 25:46 Mark 9:43-44; Luke 16:19-31 The Kingdom Realized: Revelation 22:1-5 Then he showed me a river of the water of life, clear as crystal, coming from the throne of God and of the Lamb, in the middle of its street. On either side of the river was the tree of life, bearing twelve *kinds of fruit*, yielding its fruit every month; and the leaves of the tree were for the healing of the nations. There will no longer be any curse; and the throne of God and of the Lamb will be in it, and His bond-servants will serve Him; they will see His face, and His name *will be* on their foreheads. And there will no longer be *any* night; and they will not have need of the light of a lamp nor the light of the sun, because the Lord God will illumine them; and they will reign forever and ever.

---

4. Randy Alcorn, *Heaven*, (Carol Stream, Illinois: Tyndale House Publishers, 2004), 28.

After taking in this sweeping view, what do we observe? Let's look at each cosmos.

The Original Cosmos

This is the primal era as *The Original Cosmos* (Genesis 1-2), an era of exceeding goodness. This is the setting for the original human couple, Adam and Eve, created in God's image, living as co-regents in harmony with God and nature (Genesis 1: 26-27).

Within this harmonious, unencumbered, and peaceful setting, we discover Adam and Eve in fully formed, adult perfection, although a fragile (to be tested) perfection. The harmony and peace of both the human race and their cosmos are tested, but the drama does not occur until chapter 3.

The following charts lead us to observe both the elements of the story and the story's instruction and significance. Every story has 1) characters, 2) setting, 3) plot, 4) theme(s), and more. What do you perceive here?

The Original Cosmos: An Era of Exceeding Goodness

The Narration: Who, What, When, Where?	The Declaration: Aha! Statements
The Recorded Story Read Genesis chapters 1-2. • Who? God, Adam, Eve. • What? The recorded story of creation. • When? In the beginning. • Where? Where the four rivers converged in the Fertile Crescent. The Garden of Eden. "In the beginning, God (Elohim) created...." Chapters 1-2 described the six days of creations and God's attitude toward His work. On day seven, He rests. Chapter 2 expands the summary introduction of chapter 1, providing more detail, including interaction between God and Adam. 1. Describe God, the main character. 2. Describe Adam and Eve according to Genesis 1:26-31. 3. Describe the home setting God created for His beloved image bearers: Genesis 2:8-14. 4. Within this prolific garden setting, God specifically references what tree to Adam? Genesis 2: 16-17	The Significance of the Story 1. God gave purpose(s) to His image-bearing creatures, Adam and Eve. What was it, or what were they? Genesis 1:26-28; 2:15-25 2. God gave Adam and Eve a particular directive. What was it? With that command, what broad liberty does God offer? 3. What tree has no immediate influence on the lives of Adam and Eve? Genesis 2:9; 3:22. (We find this tree mentioned in the Proverbs, and in Revelation 22:2 we see the tree is now abundantly larger.) 4. In this paradise, The Original Cosmos which is exceedingly good, God designs an element of vulnerability. As you study, consider how this original order of things *differs* from the future "paradise," The Cosmos to Come—called heaven or The New Heavens and the New Earth (Rev. 21).

The Nature of the Original Human

Let's further consider the original nature of Adam and Eve as presented in Genesis 1:26-31. The nineteenth-century, Princeton Theological Seminary professor Charles Hodge explains the original nature of humankind created in God's image exhibited "perfect harmony and due subordination" in which:

> *"His **reason** was subject to God;*
> *his **will** was subject to his reason;*
> *his **affections** and appetites to his will;*
> *the **body** was the obedient organ of the soul."*[5]

---

5. Charles Hodge, *Systematic Theology*, Vol. II (Peabody, Maine: Hendrickson Publishers, 2003), 99. Italics added.

CHAPTER 1

Dr. Hodge also stated that no outside influence was needed for the human being to stay in harmony with God.[6]

- What insight do you gain from Dr. Hodge's explanation of humankind's original nature?

This Broken Cosmos: The Era of Enmity and Grace

It is so sad to leave the lovely garden and original scene so soon! God had good reason to drive the sinful couple from the paradisal setting, lest they eat of the tree of life, becoming immutable sinners—unchangeable, untreatable, permanent in their pitiful deformation. He had a better plan. It is not an easy one.

In Genesis chapter three the storyline shows two changes. First, there is a new character, the serpent. Second, the plotline develops an element that did not previously exist. The Tree of the Knowledge of Good and Evil has always held a test and a healthy tension. But never **conflict**. We now have a new element infused into all real and fictional stories.[7] We will study this more in the next chapter.

God enters the scene by making His presence known. "Then the LORD God called to the man, and said to him, 'Where are you?'" (Gen. 3:9). This is God's first of many questions recorded in Scripture. But it is not the first in Scripture. However, God's question does relate to the very first recorded question, the one asked by the serpent, "Indeed, has God said, 'You shall not eat from any tree of the garden?'" Think about that.

Why did God call out asking "Where are you?" He is omnipresent and omniscient. Did God not witness the interaction between the serpent and Eve and Adam? Yes, He witnessed it and did not interfere. He did not stop it from happening. Why? The text does not say. But now God dialogues with the man first, then the woman, and finally the serpent.

---

6. *Ibid.*

7. Travel to the Vocab Café in the appendices to locate a definition of *conflict* and other terms you will encounter along this journey.

However, when God pronounces the consequences of their choices, God first addresses the serpent, then the woman, and finally Adam. Interesting. Can you infer any importance or meaning in the order? Read the passage carefully and think about this. Discuss or sojournal about it. We'll get back to this in the next chapter.

Explore this chart, and try to look up references, recording key points you find.

The Narration: Who, What, When, Where?	The Declaration: Aha! Statements
The Recorded Story: Genesis chapters 3 & 4 After the couple's expulsion from the garden, the narrative speeds right to the next generation. Adam and Eve's first two children are adults—adults in conflict. Violence. Murder. A guilty party. An innocent party. We will come back to this story to discover here the first two kinds (but not the first two examples) of suffering. All of the Old Testament demonstrates mankind's brokenness and neediness—sinfulness—but God previewed the coming conflict in Genesis 3:15: And I will put enmity Between you and the woman, And between your seed and her seed; He shall bruise you on the head, And you shall bruise him on the heel. 1. What is *enmity*? (Note Vocab Café) 2. Who are the characters spoken of: *you, woman, your seed* and *her seed*? 3. Whose head? Whose heel? 4. The drama of the ages is framed in this Genesis verse. All the drama of human civilization and history is marked out here, including the framework of your story and mine. Historical stories (as well as fictional) always would have involved characters, settings, themes, and plots, but now, a new element has intruded into every storyline. What is it? Yes. It is conflict.	Expanded Significance of the Story In The Original Cosmos, the focal tree was The Tree of the Knowledge of Good and Evil. In This Broken Cosmos, the focal tree is The Cross of Christ. Read the following and note key phrases: 1 Peter 2:24 Isaiah 53 Hebrews 2:14-15 Colossians 2:13-15 How is This Broken Cosmos described? Romans 8:19-22 Titus 2: 11 -15 1 Peter 4:12-19

Adam and Eve are thrust into a second cosmos, the one in which we find ourselves—*This Broken Cosmos*. In this cosmos, after the Fall of the human race, good and evil mingle. God rules over a broken world in which His image in humankind is broken, in which He subjects all creation to the captivity of corruption (Gen. 3:14-19; Rom. 8:20-25), and in which He subjects Himself to the ultimate suffering for His broken creation.

Let's observe again Dr. Hodge's description of human nature before sin altered the human disposition. Insert the word NOT into the blanks below to see the inverse change in human nature subsequent to the Fall (Gen. 3).

(Every person's) reason is _____ subject to God;
his/her will is _____ subject to his reason;
his/her affections and appetites (are _____ subject) to his/her will;
the body is _____ the obedient organ of the soul.[8]

Thus, "the perfect harmony and due subordination of all that constituted man" was lost. Previously, no influence outside of man's conscience was needed to keep humanity in harmony with God. Now, outside influences are needed. Nonetheless, some echo of the perfect original remains.

- How did the Fall change human nature? How did the Fall change human need?
- When you observe yourself, how does your nature compare to the original human nature and the fallen human nature?
- What is at the heart of God's answer to human need? Ephesians 2:1-10
- Ephesians 2:7 explains God's purpose in loving us so that "in the ages to come He might show the surpassing riches of His grace in kindness toward us in Christ Jesus." How do you respond to this truth?

The Cosmos to Come: An Era of Eternal Goodness

This directs us to the third and final cosmos, the era to come, *The Cosmos to Come*. In this era God will permanently divorce evil from good. The perfections of God's goodness

---

8. Charles Hodge, *Systematic Theology*, Vol. II (Peabody, Maine: Hendrickson Publishers, 2003), 99.

will reign in the New Heavens and the New Earth (Rev. 21-22). All evil, Satan, fallen angels, and lost humans are confined to an eternal lake of fire (Rev. 20:10-15; 21:7-8).

In this future age, *The Cosmos to Come*, human nature will be more than restored. Lacking its original fragility, our nature will be immutably resilient, the curse permanently gone (Rev. 22:1-4).

The domains of divine image bearing will again align and harmonize: human reason will concur perfectly with God's thoughts; human volition (the will) will affirm godly reason; human affections and appetites will cooperate with human reason and will; and the freshly minted imperishable body will joyfully complement the imperishable soul. Gloriously, the groaning creation will be happily restored (Rom. 8:19-25), singing again as it did on the day of its birth (Job 38:7).

In the Kingdom of God in Christ, all narrative elements will harmonize truthfully as the doxological music of the eternal eons.

This is wholeness and health. This is the cosmic beauty, the craftsmanship in which we were meant to participate and showcase as glory to our God (Eph. 2:10). *The Cosmos to Come* is on its way.

> *"And the Spirit and the bride say, 'Come.' And let the one who hears say, 'Come.' And let the one who is thirsty say come; let the one who wishes take the water of life without cost"* (Rev. 22:17).

"The best of life on earth is a glimpse of Heaven; the worst of life is a glimpse of Hell."[9]

"An Era of Eternal Goodness" is a one-sided subtitle for The Cosmos to Come. It represents only the heaven side, the side for which we are aiming. The **hell** side, we could argue, is technically not a cosmos. A cosmos requires and represents some kind of "order." Hell, the Lake of Fire (Rev. 20:10-15), will be at its very least the absence of God,

---

9. Randy Alcorn, *Heaven*, (Carol Stream, Illinois: Tyndale House Publishers, 2004), 28.

CHAPTER 1

goodness, order, relationship, and meaning for its inhabitants (note caveat below[10]). Hell is separation. It is separation from God and everything good. Hell is the result of the divorce of evil from God's good creation and from creation's Creator. Its inhabitants will be as they wished, on their own, without God's help or resources. Hell is the ultimate and consummate chaos, The Chaos to Come. However, The Cosmos to Come: The Era of Eternal Goodness offers the opposite. Pause and think on these things. Pray and be quiet before the Lord.

This pascharology (theology of suffering and joy) follows the trail of the redeemed, the upward trajectory. It focuses on the paths of Christ-followers, Pedestrian Theologians (PTs), identifying nine genres of suffering and joy preparing us for The Cosmos to Come. "All who call upon the name of the Lord will be saved" (John 10:13). Let each of us call in faith on the name of the Lord! Let us follow His paths.

Explore this chart, and try to look up references, recording key points you find. Highlight key ideas or what strikes you.

---

10. We could also argue that hell is a cosmos because its "disorder" is a kind of order, a bad order or an anti-order. Designating it a fourth category, we could call it The Chaos to Come. While those in hell will lack personal meaning for existing, hell, as a domain has meaning in that it demonstrates the conclusion of holy justice, thus bringing glory, however awful, to the Lord God. Truly, "The fear of the Lord is the beginning of knowledge/wisdom" (Prov. 1:7).
The study of hell should have its place in pascharology. Since it was outside the scope of my dissertation's objectives, I did not make it a key part of my research project; although, I necessarily referenced it in places. In this Bible study, it will be addressed at times but not developed. Here, we are examining the trajectory of the people of God, not of those who reject God, as essential as that study also is. "Draw near to God and He will draw near to you" (James 4:8).

The Cosmos to Come

The Narration: Who, What, When, Where?	The Declaration: Aha! Statements
The Recorded Story: Revelation 22:1-5 This is the era of the New Heavens and New Earth prepared for restored people living with the resurrected Lord. • Who? The triune God, the Bride of Christ, and the saints of the ages, the holy angels. • What? His Kingdom has come. • When? When it comes; "Amen! Come, Lord Jesus!" (Revelation 22:20). • Where? "And I saw a new heaven and a new earth; for the first heaven and the first earth passed away" (Revelation 21:1). "Then he showed me a river of the water of life, clear as crystal, coming from the throne of God and of the Lamb, in the middle of its street. On either side of the river was the tree of life, bearing twelve kinds of fruit, yielding its fruit every month; and the leaves of the tree were for the healing of the nations. There will no longer be any curse; and the throne of God and of the Lamb will be in it, and His bond-servants will serve Him; they will see His face, and His name will be on their foreheads. And there will no longer be any night; and they will not have need of the light of a lamp nor the light of the sun, because the Lord God will illumine them; and they will reign forever and ever" (Rev. 22:1-5).	Expanded Significance of the Story The focal tree becomes a tree we've seen before. It looks different now, having greatly matured. It is The Tree of Life (Genesis 3:22; Revelation 22:2). While The Cosmos to Come is mainly about the eternal state, not the intermediate heaven (the current paradise where believers who have died dwell with Christ until the second coming), *all these future events offer anticipatory instruction.* Meditate on the following passages, and you may want to SoJournal about them. How do these truths impact your current relationship and walk with God? Your relationship and testimony with others? Jeremiah 31:31-34: God's rule written within God's peoples' hearts. Jesus's talk about hell: Matthew 8; 10:28; 13:40-42; 25:46; Mark 9:43-44; Luke 16:19-31. John 14:2-3: A place Christ is preparing for us. 2 Corinthians 5:6-8: At home with the Lord. Hebrews 11:16: A better country.

1.3 ADJUST THE FOCUS: REFLECTION AND RESPONSE

We began with God's first recorded question. He is speaking to Adam, His first created human:

"Where are you?" (Genesis 3:9).

There are many layers of answers to this, and we can start with the most basic. Discuss or write about the following.

A. Where are we? We are here, on planet Earth, living in the twenty-first century during the reign of sin, brokenness, and satanic influence—all constrained by our reigning, good God who rains down goodness and blessing on all humanity. In this Broken Cosmos, grace abounds more than sin and brokenness. We pray in gratitude for more mercy and grace.

B. Going deeper, where are you? How do you answer God? Are you still like Adam and Eve, cowering in fear of consequence rather than responding to God in the fear of respectful agreement? Ashamed of your exposure? Aware you have offended His Majesty? What have you done about this? What has God done about this? He cares. He is not silent. You don't need to be either.

Consider the instruction of the following passages. You may want to read some or all of these passages with a friend. They walk us through the path to know God personally.

This is the main place of healing for our chronic soul-pain. You may also want to write in your sojournal about what some of these mean to you. You may want to write a prayer.

Psalm 51
John 3:16
Romans 3:23-24
Romans 6:23 2

Romans 10: 9-13
John 1:12
2 Corinthians 5:17
Peter 3:16

C. Go deeper still. Where are we? When we are Christ-followers, we are "in Christ" (2 Cor. 5:17), we are on the road growing "in the grace and knowledge of our Lord and Savior Jesus Christ" (2 Pet. 3:16). "In Christ," we experience His kingdom within us, while awaiting the consummation of His coming kingdom.[11]

Suggestion. Have you taken several study sessions to walk this far? This may be a good place to stop for today. (I will not be telling you how to divide these chapters. I think that a week per chapter, traveling around four or five pages each study session, may set up a thought-filled pace. You decide.) Next study session, spend some refreshing time traveling through sections 4 and 5.

1.4 TREK THE TRAIL: STEPS IN SPIRITUAL DISCIPLINES

What are spiritual disciplines? Spiritual disciplines are pattern-creating steps we take in cooperation with the Holy Spirit to grow spiritually.

Our Guidepost is 1 Timothy 4:7b-8 (NIV) which admonishes you and me to:

"Train yourself to be godly. For physical training is of some value, but godliness has value for all things, holding promise for both the present life and the life to come." (Note the reference to This Broken Cosmos and The Cosmos to Come.)

Spiritual disciplines are the exercises of spiritual training, strengthening you for the walk of life.

I encourage you to look up some or all of the following verses and jot down their main phrases or ideas. Think on them and pray about how you can live out this wisdom.

Spiritual disciplines will feed us (the interior work) and lead us (the exterior work, touching others). They will:

---

11. The "now and not yet" kingdom of God.

A. Nourish us "on the words of faith and sound doctrine": 1 Timothy 4:6.
B. Lead us to prayer in which we draw near to God: Philippians 4:6; James 4:8.
C. Feed the joy of the Lord in our hearts: Hebrews 12:2; Philippians 4:1,4; Luke 6:23.
D. Exercise our faith: Romans 10:17; Hebrews 5:12.
E. Train us to love in word and deed: Galatians 5:22-23; 1 Corinthians 13:1-8.
F. Motivate us to live as examples and testimonies: Philippians 4:9.
G. Build us to build up one another, as we live in connection with others: 2 Corinthians 1:3-5.

- What spiritual disciplines do you practice? Do you have a certain routine or schedule for certain disciplines such as Bible study and prayer? Also some disciplines might be exercised organically—as they are woven into your days. Do you recognize any organic disciplines in your life?
- Review our Guidepost passage above and quote it as you can to someone. Write it out here:
- When you compare and contrast our original human nature as Dr. Hodge described it to our fallen nature, do you see your need for Christ and spiritual disciplines? How do you see one or two of the above spiritual disciplines helping you, as a born-again PT, to walk in Christ?

As we traverse each chapter, we'll try to exercise our spiritual muscles in specific ways.[12]

1.5 REST STOP

It's time to be quiet. Resting, we can sit and meditate upon the reality of our lives within God's world, This Broken Cosmos. Where are we? We are here, and He is present. James 4:8 encourages us: "Draw near to God, and He will draw near to you."

---

12. Remember, there is a short journal section called *My SoJournal* in the back of this book to get you started. *This* is a place for you to exercise various spiritual disciplines, such as prayer journaling, note-taking, Scripture copying, paraphrasing, and studying and for spill over when you lack space on a page for adequate response. Because it is so short, you will need a separate journal to use as your *My SoJournal*.

Each chapter closes with a hymn for meditation. Here are three hymns, one per cosmos.[13]

Regarding The Original Cosmos, we can sing with the lyricist, Peter Ellis (1986), "Lavish Love, Abundant Beauty":	Regarding This Broken Cosmos, we can sing with the lyricist, Katarina von Schlegel (1752), "Be Still, My Soul":	Regarding The Cosmos to Come, we can sing the hymn that was my mother's favorite, composed by Carrie E. Breck, "Face to Face":

Lavish love, abundant beauty,
   Gracious gifts for heart and hand,
   Life that fills the soul and senses
   All burst forth at Your command.
 	
To confess is to say the truth.
 	
We confess our sins. We also confess God's greatness and goodness. Our confession is our expression of need, praise, and gratitude.
	Be still, my soul: the Lord is on your side; bear patiently the cross of grief or pain. Leave to your God to order and provide; in every change He faithful will remain.
	
	Be still my soul: your best, your heavenly Friend through thorny ways leads to a joyful end.
		Face to face with Christ my Savior, Face to face, what will it be? When with rapture I behold Him, Jesus Christ who died for me?
		
		What rejoicing in His presence when are banished grief and pain; when the crooked ways are straightened and the dark things shall be plain.
		
		Face to face I shall behold Him, far beyond the starry sky; Face to face in all His glory, I shall see Him by and by.

---

13. You can locate these hymns in many hymnals or online at such sites as Hymnary.org, Hymnsite.com, The Open Hymnal Project, Hymnal.net, and Hymntime.com. I recommend that you collect some physical hymnals to enrich your personal study time. These three hymns are found in *The Hymnal for Worship & Celebration* (Waco Texas: Word Music). Note the QR code on p. xxiii to access a playlist of chapter songs. They are also available on the website, KarenThomasOlsen.com.

The Nine Discoveries

Tier 3 The Unexpected Views (Chapters 8,9,10)	7	8	9
Tier 2 The Winding Way Up (Chapters 5,6, 7)	4	+ 5	6
Tier 1 The Ground Under Our Feet (Chapters 2, 3, 4)	1	2	3

Read the chart from the bottom up. The completed chart is on pages 206–207.

CHAPTER 2

WHICH COMES FIRST: SUFFERING OR JOY?

DISCOVERY 1

Which comes first—suffering or joy? At first this may seem like an odd question to begin our investigation. Its answer, of course, is not our first discovery. However, we will never get to where we're headed without first traveling through this question. The meaning of the answer holds exactly what we need in order to face what we need to face in our first discovery.

I never saw this clearly before.

So which came first? **Elohim** will show us. "Elohim?" Yes. Elohim. Let's first set up the chapter.

2.1 TRAVEL SCOPE

In part I we are sampling the soil of the ground under our feet.

We are exploring the three, ground-level "root causes" of both suffering and joy.

CHAPTER 2

In this chapter, we will explore the foundational layer of suffering and joy discovered in the Scriptures and experienced in our lives.

Each chapter has a theme verse or passage called a Guidepost.

GUIDEPOST

For the wages of sin is death, but the free gift of God is eternal life in Christ Jesus our Lord. (Romans 6:23)

In the introduction, we took in the wide-lens view in order to see where we are in history. We identified three cosmos:

1. The Original Cosmos: The Era of Exceeding Goodness with Adam and Eve in the Garden of Eden.
2. This Broken Cosmos: The Era of Enmity and Grace with the fallen sons and daughters of Adam and Eve scattered around the world.
3. The Cosmos to Come: The Era of Eternal Goodness in which The New Heaven and Earth will be the Kingdom of God in its eternal state.

The word cosmos was chosen to name the three eras because this word, often translated as world, means order. Ordering principles govern a cosmos. We live in the second cosmos, and we're aware certain invisible principles guide the direction of the world at large and our own realities. These ordering principles are the key to unlocking some of the mysteries of our world's brokenness and the resilient hope of a true cure.

It has often been said a proper diagnosis is half the cure. If we're wrong on the diagnosis, we respond by moving in a counterproductive, possibly even dangerous direction. A proper diagnosis is important. This is the first part of our journey.

To diagnose is "to identify by careful observation"; that is, "to distinguish or discern."[1] It is mainly used in the field of medicine, but we use the same probing process when we

---

1. Oxford English Dictionary.

investigate the Scriptures to diagnose the sources of suffering and joy. We don't have to go far.

Why suffering? If we stop with the first answer we find, our diagnosis will be dangerously incomplete. From our Guidepost verse, we find an answer, but the answer has important layers!

Why joy? We tend to have a puny view of joy.

What does joy have to do with suffering? The answer is stunning. We have to continue our investigation.

2.2 VIEWING THE BIBLICAL MAP

Let's return to Genesis, the first book of the Bible, the first of five books written by Moses. "Again? We looked at Genesis in the last chapter!" Yes, but we are observing something different in this chapter.

Returning to chapter one, stroll again through this chapter. Drink in the sights and sounds. One cannot help but love the Bible's first verse: "In the beginning God created the heavens and the earth." It is such a clear and clean declarative sentence opening the expansive narrative.

Over 1200-1500 years after Moses, the apostle John explains rather philosophically, "All things came into being through Him, and apart from Him nothing came into being that has come into being" (John 1:3). The Creator of the material world is the creator of the conceptual world, the world of thought and language! I love that thought. In making us in His image, He designed our consciousness, our conscience, and our communicative capacities, all so we can commune with Him. This design reveals the intention of relationship.

God is called Elohim, in Genesis 1—the Majestic, Mighty Creator, so wise and powerful He can create by speaking His thoughts. God is called Logos (Word) in John 1:1: "In the beginning was the Word and the Word was with God and the Word was God." Verse fourteen says, "The Word became flesh and made his dwelling among us, and we have seen his glory, the glory of the one and only Son, who came from the Father, full of grace and truth" (NIV).

God, the Logos, in verse one is identified as Jesus in verse fourteen. From the word *logos*, we derive the word logic—reason and intelligent discourse. John 1:1 echoes Genesis 1:1. Elohim-God-Logos-Jesus brings together these worlds of thought and matter. How? By speaking things into existence. "Then Elohim said, Let there be light, and there was light" (Gen. 1:3). "All things came into being by Him, and apart from Him nothing came into being that has come into being" (John 1:3). **Selah!**

I find it charming Elohim, the Creator, steps back, so to speak, after His work is done each day of the six creation days to eye His intricate and exquisite handiwork. He pauses to evaluate. Ahh! And what does God think of His own craftsmanship?

What was Elohim's discerning conclusion at the end of each creation day?
Genesis 1:4: "and God saw that the light was good"
Genesis 1:10: the land and seas: "God saw that it was good"
Genesis 1:12: vegetation: "God saw that it was good"
Genesis 1:18: sun, moon, and stars: "God saw that it was good"
Genesis 1:21: living creatures in the waters: "God saw that it was good"
Genesis 1:25: Animals and land creatures: "God saw that it was good"
Genesis 1:26-27;31: Humankind: "And God saw all that He had made, and behold, it was <u>very good</u>."

God observed that His work each day was _____.

What does the adjective *good* mean?
God chose through His human author, Moses, to describe His handiwork with this adjective, translated good. The Hebrew word *tob/towb/tov* is employed around thirty-four times in the book of Genesis and hundreds of times in the Old Testament.

Good as an adjective is a broad term taking in a range of meaning in the Old Testament, such as *well, pleasing, beautiful, bountiful, cheerful, at ease, fair, glad, pleasant, merry, loving,* and *best.*[2] It is the *summum bonum*[3], highest good, the ultimate beneficence. *Good* describes God's wellspring and storehouse of health, wholeness, delight, wonder, beauty, and beneficence.

So what did God mean when He scanned His work daily and pronounced His masterpieces to be good, good, good, good, good, good, and very good?

Do you think God with His perfect personality, power, and skill enjoyed the results of His designs and construction?

God admires and appreciates His own work. He approves of it! After a stroll through Genesis chapter one, aren't you smiling along with God? I'm oohing and ahhing. I want to burst out in amazed laughter! Then, I'm silent in grateful wonder! I'm feeling good, right along with God!

God is pleased! What is at the heart of God's response to His creative goodness? It is JOY.

Good, the mother of Joy, always delivers Joy.

- God is Good. God does good. God causes good. Read Psalm 119:68, Romans 8:28-29, and James 1:13-17.
- What is the relationship between *good* and *joy*?
- So which came first? Suffering or joy?
- What's the big deal about which came first?
- Since suffering is so pervasive now, why does it matter that joy came first?

Suffering is *ubiquitous*. I love that word. But I don't like that it describes suffering. *Ubiquitous*: existing everywhere, constantly encountered. I'd prefer to associate it with *chocolate* and *happy times* and *satisfaction*.

---

2. Zodhiates. *The Complete Word Study Dictionary* (Chattanooga, TN: AMG Publishers, 1992). We want to be careful to avoid the logical fallacy of employing all meanings of a word used in many contexts and apply all those meanings to a specific context. Language does not work that way. However, a look at the range of meaning helps us consider how it is used in a particular context. *Good* as an adjective contains the facets of all things beneficial.

3. *Ibid.*

If suffering, which entered creation at the Fall of humankind, is ubiquitous, is joy—which came before the Fall and is a characteristic of God Himself—is joy also ubiquitous?

"Which has a longer shelf life, suffering or joy?" How do you know?

Joy precedes suffering. Joy was there from the beginning. But when we hurt, the pain takes the lead voice while the good and joyful hang around at the back of our stage, singing in a different key, waiting to be noticed. But they are still there. Never forget this.

How Shall We Name this First Source of Pain?

We're now going to name the first category of suffering. Our Guidepost verse indicates the source of this suffering, but how do we categorize it?

I've seen lots of books about pain and affliction by theologians (liberal and conservative), Christian apologists and counselors, Christian and non-Christian psychiatrists and psychologists, by atheists, by Jewish thinkers, and proponents of other religions, and in autobiographies of personal experience. Suffering has been examined many ways; joy also but not as much. Then we look at our own stories. Many of us have multiple PhDs in suffering: Painfully Hard Days.

Suffering can be classified by personal experience:
1) loss, 2) illness, 3) violence, 4) fear and disillusionment, and 5) failure.

Each is a huge category in itself with many subcategories. There is at least one other way of categorizing.

We can also categorize suffering and joy by purpose—divine purpose. In Fred Chay's book, *Suffering Successfully*, he opens his chapter on the purpose of suffering by stating people "can endure most anything if they know the purpose behind it."[4]

---

4. Fred Chay. *Suffering Successfully* (USA: Grace Line, INC, 2014), 39. Written by a seminary professor who has been teaching graduate students for decades, this book is biblical and down to earth. The title may jar you: life hurts too much and you don't want to succeed at suffering, but you want out of it! Or if you are rolling along well enough, the title may cause you to chuckle. Dr. Chay gave me some counsel and encouragement concerning my research when he was a professor at Phoenix Seminary, so I value his wisdom. (I was enrolled in a different seminary but had a membership at the library of Phoenix Seminary, where I did some of my research for a number of years when I lived in Arizona.)

Key: We will name and classify our discoveries according to divine purposes.

Keep this in mind: In this chapter I will lead you through the process of naming our foundational category. I will not ask this of you in the coming chapters. Their names will fall into place more readily.

Look up the following verses. Jot down their main ideas. What words would fit well to describe this first and most fundamental form of suffering, the soil of suffering?

- Genesis 3:17-19:

- Genesis. 50:15:

- Proverbs 12:13-14:

- Romans 5:12-21:

- Galatians 6:7-9:

You can collect many more references involving many statements and stories, all explaining and describing the first and foundational cause of suffering: sin which resulted in the curse and death.

Sin is the transgression of God's instruction because of a change in desire and allegiance from God and toward self. It is trespassing, going off God's trail.

Sin is falling short of the glory of God (Rom. 3:23); that is, failing to reflect God as we were so designed. Wandering in our own ways, we have all fallen short, but we've never fallen out of His reach and His care.

CHAPTER 2

This kind of suffering is represented by the sow-reap principle. It is suffering brought on by one's own desires and choices. I really don't want to believe I deserve some of my suffering, but it's there in black and white, and it's there in life experience as evidence of how our current cosmos operates.

What are some possible adjectives to describe this kind of suffering?

_____

_____ Suffering

Consider (for thought, discussion, and/or sojournaling):

- Would you want to live in a cosmos where people did not reap what they sow?
- What would that be like? Why do you think God designed this cosmos that way?
- Do you see this principle at play also in the first cosmos and the third?

Is there a positive side as well as a negative side to the sow-reap principle?
What is our name for this foundational pain?
<u>Recompensive Suffering</u>. It is earned and deserved.

To recompense is to compensate—to pay. "For the wages of sin is death, but..." (Romans 6:23a).

We could use the word *retributive*. We could use the words *reciprocal* or *punitive*. I suppose these aren't words we use often. Our choice may take a while to get used to. However appropriate any one of these words may be, not one is comfortable. These words hurt just to say, to admit.

But there is good news. There's that word again: good. Good with all its warehouse of riches. Good News is the Gospel of Jesus Christ. The word *gospel* means *good news*, and we should preach the gospel to ourselves regularly, as well as share it with others![5] The gospel, when embraced, opens God's saving, unmerited goodness to us—His joy!

---

5. Two good books teach us how to preach the gospel to ourselves daily (and then we'll be set up to share it with others rather naturally): *The Gospel for Real Life,* by Jerry Bridges, and *A Gospel Primer for Christians*, by Milton Vincent.

So let's consider how JOY speaks back to Recompensive Suffering—deserved suffering.

- Look up the following verses. Jot down their main ideas. What words would fit well to describe this first and most fundamental form of joy, the soil of all joys emerging from a proper response to our own sin and brokenness?
  - Matthew 21:28-32:

  - Luke 15:7:

  - Galatians 5:19-23:

  - Ephesians 2:8-9:

  - Psalm 51:

Check out the narrative behind Psalm 51. David blesses the Lord and rejoices in Him, even when he is being persecuted undeservingly by King Saul and is running for his life (Ps. 34). Even in his desperation, you hear his confident hope in the LORD. However, after his grave sin with Bathsheba and his ordering the murder of her husband, David can feign no joy and deserves none. He is suffering under Recompensive Suffering—earned and deserved.

The prophet, Nathan, wisely confronts David about his sin (2 Sam. 12). He has been suffering, deservedly, recompensively. Under conviction, he admits God "desires truth in the inmost being" (Ps. 51:6).

Asking God to purify and wash him until he is "whiter than snow," David asks God to "make me to hear joy and gladness; let the bones which You have broken rejoice" (Ps. 51: 7-8).

Read the rest of this psalm. The entire psalm is a prayer of repentance, confidence in God's love, justice, and power to forgive, and an expectation of restoration for him and for Zion. Yes, David faces that he still has significant consequences from his sins (2 Sam. 12:10), even though his sins are forgiven. Yet, he envisions God's delighting in His people again. His expectation of restoration, even though he knows he deserves to suffer, shows he knows the vastness of God's longsuffering grace. Such assurance gives him confidence joy will return.

Reviewing the above verses and David's story, think about some adjectives that might describe the first category of joy as an answer to the first kind of suffering, Recompensive Suffering.

What are some possible adjectives to describe the kind of joy emerging from repentance?
_____
_____ Joy

It is hard to find good options, isn't it?
    This joy is the response to being cleansed.
  This joy is the lightness one senses after the total burden is lifted.
    This joy is the dignity of purity. Christ's purity in me.

What is our name for this foundational joy responding to Recompensive Suffering?
    Repentive Joy

These two adjectives, *recompensive* and *repentive* are based upon their forms as verbs and nouns.

Verb	Noun	Adjective
Recompence	Recompence	Recompensive
Compensate	Compensation	
Repent	Repentance	Repentive

Thus, we've have named our first category: Recompensive Suffering and Repentive Joy.

In your own words summarize the meaning of this category.

For further thought:

Hebrews 12:15-17 present a negative example of a sinner who couldn't make himself repent: Esau. This passage offers interesting insight into Esau and how repentance works. Here's a grown man crying. That sounds good! It sounds like humility and repentance! But it's not. He's crying for the inheritance he has lost. He regrets this loss. He is not wanting the Blesser but the blessing. God knew Esau's motives. God knew David's.

Truly, the answer to Recompensive Suffering is repentance, which offers us our first taste of spiritual joy. This joy tastes like overwhelming gratitude. What do you have to say or write about that?

2.3 ADJUST THE FOCUS

Let's take a deeper look at **repentance**. We've watched it in action, but we haven't defined it. Repentance involves "regret accompanied by a true change of heart toward God."[6] This change of heart causes change of behavior.

The Greek word translated repentance *metanoeo* means "to know after."[7] Interestingly, it was the eating from "The Tree of the Knowledge of Good and Evil" that introduced this kind of knowledge. This experiential knowledge is knowledge gained through defiance

---

6. Spiros Zodhiates. *Hebrew-Greek Key Word Study Bible.* "Lexical Aids to the New Testament" (Strong's # 3340, *metanoeo*).

7. *Ibid.*

CHAPTER 2

or foolishness in which a certain understanding producing regret and shame comes after the action.[8]

Metanoeo, "to know after," contrasts with *pronoeo*, which means "to know before." Knowledge known before action is providence and prudence (wisdom), which leads to following the right path.[9] This is the knowledge of faith (Heb. 11:3; Ps. 46:10; Prov. 1:7). While regret and shame innately accompany *metanoeo* knowledge, satisfaction and joy innately follow *pronoeo* knowledge. Do you recognize the sow-reap principle at work here?

Knowledge acquired after disobedient action produces regret and shame. Repentance is the right response to knowledge gained after following the wrong path. Regret and shame are there to lead a person to turn around and change direction, to repent. Here, we witness a good use for pain. The relief of the burden births a new and different kind of joy.

"The fear of the LORD is the beginning of knowledge," Proverbs 1:7 says, explaining *pronoeo* knowledge, which was scorned by our primal parents. "Fools despise wisdom and instruction," concludes this verse, describing those who won't gain *metanoeo* knowledge. That is, they won't learn from their sin, after the fact, thus confirming themselves as fools and forfeiting the merciful joy God offers through repentance.

Consider (for thought, discussion, or writing):

- Describe your growing insight into repentance, knowledge, and joy.
- What does this mean to you?
- Compare and contrast knowledge by faith and prudence (Heb. 11:3; Ps. 46:10; Prov. 1:7) and knowledge by disobedient experience (above references and others from your research).

---

8. Experiential knowledge is not always motivated by defiance/sin. God gave Adam the job to name the animals (Gen. 2:18-24). Obediently, and I'm sure joyfully, Adam did so. From this experience, he learned that just as the animals had partners, he needed a suitable helper for himself. This was experiential knowledge. Wisdom was gained from it. Adam became the first scientific taxonomist. God loves for us to explore His creation.

9. *Ibid*. 4306-4307. *Pronoeo*: to think, know, understand before. Providence, care, prudence.

- How does this apply to you?
- Prudence learned by faith is a knowledge gained before action.
- Prudence learned by disobedient experience is a knowledge learned after the action.

Why does prudence produce joy?

2.4 TREK THE TRAIL

Can you think of examples in your own life when you experienced Recompensive Suffering and Repentive Joy? We don't want to think about this, but our sin begins with our own attitude that doesn't want to listen to God. Where is our allegiance? Each and all of our sins separate us from God and good and joy. How do I respond?

Do you remember Psalm 51:6?
"Behold, you delight in truth in the inward being,
and you teach me wisdom in the secret heart" (ESV).

"Behold, You desire truth in the innermost being,
And in the hidden part You will make me know wisdom" (NASB).

The question in the title at first did not seem to fit the foundational discovery of the chapter.

"Which came first, suffering or joy?"
(Add, *"Which has a longer shelf-life?"*)

Let us turn to Romans 2:4 to witness the connection between good, recompense, repentance, and joy.

"Or do you despise the riches of His goodness, forbearance,
and longsuffering, not knowing that the goodness of God
leads you to repentance?" (NKJV).

CHAPTER 2

"Or do you think lightly of the riches of His kindness and tolerance and patience, not knowing that the kindness of God leads you to repentance?" (NASB).

We have seen from God's first act of creation His expressions of pure goodness. We have noted God's goodness is His storehouse of blessing. We witnessed God's response to His own goodness: joy. In this New Testament text, we see His goodness expressed toward His fallen creatures. We see that it is His joy-filled virtue wooing us to Him.

Were it not for God's rich goodness, God would have no repentance to offer us. The gospel (good news) does not begin with "for all have sinned" (Romans 3:23) but with "the goodness of God leads you to repentance" (Rom. 2:4). This is the biblical witness from creation to His coming kingdom.

Read Romans chapter 8 which ends with this powerful sentence: "For I am convinced that neither death, nor life, nor angels nor principalities, nor things present, nor things to come, nor powers, nor height, nor depth, nor any other created thing, shall be able to separate us from the love of God, which is in Christ Jesus our Lord" (Romans 8:38-39).

If God were not good, this would not be so. But God is good, and the divine response and proper human response to God's goodness in His person and work is joy.

Consider (for thought, discussion, and/or sojournaling):

- When it comes to dealing with our own Recompensive Suffering, do you see why repentance which results in Repentive Joy is the proper response? Explain.
- The sense of shame, the feeling of guilt, and the disturbance of our consciences uncover to us our own misery. When is this hurt a healthy and good hurt that can be a path to joy?
- How strong and sturdy is joy?
- How kind, longsuffering, and patient is joy?
- How loving is joy? The love described in Scripture as "agape" love is a love of the will that finds its joy (delight) in seeking what is beneficial (good) for others.

Now we can see the nourishing encouragement God gives us when He shows us His joy exuding from His creative, loving goodness.

Remember: Joy is God's divine response to His own goodness. Joy is our proper response to God's goodness which He expresses in infinite ways. His good forgiveness is one of those ways.

Joy will always outlive sorrow. If we follow the repentive path, this will be our own experience.

2.5 REST STOP

Ah. Here we are. We've walked quite a way! See the park bench? Time to rest, isn't it? Meditate upon this chapter's Guidepost.

> *For the wages of sin is death, but the free gift of God is eternal life in Christ Jesus our Lord.* (Romans 6:23)

Are you holding your gift?

You may want to sojournal your prayer. Or you may want to sit quietly by the window and meditate on this chapter's journey.

We have named the pain, having discovered our first category of suffering, Recompensive Suffering. We have named its needed partner, Repentive Joy—that gracious voice of joy, calling us to the purifying, satisfying joy of repentance.

Now let's meditate on the sweet name of Joy incarnate—the Alpha and the Omega, the first and the last. A slave trader rescued by Christ who became a Christian minister, author, and poet penned these words which were published in 1779.

How Sweet the Name of Jesus Sounds[10]

How sweet the name of Jesus sounds in a believer's ear!
It soothes his sorrows, heals his wounds, and drives away his fear.

---

10. John Newton. "How Sweet the Name of Jesus Sounds." *The Trinity Psalter Hymnal* (Willow Grove, PA: Trinity Psalter Hymnal Joint Venture, 2018), 492.

It makes the wounded spirit whole and calms the troubled breast.
'Tis manna to the hungry soul, and to the weary [it is] rest.
Dear Name! the rock on which I build, my shield and hiding place,
My never-failing treasury filled with boundless stores of grace.
Jesus, my Shepherd, Brother, Friend, my Prophet, Priest, and King,
My Lord, my Life my Way, my End, accept the praise I bring.

So we pray:

Sweet Jesus,
You are the Alpha and Omega, the first and the last.
We thank You that Joy is both first and last,
Able to consume our sin and destroy our sorrow.
We thank You that Joy is the eternal expression of your goodness,
And suffering is the temporary expression of our fallenness.
Incarnate Goodness, Divine Joy,
You woo us to turn toward You in repentance
To accept your cleansing that makes us pure in You.
We humbly embrace your cross-paid, grace-filled gift.
Through Your Name,
Amen.

CHAPTER 3

HOW DO I MAKE SENSE OF THE SENSELESS?

DISCOVERY TWO

How do I make sense of the senseless?

Richard Wurmbrand retells a fascinating Jewish legend in his book, *100 Prison Meditations.* Moses is sitting at a well when three men, one at a time, stop by. (Apparently, Moses is simply an observer, out of sight.)

The first man unknowingly loses his purse of money in the sand. After he leaves, a second man passes through, finds the purse lying in the sand by the well and gladly takes it with him. Later, a third man comes to the well, drinks, and falls asleep there. The first man returns for his purse and kills the innocent, third man, believing him to be the thief.

Moses questions God. God answers, "For once and only once, I will give you an explanation. I cannot do it at every step. The first man was a thief's son. The purse contained money stolen by his father from the father of the second, who finding the purse, only found what was due him. The third was a murderer whose crime had never been revealed and who received from the first the punishment he deserved. In the future, believe that there is sense and righteousness in what transpires even when you do not understand."[1]

---
1. Richard Wurmbrand, *100 Prison Meditations* (Bartlesville, OK: 2000), 17.

CHAPTER 3

This is a legend, but it illustrates the human mind finds rationality in suffering only when a recompensive (sow-reap) cause is evident. This is fair play. Under these circumstances we may gain the ability to come to terms with suffering.

Without some reasonable cause, the suffering becomes confusing and mysterious. It feels unjust and cruel. Sometimes it truly is unjust and cruel. It makes us angry.

3.1 TRAVEL SCOPE

In this chapter we will explore the second layer or genre in the foundational tier, discovered in the Scriptures and experienced in our lives: Collateral Suffering and Redemptive Joy.

GUIDEPOST

And they that know Thy name will put their trust in Thee. (Psalm 9:10a)

Consider these scenarios:

Prison	Collision	Natural Catastrophe
1. You are in prison for a stealing someone's identity and property. You did it, and now you're paying. What are you thinking? 2. You are in prison for stealing someone's identity and property. You did not do it. You can't prove it. You are now paying for someone else's crime. What are you thinking? What Cosmic laws do you see written on your own heart? Note Romans 2:14-15; 1:19	It all happened so fast! She was driving home from church on a country road Sunday evening at dusk. Heading over a small rise in the road, Silvia sees oncoming lights raging toward her. When she awakes, she awakes alone in a sterile environment. Her two children have left this world, never to be held by Silvia again. Physically, she is bruised but fine, but emotionally, mentally, spiritually, she is numb. What	Two rangers knocked at the Daly's door. "You have to leave now. You've been warned. Come with us." The next day the Daly family learns their house was consumed within hours after they fled it. All their possessions are gone. Most of their housing development is gone. It was a very dry season, and the forest behind the development had become dangerous. How did the fire start?

Continued on next page.

Continued from previous page.

	process of thinking and feeling will she go through in the coming months and years? How can she come to terms with reality?	Is this fair? Why natural disasters?

These are contemporary scenarios of various types of suffering which also share some key similarities.

We can also consider biblical examples, each unique in detail yet also carrying similarities. What do you remember about the following? For now, just think about these parties, and we'll come back to most of them.

- Abel. Joseph. Job. Hagar. Hannah. Dinah.
- How about that unnamed concubine in Judges 19-21?
- Preceding all of these, what about all of Creation (Romans 8:19-22)?
- Consider that animal in Genesis 3:21, skinned for clothing. By whom? For whom?

Let's return to Wurmbrand's retelling of the Jewish legend. Most interestingly, Wurmbrand's point in telling this story in his book is not to illustrate man's longing and search for fairness behind suffering, but to present God's right, His authority, *not* to justify Himself to His creatures. How humbling. And how do you respond? Wurmbrand addresses the age-old mystery: *"How can an all-powerful, all-knowing, all-wise and good God permit evil?*[2] *Injustice? Suffering?*

This line of questioning has been framed in various ways over the centuries. It is a part of any study in Christian Apologetics. A professor insisted I research and write a chapter on it to be included in my dissertation. I had to address it: fifty-two pages of logic, syllogisms, Scripture, philosophy, and footnotes. But Richard Wurmbrand's silent life screamed for an answer. I'll give you his answer.

---

2. This line of questioning falls under the study of *theodicy*. Probably most people ask this type of question at some time, but philosophers and apologists have dug deeply into it. If you want to explore theodicy, mystery, and the paradoxical points of faith and knowledge, free will, and God's sovereignty and goodness, you may want to start with D.A. Carson's book, *How Long O Lord?* Note his chapter on the book of Job and part 3 entitled "Glimpses of the Whole Puzzle: Evil and Suffering in the World of a Good and Sovereign God."

CHAPTER 3

First, you must know Wurmbrand was a twentieth-century Romanian, Jewish Christian who was persecuted under the Nazis and then spent fourteen years in prison under Communist rule. He spent years in solitary confinement in total blackness and soundlessness, meant to drive him insane.

Instead of going insane, although he nearly did, he wrote sermons in his brilliant head, repeated and memorized them, and his book, *100 Prison Meditations*, is one of the products of that tenacious, God-protected mind. He spoke nine languages, had read literature from many peoples, and was well read in the Scriptures. His mind had food on which to live.

In 1965 after over fourteen years in prison, it took the work of two organizations and $10,000 to get Richard, his wife, and son out of Romania. Brought to the USA, Richard wrote what has become a classic, *Tortured for Christ*, and started the organization that has become The Voice of the Martyrs. When Richard Wurmbrand speaks to the issues of persecution, undeserved suffering, and the evil of our world, we should listen. Richard writes:

"Faith in God is the sole answer to the mystery of evil."[3]

And we know evil is at the root of all suffering. My fifty-two pages may be interesting to some people, but Wurmbrand's one sentence is something we all can grab and grow by (Rom. 10:17; Heb. 11:6; Deut. 29:29).

Option: If you are doing this study in a group, maybe one of you would like to research Wurmbrand and report on your findings. The bibliography in the appendices will direct you to other authors, books, and sub-topics to provide everyone in your group ideas for exploration to share with each other. (Sidebar content)

---

3. Richard Wurbrand, *100 Prison Meditations* (Bartlesville, OK: Living Sacrifice Books, 2000), 17.

3.2 VIEWING THE BIBLICAL MAP

Earlier, I mentioned Job, Abel, Hannah, Hagar, Joseph, Dinah, Shechem, an unnamed concubine, all of creation (Rom. 8:19-22), and an animal referenced in Genesis 3:21. Let's think about what they have in common. Check out the following chart for an overview. I am not asking you to read all these references but to gain first the big picture.

Collateral Suffering: Eight Biblical Examples

Example & Reference	Narrative Summary	Commentary Note
1. All Creation Romans 8:19-22 The animal in Genesis 3:21	All creation groans and suffers. God killed and skinned an animal to make clothing for Adam and Eve.	Creation pays a price for Adam and Eve's sin. The skinned animal is the first within creation to experience collateral suffering.
2. Abel Genesis 4 Hebrews 11:4	Righteous Abel is slain by evil Cain.	Abel acts by faith, offers a proper sacrifice, and is described as righteous. God testifies about his acts and faith. "Though he is dead, he still speaks."
3. Hagar & Ishmael Genesis 16; 21:17-18; 25:7-10	The bondservant of Sarah, Hagar bears both Abraham's child and Sarah's mistreatment. Hagar & Ishmael suffer rejection, abandonment, and destitution.	Hagar and her son experience great mistreatment by no fault of their own. However, God intervenes on their behalf, provides for them, and makes Ishmael a leader of his own clan.
4. Dinah & Shechem's people Genesis 34	Dinah, daughter of Jacob and Leah, is raped by Shechem, the son of a tribal king. Dinah's brothers take revenge upon the entire city of Shechem.	Dinah is a true victim, and so are the people of Shechem who did not harm her. Dinah's brothers make Jacob's people and God odious to the people of Canaan.
5. Jochebed Exodus 2 Numbers 26:59	Mother of Moses, Jochebed and her family endure the mistreatment of Pharaoh and his policies toward the growing sons of Israel.	Jochebed and her family suffer the horrible anxiety of having to protect their baby boy from being killed. Descendants of Jacob, they live in Goshen in Egypt under slavery and oppression by no fault of their own, even because of their strength and wise living.

Example & Reference	Narrative Summary	Commentary Note
6. Hannah 1 Samuel chapters 1-2	Positioned as one of two wives, barren Hannah is provoked by the rival wife who has children. She weeps bitterly in distress, calling on God to answer her prayers.	While Hannah's prayers are happily answered, her period of suffering involves her identity, life purpose, and "dysfunctional" family relationships and culture.
7. Mephibosheth 2 Samuel 4:4; 9:3-9; 21:7	Son of Jonathan, grandson of King Saul, he is crippled at age five, fleeing with his nurse after the death of his father and grandfather.	Mephibosheth is caught within the web of his family's story, crippled because his nurse's fumbling. He is lame and powerless for life.
8. An unnamed concubine Judges chapters 19-21	During the periods of the judges when everyone does what is right in his own eyes, a concubine is group raped, killed, and cut into twelve pieces to be distributed among the tribes of Israel.	Descent into malevolence characterizes this period in which women are already demeaned and mistreated. In this case, a woman is acted upon demonically.

Just reading the list, summaries, and short commentary is overwhelming to me. This study is heavy, so listen to the Holy Spirit regarding how much energy you can invest.

Pray while you study. For now, getting the big picture is enough, and then you have all of this material to come back to when you need it or are ready to return to it.

Ask God: What perspective are You wanting me to gain?
What strength/encouragement are you offering me?
Where is the good/joy/hope coming out of this tragedy?

From the above list, we will look at just one example.

A. Let's consider Abel. Scripture offers very little information about him.

- Read Genesis 4:1-16 and record what facts or details are known about Abel.

- Compare Genesis 4:10 and Hebrews 11:4. Interestingly, both passages say Abel "speaks" even after he is dead. It is not the vocal cords or the pen of Abel speaking.

- In Genesis 4:10, what does God say is crying to him from the ground?
- According to Hebrews 11:4, how does Abel still speak?
- Note Luke 11:50-51. Here, Jesus lists Abel as the first prophet slain! Hebrews 11:4 describes Abel as righteous, and Genesis 4:4 says that "the LORD had regard for Abel and his offering."
- How would you describe his witness?
- As "the first prophet slain," what is his prophetic message?

In Genesis 4:6-16, the LORD speaks directly to Cain, questioning his attitude and countenance, advising and warning him. So Cain has no excuse for his actions.

Let's compare and contrast Adam and Eve's first sin which initiated the Fall of humankind and Cain's sin against Abel, murder.

The first act of disobedience was the eating of a fruit. It seems small to us (sinners seeing through warped lenses). However, it was defiance against God because their inner allegiance had changed. Certainly, many sins were perpetrated between the expulsion from the Garden to this point when Adam and Eve's first sons named in the Bible come into conflict. Note Genesis 4:3: "So it came about in the course of time...."

Cain's sin, the second recorded sin, is a huge behavioral leap of defiance from dietary disobedience. We have the far ranges of sinful behavior here—from wrongful eating to the violence of murder! Taking a human life! Behind all behavior is a personal mindset and an orientation to an allegiance. Allegiance to their Creator-God or to the god of self.[4] The entire range of sin demonstrates variegated expressions of idolatrous defiance.

Cain's life illustrates the first form of suffering, *Recompensive Suffering, deserved suffering.* Even then, God's punishment on Cain is less than he deserved. God mixes grace with judgment. God does not end his life but lets him live with the guilt and consequences as a "vagrant and wanderer" (Gen. 4:11-20). Cain receives a curse, yet blessings too, for he lives to marry and have children and grandchildren.

---

4. The Fallen nature is the sin nature, which we all have. Our sin nature is our fallen, "default setting," and orientation in which we are allies of self and are separated from our Creator to whom our allegiance is owed. Refer to the Vocab Café in the appendices.

CHAPTER 3

Abel did not have these opportunities. Even in God's judgment, there appears unfairness. Abel suffers the loss of his life and all the opportunity and potential it held. Abel walked in the will of God, but that did not protect him from a jealous and angry brother. Abel's life illustrates the second form of suffering: Collateral Suffering—undeserved suffering.

In This Broken Cosmos, God permits Collateral Suffering. Abel's life clearly shows this to be true. God did not force Cain to do right but gave him opportunities to choose. The consequences of Cain's choice became Collateral Suffering for Abel. Abel did not deserve to suffer. There is mystery here.

Cain's experience of Recompensive Suffering was God's justice applied to him. In Cain's life we see God's grace mixed with His justice.

We see that Abel, who "obtained the testimony that he was righteous" (Heb. 11:4), was listed in Hebrews 11 as among "all these, having gained approval through their faith" who will be made complete along with all God's other saints (verse thirty-nine).[5]

> B. How do you process the Cain and Abel story? What does it tell you about God and His ways? What encouragement do you gain from Abel?
>
> C. How do the following three realities demonstrate that justice is certain?
>
> - The resurrection (Eph. 2:5-7; John 11:25-26)
> - Future judgments (Eccles. 12:14; Rom. 2:4-8, 1 Corinthians 4:5; Revelation 20:11-15)
> - The future New Heavens and New Earth (Revelation 21-22)

Justice is coming:

> *"For God will bring every act to judgment, everything which is hidden, whether good or evil"* (Ecclesiastes 12:14).

---

5. We will return to the meaning of Abel's life in chapter 8 on Eschatological Suffering and Joy.

> *"Therefore, do not go on passing judgment before the time,*
> *but wait until the Lord comes who will both bring to light the things hidden*
> *in the darkness and disclose the motives of men's hearts;*
> *and then each man's praise will come to him from God"* (I Corinthians 4:5).

Owning this perspective will relieve the weight of some of our suffering.

Sojournal Suggestion: Copy the above two verses. Then describe how these verses impact your perspective and help you better manage some nagging experience of Collateral Suffering in your own life.

We can see Collateral Suffering has two or three elements:

1. *Collateral Suffering is not directly deserved.*
2. *Collateral Suffering is a result of secondary causes.*
3. *Sometimes, Collateral Suffering is mysterious.*

Yes, since "all have sinned" we all deserve to suffer for our sins. In This Broken Cosmos, in which we all by nature and by action are sinners, our sins impact others. Thus, there is plenty of collateral damage. Life is messy. Life is unfair. Often in This Broken Cosmos, justice is absent or distorted.

Sometimes we find ourselves in situations where our suffering, not brought on by ourselves directly, seems so mysterious. How could this have happened? Why to me? To us?

That was the case for Jerry Sittser who was driving his car home one fall evening from a home school field trip. What a lovely day he had experienced with his wife, mother, and four children. Contentedly they hummed along until headlights flashed in front of them and the car crashed. He wrote, "I remember the feeling of panic that struck my soul as I watched Lynda, my mother, and Diana Jane all die before my eyes."[6] His wife, mother, and his four-year-old daughter—gone.

---

6. Jerry Sittser, *A Grace Disguised* (Grand Rapids, Michigan: Zondervan, 2004), 31.

CHAPTER 3

Jerry and three traumatized children lived through this accident. Accident. The other driver was quite drunk. Collateral Suffering. Catastrophic suffering. Undeserved. The fallout from someone else's evil addiction to alcohol. Jerry and his remaining family would never be the same.

This makes you angry, doesn't it? You can tell tales from your own life or your loved ones' lives illustrating Collateral Suffering. What do we do with it? How do we live through it?

A Grace Disguised by Jerry Sittser is a heavy but encouraging book that you may want to read.

As you continue reading the Bible, I hope you will mentally mark illustrations (narratives) involving Recompensive and Collateral Suffering. Every biblical story involves various forms of suffering and joy. In places, the Bible can be very disturbing. Often, we'd prefer less "reality," but there's no remedy in denial or fantasy.

Sojournal Suggestion: Your sojournal is also a place to lament: to write out your sorrow as prayers to God.[7] Collateral Suffering calls for us to lament before God in communion with Him. We will briefly look at lament in the next chapter.

Let's illustrate Collateral Suffering and then add Redemptive Joy through one final illustration, the most unbelievable narrative of them all. It will help us to come to terms with suffering and to embrace available joys.

Our Suffering Sovereign

You remember Wurmbrand claimed, "Faith in God is the sole answer to the mystery of evil." This can only be true if your God is a good God.

---

7. In dealing with Collateral Suffering, a resource that will take you far beyond what this framework can go is the book *Between Pain & Grace* by Gerald W. Peterson and Andrew J. Schmutzer (Chicago: Moody Press, 2016). It has an excellent chapter on lament. It contains helpful material on sexual abuse, toxic relationships, mental illness, and more.

A.W. Tozer observes:

> "We wonder why we don't have faith; the answer is [that] faith is confidence in the character of God and if we don't know what kind of God God is, we can't have faith."[8]

Note the important correlation between proper knowledge of God and faith.

Tozer quotes Psalm 9:10: *"And they that know Thy name will put their trust in Thee."* Explaining the word *name* means "character plus reputation," Tozer claims faith will become "automatic" or "natural" when we come to know God's character.[9] "And if you're listening with a worthy mind, you'll find faith will spring up."[10]

If we are to address Collateral Suffering (and yes, Recompensive Suffering) in any useful and satisfying way, our journey will lead us back to our theology of God—searching what we know about God—as He has revealed Himself in His creation, His Word, and our born-again consciences.

If we did not have the Scriptures, where would we be? But God is Personal Being; He is not a cosmic force or principle. And He chose to design human beings in His image and with capacities through which He can reveal Himself to us, pouring a pitcher full from His infinite reservoir into the cups of our human hearts. Why? So that we could have fellowship with Him and each other. So that we could communicate, commune, and worship.

Who is this God in whom we put all our faith and trust? How does such knowledge help us come to terms with suffering?

A classical answer provides us with an outline of God's attributes (at attention, left hemisphere of the brain!). The Scripture provides us with narratives through which God

---

8. A.W. Tozer, *The Attributes of God, Vol. 2*, (Chicago: WingSpread Publishers, 2003), (WingSpread Publishers is an imprint of Moody Publishers), 5.
9. *Ibid.*
10. *Ibid.*

CHAPTER 3

reveals Himself (ready, right hemisphere of the brain!). Theologians gather data from both the biblical narratives (stories) and the declaratives (statements), making it easier for us to grasp truths.

Let me give you some succinct lists of attributes of God.

- The God revealed in the Bible is 1) Self-revelational, 2) Personal, 3) Unity-Trinity, 4) Great, 5) Good, 6) Incarnational in Christ.
- God's Greatness is revealed in His 1) Self-existence 2) Omnipotence, 3) Omniscience, 4) Omnipresence, 5) Eternality, 6) Infinity, 7) Incomprehensibility, 8) Immutability (unchangeable).
- God's Goodness shows Him to be 1) Holy, 2), True, 3) Love, 4) Righteous, 5) Faithful, 6) Merciful, and I'm sure we could add to this list!

Ah! If only your brain reads these words, your mind may go numb. The words can stay abstract and flat. We don't get it. We only get it when we witness these characteristics in the works and words of God the Father, Son, and Holy Spirit—in action—in narratives, including our own lived stories. Then such truths become lively treasures.

We are going to consider what it means for God to be personal—expressing all of His sovereign, majestic perfections through personality, aimed at calling a people unto Himself.

A. Read the following verses and record the key phrases. Check the contexts as you are able.

- Genesis 6:6
- Psalm 78:40-41
- Isaiah 63:7-10

In all of these verses, we see that God suffered collaterally because_____
_____
_____

- Isaiah 53:3-5; 6-12

- Mark 3:5
- Luke 19:41
- John 11:35

In all of these verses, we see Jesus suffered collaterally for _____

_____

_____

- Ephesians 4:30
- Isaiah 63:10

In these verses, we see the Holy Spirit suffers collaterally because_____

_____

_____

God is Sovereign. He is in control. His decrees have and will be fulfilled. Equally true, our Sovereign God is personal. That is one reason He chose the name I AM who I AM or YHWH (Jehovah, often translated LORD in the Old Testament).

We tend to focus on the verb part of His succinct name: "AM" revealing eternality—underived existence, transcendent being, the eternal "now." We overlook the "I"—the personal pronoun. God invented language, and one of His purposes was to communicate with those He created in His own image, for fellowship with Himself.

So when God chooses a personal pronoun to identify Himself, we must take note. This is more than His condescending to our limitations. The Old Testament records "YHWH" as God's name 6,828 times.[11] The book of John records Jesus employing it eleven times.[12]

---

11. E. Jenni, C. Westermann, *Theological Lexicon of the Old Testament*, (Hendrickson Publishers 1997), 685. From the Masoretic text of the Hebrew Scriptures.

12. Seven of the eleven times Jesus calls Himself "I am," He turns the name (subject + linking verb) into a sentence: "I am the bread of life (John 6:35); "I am the light of the world" (8:12); "I am the gate for the sheep" (10:7); "I am the good shepherd" (10:11); "I am the resurrection and the life" (11:25); "I am the way, the truth, and the life" (14:6); "I am the true vine" (15:1). Thus, we see Jesus is just what we need. He completes my sentence. Four times, Jesus uses the name alone, an incomplete sentence, God's name: ". . . If you do not believe that I Am, you will die in your sins" (8:24); "When you have

Our God is not some cold force. God is not a principle. He is the Perfect Person. As such, He has absorbed all of our suffering in Himself, on the cross.

Discuss or sojournal: "My God, the Perfect Person Who Suffered for Me." In your current circumstance and stage of life, what does this mean to you?

3.3 ADJUSTING THE FOCUS

Do you remember when you asked Jesus to be your Savior? We respond to God's wooing us in so many different ways, but all of His children have responded positively to Him. Some people speak of Jesus as our "personal Savior." I remember many pastors and evangelists asking, "Have you invited Jesus into your life to be your personal Savior?" Some have objected to this language, but how right it is to call Jesus our "personal Savior!" Do remember the entire trinity is our personal Savior, for all three persons of the trinity are involved.

James 4:8 says, "Draw near to God and He will draw near to you." Some translations say, "Come near to God and He will come near to you."

Jesus urged, oh so consolingly, "Come to me, all you who are weary and burdened, and I will give you rest. Take my yoke upon you and learn from me, for I am gentle and humble in heart, and you will find rest for your souls. For my yoke is easy and my burden is light" (Matt. 11:28-30).

You see, Elohim, the Mighty Creator in Genesis 1:1, is YHWH, the I AM who I AM, who reveals Himself as a personal being to Moses in Genesis 3:13-14. He reveals Himself as "I AM the good shepherd" in John 10:11. "I am the good shepherd who gives his life for the sheep."

---

lifted up the son of man, then you will know that I AM (8:28); "...Before Abraham ever was, I AM" (8:58); "I tell you this now, before it happens, so that when it happens you will know that I AM" (13:19). Thus, we see Jesus truly is one with the Father, the Son within the Trinity. And we are in awe.

We don't have all the answers to our pain, but we do have a personal God who is good, who is afflicted with us and collects all our tears (Ps. 56:8), who gave His life on Calvary for my sin and for yours, and who ultimately will fix everything. *"Thy Kingdom come..."*

Another Kind of Good and a New Kind of Joy

C.S. Lewis explains a change in the way "good" shows itself and operates after the Fall of the human race, which helps us to recognize a different kind of joy awaiting us after the Fall.

> ...God saw the crucifixion in the act of creating the first nebula. The world is a dance in which good, descending from God, is disturbed by evil arising from the creatures, and the resulting conflict is resolved by God's own assumption of the suffering nature which evil produces. The doctrine of the free Fall asserts that the evil which thus makes the fuel or raw material for <u>the second and more complex kind of good</u> is not God's contribution but man's.[13]

This more complex kind of good in This Broken Cosmos is good working through evil, sin, and all the twisting and tangling convolutions of such mixture into the reality of our lives, personally and collectively, but now amazingly, purposefully (Rom. 8:28-29). When you see the Heroic Good, mudded, tarred, and feathered, but never extinguished and never vanquished, you experience a new kind of joy—a second and more complex kind. It never gives up.

3.4 TREK THE TRAIL (AND WATCH YOUR STEP)

How Regenerative Agriculture Illustrates "The Second and More Complex Good"

Regenerative farming works with God's good earth and sovereign plan in order that, as Daniel Trevor explains, "the waste of one part of the farm becomes the energy for another."[14] This is biodiversity. A more complex good. "For example, animal poop creates rich,

---

13. C.S. Lewis, *The Problem of Pain* (San Francisco: HarperCollins Publishers, 1940), 80. Underline added.
14. Daniel Trevor, *The Unholy Trinity: How Carbs, Sugar & Oils Make Us Fat, Sick & Addicted and How to Escape Their Grip*, www.DanielTrevor.com, 2024, 201.

CHAPTER 3

fertile soil that captures, sequesters, and draws down carbon. This results in an increase in the farm's capacity for self-renewal and makes the farm fully sustainable."[15] Is this not good? "This is where the raising and production of livestock will not only *not* harm the environment in any way but will instead greatly benefit it."[16] Benefit. This is one of those words meaning *good*.

The natural world, as Jesus often demonstrated, enlightens us spiritually. God will use the waste produce of our Collateral Suffering as *"the fuel or raw material"* to fertilize the broken soil of our hearts and lives when we cooperate with His farming techniques. Fertilizer is food made of all kinds of dirt to enrich the soil. "And the one on whom seed was sown on the good soil, this is the man who hears...understands...and bears fruit" (Matthew 13:23). This good soil is the soil of the heart. Read the whole parable in Matthew 13, Mark 4, and Luke 8.

- How have you witnessed Collateral Suffering used beneficially—to feed, nourish and energize you and others? What more complex good has come from it?[17]
- How have you witnessed Collateral Suffering used harmfully—as manmade chemicals and pesticides by the rejection of suffering as divinely useful waste?
- When you look beyond your own personal situation, how do you see Collateral Suffering impacting the kingdom of God? When does it advance the kingdom of God?

No human Collateral Suffering compares to Christ's in His incarnation and crucifixion. Here we see the Father as the ultimate Regenerative Farmer, and we see the Son as the seed and the blood sacrifice. *"Unless a grain of wheat falls into the ground and dies, it remains solitary, but if it dies, it brings forth much produce"* explains Jesus (John 12:4—study the context). God is farming for us.

---

15. *Ibid.*

16. *Ibid.*

17. Much suffering is rooted in Christians not understanding or following their callings and vocations as means to love and serve their neighbors. Explore this study through Gene Edward Veith Jr.'s outstanding book, *God at Work* (Wheaton, IL: Crossway Pub., 2002; 2011).

So now we have Christ in us, the Wounded, Slain, Risen, and Victorious Lamb of God, residing in us through the indwelling Holy Spirit. We are "in Christ" (Romans 6; Ephesians 1).[18]

Your Redemptive Joy springs from your Collateral Suffering, just as Jesus' did: "who for the joy set before Him endured the cross . . ." (Heb. 12:2). Probably you have one or a few cases of Collateral Suffering in your life that you've never been able to come to terms with and find peace. You may need to lament in prayer about it in your *My SoJournal*. You may need to talk it over with a trusted friend. May the Lord comfort you.

This chapter may not have spoken to your specific experience of Collateral Suffering. However, we are looking at suffering through the lens of divine purpose. Your unjust, mysterious, seemingly absurd, and seemingly "gratuitous" sorrow need not be gratuitous or meaningless after all. Your suffering is absurd only if you choose not to let God be your Regenerative Farmer raising meaningful produce through your pain. He does so by entering into every ounce of our pain, anguishing ultimately and finally for us, and He rises victorious. In Him, we die; with Him we rise.

Richard Wurmbrand says: "Faith in God is the sole answer to the mystery of evil."

A.W. Tozer says: "We wonder why we don't have faith; the answer is, faith is confidence in the character of God and if we don't know what kind of God God is, we can't have faith."

Faith in God is the sole answer only if God's character is good.

The Psalms report His good character:

> *"Good and upright is the Lord;*
> *Therefore, He instructs sinners in the way"* (Psalm 25:8).

---

18. David K. Spurbeck Sr. *The Christian "In Christ"* (Forest Grove, Oregon: Know to Grow Pub., 1999). An excellent reference in studying "the believer's position and possessions in Christ.

*"He loves righteousness and justice; The earth is full
of the loving kindness of the LORD"* (Psalm 33:5).

*"O taste and see that the LORD is good;
How blessed is the man who takes refuge in Him!"* (Psalm 34:8).

*"You are good. And what you do is good.
Teach me your decrees"* (Psalm 119:68).

The Dexterity and Resilience of God's Goodness

The book of Genesis reveals the dexterity and resilience of God's goodness. The book begins with the breathtaking description of God's goodness expressed in His creation of the universe. Here we witness The Original Cosmos in its majestic purity. God creates "ex nihilo," out of nothing! *What brilliant, benevolent power!* Then we witness the more complex expression of His goodness in the second cosmos, This Broken Cosmos, through the narratives about Adam and Eve and the lineage down to Abraham, Isaac, and Jacob.

The book of Genesis ends with the record of Joseph's life. Joseph, the eleventh son of the twelve sons of Jacob, was sold into slavery by his jealous and angry brothers. Here, we witness the goodness of God woven through the muck of sinful human acts causing much Recompensive and Collateral Suffering. Yet the good prevails. *"You meant evil against me,"* spoke Joseph to his fear-filled, repentant brothers, *"but God meant it for good in order to bring about this present result, to preserve many people alive"* (Genesis 50:20). What dexterity God's goodness exhibits! What re-creativity. What doubly brilliant, benevolent power. This story and much of Scripture reveal threads of purposefulness woven through the tapestry of history actuating God's ultimate plan.[19]

We will return to Joseph's story in chapter 10 of this study guide. If you want to explore this story now, you'll need to read most of the book of Genesis, beginning at chapter 12. What a saga!

---

19. Josef Ton, *Suffering, Martyrdom, and Rewards in Heaven* (Wheaton, Illinois: The Romanian Missionary Society, 2000). In chapter 7 on Exemplary Suffering and Joy, we will see that God uses Collateral Suffering and Joy to advance His kingdom. This is the creative, mysterious, divine exercise of the "more complex good" for the ultimate good.

- Consider your own life. What does God's goodness, woven through the messiness of your life, look like to you?

- Do you recognize that God is investing meaning into your situation and suffering through His "farming techniques," which activate "a more complex good?"

- Can you trust that meaning is being mixed into what has seemed senseless?

- How can you today and this week activate an attitude of confidence in the goodness of God, His purposes, and His plan in your circumstances?

- How can you lean into God and accept some JOY, redeemed (purchased) by God's own suffering for you and with you?

3.5 REST STOP

GUIDEPOST

And they that know Thy name will put their trust in Thee. (Psalm 9:10a)

You know, the Jews do not say the name, YHWH (Jehovah in the KJV). The name is so sacred they substitute the name, Adonai (LORD in many translations). Or, they use the expression, "The Name."

It is interesting that most of us end our prayers with "in the name of Jesus, Amen." Many of us don't know what we're saying. It's just the way it's done.

In the name—according to the character of.
In the name—according to His will and in His stead or place (how bold of us).
Amen—Truly, let it be.

CHAPTER 3

In this quiet time of rest, let's meditate on this verse. You may want to recite Psalm 9:10a aloud. Next, read verses nine through ten together, and then read the entire psalm. Sit quietly with Psalm 9.

Finally, review some of the other Scriptures you have read in this chapter and pray over them, talking to the LORD about them, thanking Him for who He is, what He has done, and what He is doing in your life and world. In the name of Jesus.

Let's close this chapter with a beautiful hymn penned in the late twentieth century.

Meekness and Majesty[20]

Meekness and majesty, manhood and Deity,
In perfect harmony, the Man who is God.
Lord of eternity, dwells in humanity;
Kneels in humility and washes our feet.

Father's pure radiance, perfect in innocence;
Yet learns obedience to death on a cross.
Suffering to give us life, conquering through sacrifice;
And as they crucify prays, "Father, forgive."

Wisdom unsearchable, God the invisible;
Love indestructible in frailty appears.
Lord of infinity, stooping so tenderly;
Lifts our humanity to the heights of His throne.

Chorus: O what a mystery, meekness and majesty;
Bow down and worship, for this is your God.

---

20. Graham Kendrick. *"Meekness and Majesty."* Praise Chorus Book (USA: Maranatha! Music, 1990), 41.

CHAPTER 4

WILL I EVER BE THE SAME?

DISCOVERY THREE

My first awareness this morning when I awoke was the pain in my face, then my stomach, and my right leg, but oh, my feet. My headache. The rushing noise in my ears. Then I had a lovely thought. "God." Today, my first worded thought was this simple prayer: "God." This most simple of divine names. "God." And my heart smiled. Lying there, I rested in His name.

Now, hours later, I connect this morning's experience with our last theme verse. "They who know Thy name will put their trust in Thee" (Ps. 9:10a). That's why I could smile when I was miserable. I know His character, and it is good. Yet He lets me live every day in pain.[1] I also know it is true of many of you! There was nothing new about my experience awakening this morning. It is typical of decades of mornings. However, in the last year my pain levels have decreased to some degree and my stamina has been increasing in varying degrees. God is giving me a window to finish this project and whatever else.

---

1. The pain was initiated by structural injury in childhood which led to neurological injury and body-wide chronic pain and fatigue. New injuries often do not heal well. Cleveland Clinic concluded back in 1986 the good news is "it" won't kill me, but the bad news is I'll never get over it. Learn to manage it. Ha! How? Fibrositis, they labeled it then, which came to be called fibromyalgia. So began my "fight for my life plan," which is still going, plus some other issues. My research and this book are a part of that "fight for my life plan," which I view as God's sovereign plan for my life that provides me with batons to pass on to the next generation.

CHAPTER 4

What happened this morning? A mixture of Recompensive and Collateral Suffering beat me up. I know I made some unhealthy food and activity choices recently. I can make all kinds of excellent excuses. I'm not at home right now, so I need to be flexible, and I need to participate with the work at hand... but I also made some wrong and some poor choices. It was my decision to go ahead and eat what I know I should not. I pay. Recompense. Does God still love me? Forgive me? Is He still with me? Yes!

How is Collateral Suffering mixed in here? The food additives, the toxins in our air and water. Maybe some of these exacerbate my issues. I think of the bad fats, the sugars, and chemicals the food industry uses to make us addicted to "fake food," which I try to avoid. The list goes on. Sigh. These harmful elements are not of my doing. But they are a part of my environment. Does God still love me? Is He still with me? Yes! Yes!!

Big business, big pharma, and big government are more sources of abuse and injustice, as well as blessing. In our times we all live with these dilemmas and stresses. Many of our burgeoning chronic health issues are due to or are exacerbated by human mismanagement of the responsibilities God gave mankind to steward the earth and care for each other.[2] Recompensive and Collateral Suffering marble together.

Your troubles may differ from mine, but no matter, it is normal to want out of our hurt. It is also typical to want the circumstances to change, maybe to go back to where they were before the incident, accident, or trial without ourselves having to make changes.

"Will I ever be the same?" we ask if we remember a time when we didn't hurt, when things weren't crazy. What we want is to be out of our affliction. Ask this question at the end of this chapter. Would a positive answer produce a positive result? With a negative answer, where is the hope?

---

2. In the last chapter I referenced Daniel Trevor's *The Unholy Trinity*. Let me add *Good Energy* by Casey Means. These two well researched books confront chronic illness, its dramatic increase, causes, and changes needed. Casey Means' spirituality is not Christ-centered, but her research findings are essential for us to face in order to correct the mismanagement of God's resources, resulting in much of our current suffering.

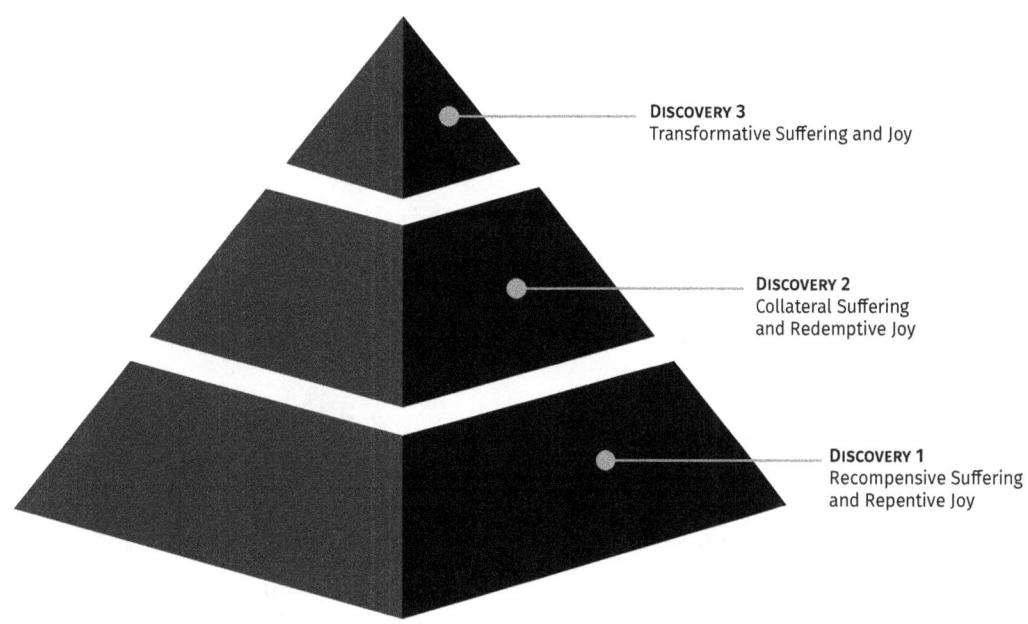

Foundational Tier: Discoveries 1-3

4.1 TRAVEL SCOPE

In this chapter we will discover the third layer in the foundational tier: Transformational Suffering and Joy.

This triad comprises the ground and soil under our feet in This Broken Cosmos. The Bible employs many metaphors to describe the Christian life in this world: a walk, a plant, a building, a field, a house, a temple, a Shepherd with His sheep and more. In this traveler's guide, we major on the "walk" theme, but God's Word makes it clear we need all the metaphors as the Holy Spirit employs them to inform and transform us.

GUIDEPOST

Consider it all joy, my brethren, when you encounter various trials, knowing that the testing of your faith produces endurance. And let endurance have its perfect result, that you may be perfect and complete, lacking in nothing. (James 1:2-4)

CHAPTER 4

Transformative Suffering and Joy

Stop and think about what you know of Scripture. Can you recall some verses including these words—form, conform, and/or transform?

4.2 VIEWING THE BIBLICAL MAP

A. Through the Lens of Statements:

Below you will find key verses containing our key words. Please highlight the key words and underline the main phrases or clauses in which the key words are found. You may want to study the contexts of some of these verses. Think carefully. What concepts are cumulating?

Key Word: Form (to fashion or shape)

> Genesis 1:2: *"And the earth was formless and void, and darkness was over the surface of the deep; and the Spirit of God was moving over the surface of the waters."*

> Genesis 2:7: *"The LORD God formed man of dust from the ground, and breathed into his nostrils the breath of life; and man became a living being."*

> Psalm 139:13: *"For Thou didst form my inward parts; Thou didst weave me in my mother's womb."*

> Zechariah 12:1b: *"... The LORD ... forms the spirit of man within him."*

> Galatians 4:19: *"My children, with whom I am again in labor until Christ is formed in you."*

In the New Testament, *form* is derived from the Greek, <u>morphe</u>: characteristic form, feature, nature, or essence of a person or thing.[3]

---

3. W.E. Vine. *Vine's Complete Expository Dictionary of Old and New Testament Words.*

As a noun, *morphe* is used to describe Christ's life as God and as human in Philippians 2:6-7:

> [Christ Jesus], although He existed in the *morphe* of God did not regard equality with God a thing to be grasped, but emptied Himself, taking the *morphe* of a bond-servant, and being made in the likeness of men.

As a verb, *morphoo* "refers not to the external and transient, but to the inward and real"; it is used in Galatians 4:19, expressing the necessity of a change in character and conduct to correspond with inward spiritual condition, that there may be moral conformity to Christ.[4]

Key Word: Conform (being like, being made like)

Romans 8:29: "For whom He foreknew, He also predestined to become conformed to the image of His Son that He might be the firstborn among many brethren."

Philippians 3:10: "That I may know Him, and the power of His resurrection and the fellowship of His sufferings, being conformed to His death."

Key Words: Transfigure and Transform (to change); Conform (being like).

Matthew 17:2: "And He was transfigured before them; and His face shone like the sun, and His garments became as white as light."

Romans 12:2: "And do not be conformed to this world, but be transformed by the renewing of your mind, that you may prove what the will of God is, that which is good and acceptable and perfect."

2 Corinthians 3:18: "But we all, with unveiled face beholding as in a mirror the glory of the Lord, are being transformed into the same image from glory to glory, just as from the Lord, the Spirit."

---

4. *Ibid.*

CHAPTER 4

Philippians 3:21: *"Who will transform the body of our humble state into conformity with the body of His glory, by the exertion of the power that He has even to subject all things to Himself."*

Interestingly, *transfigure* in Matthew 17:2 is a translation of the same Greek word that is used in the above three verses, translated as *transform*.

Transform/Transfigure: *metamorphoo*: to change into another form. *Meta* = change; *morphe* = form. Romans 12:2: "The obligation being to undergo a complete change which, under the power of God, will find expression in character and conduct." "2 Corinthians 3:18: describes believers as being 'transformed into the same image' (i.e., of Christ in all His moral excellencies), the change being effected by the Holy Spirit."[5]

Inform: Hebrew meaning: to perceive, discern; understanding, insight.[6] Latin meaning: in + form = to put form or shape to; that is, to form the mind or character by imparting instruction. Daniel 9:22: "And [Gabriel] gave me <u>instruction</u> and talked with me, and said, 'O Daniel, I have now come forth to give you insight with <u>understanding</u>.'"

These passages are pretty powerful, aren't they? I hope you can meditate on some of them.

B. Through the Lens of Story, seeing concepts in action:

What do these "form" to "transform" words have to do with suffering, deserved and undeserved? For better vision, let's look through both lenses, the lens of Statement/concept and the lens of Story.

We can turn to any person in the biblical record for illustration, beginning with Adam and Eve. King Saul and King David provide a clear contrast.

---

5. *Ibid.*
6. Hebrew-Greek Key Word Study Bible.

Consider (think, discuss, write):

How did the trials and testings of Saul and David change/form them (1 Samuel 9 through 2 Samuel; Psalms, such as Psalm 23 and 51)? Under pressure, did Saul become more godly or more self-willed and manipulative? Under pressure, sometimes David grew in character. When David gave in to pressure (temptation), what happened to his heart, character, and testimony? But what made David different from Saul in God's eyes? What is the impact of "life" upon each man's heart, life, and legacy? Describe their metamorphoses.

Consider (think, discuss, write):

Ponder one of your own stories—one incident of suffering in your life, maybe the first one that emerges in your thoughts. It may be an inconvenience, a loss, a tragedy, or a conflict (or combination). It impacted you. Are you different in any way from how you were before this? Probably this incident changed you. In what ways?

The incident. The time period.

Estimate:

The suffering: Deserved? Yes/No; Undeserved? Y/N; Mixture? Y/N.

Percentage: Deserved _____%; Underserved_____%; Mixture: _____%.

Personal contribution to the trouble: _____%.

Consider the incident's impact upon the following:

- Your attitudes, anxiety-fear-peace-rest factors.
- Your worldview, the way you frame this and other relationships now.
- Your responses, decisions and actions. Its impact on others.
- Your character growth/change.
- Describe your own metamorphosis.

Suffering changes us. Calamity changed Job and Joseph. An unfulfilled promise tested Abraham and Sarah. Longings for motherhood tormented Hannah. Unjustified persecution tested David. Sexual temptation defiled David and greatly harmed others. The list goes on.

CHAPTER 4

In all these narratives, each person was changed by the challenges he or she faced. The same is true for us. Each experience of disappointment, conflict, inconvenience, or tragedy will change us for the better or for the worse. Our character will be informed and formed. We can become deformed or transformed. But we are never unchanged.

The Psalmist claims, *"It was good for me that I was afflicted, that I may learn Thy statutes"* (Psalm 119:71). This verse helps me understand an observation Martin Luther made. Luther claimed three things are required in order to make a theologian (and we are PTs!): prayer, meditation on God's Word, and affliction.[7] Affliction mixed with prayer and Scripture shows us our immediate and continuous need for His guidance, and convinces us to change direction now (repent) and to follow after Him. This process is the learning process.

This is that "more complex kind of good" which C.S. Lewis wrote about. This kind of good does not create good from nothing, *ex nihilo*, as God did during the creation week. That was in The Original Cosmos in which 1 + 1 equaled 2. Straightforward. No interception. No added factor.

> **However, in This Broken Cosmos, our Good God works**
> **through life's twisting maze to bring good out of garbage:**
> my sin, your sin, the mix of our sin,
> including the travail of captive creation
> (hurricane, tornado, tsunami, wildfire, flood, pandemic...),
> the insane tragedy of bizarre accidents
> (a person killed by a drunk driver; a forgotten child dying in car seat in hot car),
> the malevolence of terror, war...
> all these mixed together,
> making life messy, messy, messy,
> but never meaningless.

---

7. Here are two secondary sources: https://www.desiringgod.org/articles/luthers-rules-for-how-to-become-a-theologian. Piper provides you the primary source at the end of his delightful article. Here is another online essay: https://scriptorium-daily.com/how-to-be-a-theologian-by-martin-luther.

Through This Broken Cosmos, God demonstrates His character and competence through His goodness transformed into "complex good." Do you trust God's competence?

Through our suffering we have profound opportunities to be exposed to God's glory. Our understanding of and respect for God can explode—if we let God's Word invade our life experience.

We need to observe and trust that God is at work. Providentially. Patiently. Longsufferingly. Sovereignly. And if we don't "see" God working, we trust His wise leadership. He sees what we don't.

Interestingly,
just as faith is a function of knowledge ("By faith we understand..." [Heb. 11:3]),
so trust is a function of transformation.
Trust is the caterpillar's midwife.

Biblical Statements that Explain Our Stories

Before asserting it was good he was afflicted, the Psalmist admits what he was like before he suffered.

"Before I was afflicted, I went astray, but now I keep Thy word" (Ps. 119:67). Isaiah 53:6 reminds me that *"all we like sheep have gone astray; we have turned everyone to his own way."* Going astray is sinning. We sin because our natural allegiance is to ourselves: we *want* our own way. This is the substance of our fallen nature. Suffering brings us to the crisis of change.

If we learn by affliction to turn to God (repentance) and keep His word (obedience), then our suffering works for good. In theology, we call this the process of "sanctification" (Rom. 6:22; 1 Thes. 4:3; Heb. 12:14). We call this forming work of the Holy Spirit transformation and character building: Christ's character being formed in us. However, it is even more than this! But first, write out these verses or the key ideas in these verses:

- Romans 8:28-29
- Romans 5:3-5

List some adjectives describing the character of Christ being formed in us.

4.3 ADJUSTING THE FOCUS

Though we may never fully understand why,
the road to transformation
always goes through the tunnel of trials.
If you are on a road that does not include trials,
it is not the road to transformation.
God wants us to be changed
into the character likeness of Christ,
so He allows pain to come into our lives,
then He uses that pain to make us more like His Son.[8]

For the JOY He Endured the Cross

Dr. Ander's encouragement introduces the element of joy by showing us God's excellent purpose. You remember that Jesus, *"for the joy set before Him endured the cross, despising the shame, and has sat down at the right hand of the throne of God"* (Hebrews 12:2b).

Do you see how JOY is a perspective, a vision? Do you see how it infuses us with strength, resilience, and tenacity? Joy is not a silly, fluffy thing. It is not an insult to our pain.

Joy is a lifeline, graced from God's near hand.

---

8. Max Anders, *21 Unbreakable Laws of Life* (Nashville: Thomas Nelson, Inc., 1996), 180. Centering and line division added.

There are many flavors of joy suitable for various afflictions. Our need at times may be for a joy that is the gentle joy of quiet humility. We need this when facing our Recompensive Suffering. When facing our Collateral Suffering, we'll need that quiet humility, but we may also need the noisy, releasing comfort flowing from lament. Comfort is a flavor of joy, and God is "the God of all comfort" (2 Corinthians 1:3-4). Whatever the flavor of divine joy, it is a gift. All joy gifts are strong and transformative.

Transformed through Lament

The Irish poet Thomas Moore (1779-1852) penned the following words which remind us an important way to draw close to God (James 4:8) is through the process of lament.[9] Lament expresses grief, sorrow, regret, and anguish through prayer and tears. Listen to Moore's words:

"Come, ye disconsolate, wherever ye languish. Come to the mercy-seat, fervently kneel. Here bring your wounded hearts. Here tell your anguish. Earth has no sorrow that heaven cannot heal. Joy of the desolate, light of the straying, hope of the penitent, fadeless and pure. Here speaks the Comforter, tenderly saying, Earth has no sorrow that heaven cannot cure."[10]

- How does this vision of heavenly cure change your view? How does it comfort you?

Comfort is a flavor of joy. Note the joy chart in the appendices. How ironic that lament, our expression to God of anguish, can open our heart's door to let God draw close to us through His comforting presence. Do you see how sorrow and joy can healingly dance together? Selah.

- Reread Moore's lyrics. Can you identify with the need, respond to the invitation, and accept the comfort?

---

9. In chapter 5 of Gerald W. Peterman and Andrew J. Schmutzer book, *Between Pain & Grace* (Chicago: Moody Press, 2016), Schmutzer explains the importance of lament. This chapter entitled "Longing to Lament: Returning to the Language of Suffering" may help you develop your language of lament as you respond to the Lord's presence. In this travel guide, we will return to lament at times, and you can whenever you feel the need.

10. While Thomas Moore wrote the poem, Thomas Hastings (1784-1872), a church musician, altered some of the words and changed the third stanza.

CHAPTER 4

The following is the best vision that "speaks" to our lament and brokenness and transforms us. It sums up everything I've written thus far and propels us into the best that suffering and joy offer.

You may want to take a break and come to the following with fresh eyes. In one sitting, read meditatively the following. Also read as many of the given references you can. What light does this shed on Transformative Suffering and Joy?

Such Glorious Radiance and Representation

When we look at Jesus, we see no strong points. None.

What?

"Strong points necessarily presuppose weak ones, but no weaknesses can be alleged of Him.... He was without flaw or contradiction," writes J. Oswald Sanders in his excellent book *The Incomparable Christ*.[11] "The character of our Lord was wonderfully balanced, with neither excess nor deficiency" explains Sanders. Christ's character "stands out faultlessly perfect, so symmetrical in all its proportions that its strength and greatness are not immediately obvious to the casual observer." Take a deep breath. Ponder such a Savior.

Then consider we are not called to be casual observers of Jesus. We are called to be His followers *"looking unto Jesus, the author* [archegos: originator] *and finisher* [teleiotes: end, goal] *of faith; who for the joy set before Him, endured the cross, despising the shame..."* (Heb. 12:2). Moreover, we are called to become like Him (2 Cor. 3:18; Rom. 8:28-29; 1 Pet. 2:21). I need some more deep breaths! Such overwhelming realities! Clearly, I see purpose and meaning in life in this fallen world. I see beauty and truth. I hold on to hope.

J. Oswald Sanders reminds us Christ's person is utter perfection: perfectly balanced and symmetrical; no strengths stand out because strengths necessitate weaknesses. Christ has no weaknesses, but our weaknesses provide cavities for His strengths to fill (2 Cor. 12:9-11).

---

11. J. Oswald Sanders, *The Incomparable Christ*, (Chicago: Moody Press, 1952), 2.

Jesus is *"the radiance of His glory and the exact representation of His nature..."* (Heb. 1:3). How stunning it is to realize God's plan, working through our trials, is to make us like the second Adam—Christ. However, we are not a remedial, "character-education" project. This is a "Christ-living-in-me" relationship: *"To live is Christ and to die is gain"* (Phi. 1:21). As we begin to grasp this, we discover increasing endurance, hope, and joy. *"But we all, with unveiled face beholding as in a mirror the glory of the Lord, are being transformed into His image from glory to glory..."* (2 Corinthians 3:18).

Disharmonious and frail as we presently are, we are being transformed. God in the radiance of Christ is recovering His image in us, shaping us into His Son's beautiful bride. Deep breath. Ponder such glorious radiance and representation—shared with us.

4.4 TREKKING THE TRAIL

"Consider" is an accounting term. We have three thoughts to consider: 1) the worth, 2) the joy, and 3) the providential irony. Discuss, write below, or sojournal some responses to the following:

1. The Worth:

"For I consider that the sufferings of this present time are not worthy to be compared with the glory that is to be revealed to us" (Rom. 8:18). Your Recompensive and Collateral pain are real, mixed together, and they seek to transform you.

"Will I ever be the same?" we asked at the beginning of this chapter. What we want is to be out of our affliction. Would a positive answer produce a positive result? Would you want to be the person you were before troubles? Probably not. Where is the hope? It is not in who or where we were, but in who you and I are becoming.

Is it worth it to you to become as lovely as Christ so to become fit to be His bride?

2. The joy: This is our theme passage:

"Consider it all joy, my brethren when you encounter various trials, knowing that the testing of your faith produces endurance. And let endurance have its perfect result, that you may be perfect and complete, lacking in nothing" (James 1:2-4).

Reread J. Oswald Sander's description of our Savior who has no strengths because He has no weaknesses. This is completeness.

Can your "various trials" discover a good home in the "joy column," not the "meaningless suffering column," because you now see the deep meaning in them?

Can you receive the joy from the glorious vision of our Incomparable Bridegroom?

Can you receive the joy from such a daring vision of who *we* are to become as His Christly Complement? How do you respond?

3. The Irony:

Since Christ is complete, He needs no complement. So why would He want us as His bride? Such irony. Such love. How do you respond?

"For we are His workmanship [Christ-formed masterpiece] created in Christ Jesus for good works, which God prepared beforehand that we should walk in them" (Eph. 2:10).

Consider this irony.

When I aim to straighten out some injustice (Collateral Suffering) or fix some folly (Recompensive Suffering), my aim may largely be toward circumstances and players within those circumstances. My aim is probably toward some project or mission. But when I see the mission as God's work of forming Christ in me and in you, then I realize the injustice and folly are the tools God is using to do so.

I am God's mission and masterpiece-in-making. You are His mission and masterpiece.

The more I "fix my eyes on Jesus" (Hebrews 12:2) and pour out my heart to Him continually, the less I fixate on what I cannot fix. With our eyes on the Lord who is shaping Christ in us through our circumstances, we discover good work to do—to the benefit of others—which ironically may possibly help to correct some injustice upon which I once fixated and folly I could not fix. In this process, suffering of every stripe is succored. Meaning and joy blossom.

Have you experienced an irony like this? Explain.

4.5 REST STOP

Yes, let's rest. Let's meditate on our Guidepost.

GUIDEPOST

*Consider it all joy, my brethren when you encounter various trials,
knowing that the testing of your faith produces endurance.
And let endurance have its perfect result, that you may be perfect
and complete, lacking in nothing.* (James 1:2-4)

Maybe there are some other Scriptures you've traveled through in this chapter you'd like to review. You may want to sojournal about the passages or write out a prayer response.

In closing I'll give you a lovely hymn with lyrics by Jean S. Pigott to read or sing in worship and rest.

*Jesus, I am resting, resting in the joy of what Thou art;
I am finding out the greatness of Thy loving heart.
Thou hast bid me gaze upon Thee, and Thy beauty fills my soul,
For by Thy transforming power, Thou hast made me whole.*

The Nine Discoveries

Tier 3 The Unexpected Views (Chapters 8,9,10)	7	8	9
Tier 2 The Winding Way Up (Chapters 5,6, 7)	4	+ 5	6
Tier 1 The Ground Under Our Feet (Chapters 2, 3, 4)	1	2	3

Read the chart from the bottom up. The completed chart is on pages 206-207.

Part II

Exploring New Territory:
THE WINDING WAY UP

In part I (chapters 1-4), we examined the ground under our feet, sampling the soil of the first tier of suffering and joy: Recompensive Suffering and Repentive Joy; Collateral Suffering and Redemptive Joy; and Transformative Suffering and Joy. In part II (chapters 5-7), we will explore the territory that Transformative Suffering and Joy have opened to us.

Our afflictions of all kinds—deserved, undeserved, and mixed—these afflictions present opportunities. God utilizes them as educational, disciplinary, and formative tools and opportunities (note 2 Timothy 3:16-17; Hebrews 12:10-11).

Most interestingly, in this second tier, a deeper dimension of transformative, maturing sorrow takes purposeful focus: the relational dimension. Winding our way up from the soil of sorrow mixed with blessing, we will explore new territory: Compassionate Suffering and Joy, Sacrificial Suffering and Joy, and Exemplary Suffering and Joy.

We will never experience the best that affliction has to offer us through God's "more complex" kind of good, until we open ourselves to being formed and transformed by our suffering.

CHAPTER 5

WHAT GOOD IS MY SUFFERING?

DISCOVERY FOUR

"Oh, I have suffered with those that I saw suffer!"[1]

What good is my suffering?

What happens within me that makes me open to being formed and transformed by the Holy Spirit through my limitations, disappointments, hurts, and wounds? Consider passages such as Romans 5:3-5.

Keep these questions in mind as you work through this chapter.

---

1. William Shakespeare, *The Tempest* (Act I, Scene 2), Miranda dialoguing with her father.

CHAPTER 5

5.1 TRAVEL SCOPE

We will discover the fourth category or genre, Compassionate Suffering and Joy, which introduces the second tier, the deeply relational triad, discovered in the Scriptures and experienced in our lives

GUIDEPOST

Blessed be the God and Father of our Lord Jesus Christ, the Father of mercies and God of all comfort, who comforts us in all our affliction so that we will be able to comfort those who are in any affliction with the comfort with which we ourselves are comforted by God. (2 Corinthians 1:3-4)

We can ask ourselves "What good is my suffering?"

To start with, it is the fellowship of suffering with others. Compassionate suffering is the fellowship of suffering with others, sharing in their grief and owning it collectively—not totally, but to degrees (Gal. 6:1-10)—as Christ has owned mankind's afflictions—totally, not in degrees (Col. 2:13-15).

While many nonbelievers and many immature believers will opt out of sharing other's sufferings, believers growing in Christ and Christ-likeness will embrace it. Biblical compassion is rooted in God's mercy, which is rooted in His agape love.

The English word *compassion* comes from the Latin prefix *com*, meaning *together* and *passion*, meaning *pathos* or *suffering*. Interestingly, the word is related to *compass*, which is composed of *com*, meaning together, and *pass*, meaning step. Of course, when most people hear the word *compass* they think of a tool providing direction. The root meaning is to step together. Such is also the nature of compassion—to step together with someone in his/her sorrow, sharing that sorrow, carrying some of the weight. To speak of compassion is to speak of both suffering and joy, so this category, Compassionate Suffering and Joy, is actually redundant. Compassion says it all, but we will use the full term.

5.2 VIEWING THE BIBLICAL MAP

Biblical Declaratives and Imperatives

Let's explore Jesus's invitations recorded in Matthew 11:28-30.

Come to me, all you who are weary and burdened, and I will give you rest. Take my yoke upon you and learn from me, for I am gentle and humble in heart, and you will find rest for your souls. For my yoke is easy and my burden is light.

We have just read eight clauses. Three are imperatives. Five are declaratives. Let's look again.

Imperative clauses/sentences (giving directions or commands):

1. Come to me, all you who are weary and burdened.
2. Take my yoke upon you.
3. Learn from me.

Since the subject of these sentences is the assumed "you" (the hearer), the sentence begins with the verb.

Declarative clauses/sentences (stating claims, making affirmations, or giving information):

1. I will give you rest.
2. I am gentle and humble in heart.
3. You will find rest for your souls.

4. My yoke is easy.
5. My burden is light.

When pedestrian theologians are in step with Christ, He compassionately carries the bulk of the weight, if we will let Him.

Christ participates in our suffering, just as we are invited to participate in the sufferings of Christ.

Is this shared suffering? Compassionate Suffering? Can you identify quiet joys in rest, comfort, and compassion?

Sojournal Suggestion: Copy Matthew 11:28-30. Then explain how this works out in your life. How do you yoke up with Christ? How do you share the load and accept some quiet joys?

More Scriptural Statements:

Circle "I" or "D" to identify an **Imperative** or **Declarative** clause/statement in bold print.

- 1 Peter 4:13: "But to the degree that you share the sufferings of Christ, **keep on rejoicing. . . ." I or D**
- Philippians 3:10: "**That I may know Him,** and the power of His resurrection and the fellowship of His sufferings, being conformed to His death. . . ." **I or D**

The first is an imperative statement: "keep on rejoicing." Do this!

The second is a declarative statement: "that I may know Him. . . ." It affirms a truth aim or claim.

Now read the following passage straight through. Read it a second time and mark declarative clauses or statements with parentheses ( ). I don't think you will find any imperatives. I marked verses three through four for you. Use a colored pen or pencil. You may divide verses into clauses differently, but you are breaking down clusters of meaning into thought-bites on which to chew.

2 Corinthians 1:3-11

³ (Blessed be the God and Father of our Lord Jesus Christ, the Father of mercies and God of all comfort,) ⁴ (who comforts us in all our affliction) (so that we will be able to comfort those) (who are in any affliction with the comfort with which we ourselves are comforted by God.) ⁵ For just as the sufferings of Christ are ours in abundance, so also our comfort is abundant through Christ. ⁶ But if we are afflicted, it is for your comfort and salvation; or if we are comforted, it is for your comfort, which is effective in the patient enduring of the same sufferings which we also suffer; ⁷ and our hope for you is firmly grounded, knowing that as you are sharers of our sufferings, so also you are sharers of our comfort.⁸ For we do not want you to be unaware, brethren, of our affliction which came to us in Asia, that we were burdened excessively, beyond our strength, so that we despaired even of life; ⁹ indeed, we had the sentence of death within ourselves so that we would not trust in ourselves, but in God who raises the dead; ¹⁰ who delivered us from so great a peril of death, and will deliver us, He on whom we have set our hope. And He will yet deliver us, ¹¹ you also joining in helping us through your prayers, so that thanks may be given by many persons on our behalf for the favor bestowed on us through the prayers of many.

Paul rolls out lots of clauses (whether a series of clauses in a sentence or a stand-alone sentence), but you can see that all these clauses are declaratives: making claims, giving affirmations, or stating information. Ahh.

These verses could be further broken down into phrases with key words highlighted. This is a good way to meditate on Scripture. Let's try the following.

Take the primary colors red, blue, and yellow.

In the above passage highlight the key words listed below (in any form you find them, such as suffering, suffer, suffered). How many times is each of the following used?

CHAPTER 5

- Comfort: _____ times
- Affliction/Suffering: _____ times
- Share/Join: _____ times

After identifying Paul's focal points in this passage of cascading declaratives, what do you see as God's message to us?

Let's look more closely at the word translated comfort *paraklesis* the noun; *parakaleo* the verb: *para* = alongside or near, plus *kaleo* = to call. To call near. To encourage, strengthen, or admonish. The comforting referenced in our passage is not a shallow, "Oh, there, there. It'll be all right!" response. God is not offering us a "security blanket," such as Charles Schultz provided for Linus in his Peanuts comic strip.

No, this comfort is an encouragement (to infuse with courage) that strengthens. This process only happens in the truth and the spirit of the Spirit of the Lord. This comfort from God to us and through us to others is a spiritual strengthening producing over time spiritual, mental, emotional, volitional, and behavioral resilience. This is a fruit of the Spirit (Gal. 5:22-23).

Remember that courage is a flavor of joy.[2] This comfort conjoins joy with suffering. The joy is confidence in God's nearness to us and faith in God's goodness working through "this."

This comfort is Compassionate Suffering and joy. How do these ideas impact you? Would you live to give this kind of comfort? Would you like to receive it?

Biblical Story

Let's consider some examples of Compassionate Suffering and Joy. This is a very moving journey. It may quiet your soul (Ps. 46:10). We've viewed God's suffering before. We'll never see all there is to see.

---

2. Travel to the appendices to look up *joy* in the Vocab Café and *joy* in the charts. *Courage* is listed as a *joy* word under the Greek *tharsein*. It would be good to add *parakaleo* to the list as part of the semantic range of joy terms.

The Godhead suffers alongside, with, and for his own creation.[3]

Elohim, you remember, is the initial name for God that Scripture identifies. "In the beginning, Elohim created the heavens and the earth" (Gen. 1:1). Elohim is the Creator. Elohim, the generic name for God, is combined with YHWH, a personal name, beginning in Genesis 2:4, and is translated LORD God.

In Genesis, the story unfolds.
The characters: God, the first couple, and the serpent.
The time: in the beginning.
The setting: the cosmos, then zooming in on the Garden of Eden.
The story begins spectacularly, regally, splendidly, smoothly.

Then a new element of "story" is introduced. Today, we do not recognize a story (fiction or historical) without this element. It has become as essential to storytelling as are characters, setting, plot, and theme. Actually, it is an element of theme and plot. We call it *conflict*. The involvement of the supernatural realm, the spiritual warfare realm of conflict is another dimension that should be explored in this theological journey, but I can only point to it now and encourage you to consider the ramifications as you develop your theological framework.

Conflict changes the texture of story itself. It changes the journey of human development. However, the impact of conflict is that it exposes more facets of His infinite and true identity to His finite creatures. You know the story. Read again Genesis's first three chapters.

At the very first opportunity to suffer, God grieves.

"Where are you?" the Lord God (YHWH Elohim) calls to the man and woman (Gen. 3:9). In their relationship, there has been no disunity. No estrangement. Yes, no conflict. The

---

3. To study further the topic of the suffering Godhead, you will find two helpful chapters in *Between Pain & Grace* by Gerald W. Peterman and Andrew J. Schmutzer. Chapter three: "The Suffering of God: Compassion in Vulnerability" and chapter four: "A Man of Sorrows: Emotions and the Suffering of Jesus."

couple has always been there in the garden ready to commune with God "in the cool of the day" or at any time! No alienation. No separation. But this day, neither is ready to see God. They hear God's question and hide. Why?

The couple has contradicted the very command of God. Their opposition, instigated by the serpent-enemy of God, has broken the unity and has introduced conflict.

Omniscient God knows where the primal couple is, that Adam and Eve have succumbed to this cosmic-altering temptation, and that their hearts have welcomed an oppositional inclination, an alternative loyalty. An allegiance not to Him, who designed them and infinitely loves them. They don't know how they've changed. They don't know exactly what it is that has died within them, but they now know shame and regret. There is no going back. Conflict, the interloper, is now an unavoidable constant.

God knows—in His infinite existence in the simultaneous past, present, and future—He knows their pain more than they do or ever will. God's question reveals God's perfect sadness. "Where are you?' They are not where they should be. More divine questions follow.

"Who told you that you were naked?" (Up to now, this was not an innate knowledge.) "Have you eaten from the tree of which I commanded you not to eat?" "What is this you have done?"

God does not need to ask any questions. He knows. Nor does He need to offer a redemptive course. He could have issued, then and there, the complete consequence He has promised for disobedience: "for in the day that you eat from it you shall surely die" (Genesis 2:17).

God's providential plan was made before the foundation of the world. However, that blueprint could have included a plan to destroy, should His creatures rebel, and to recreate a subsequent cosmos, doing this again and again until a vulnerable cosmos (one that must pass a test of loyalty) chose invulnerability through constant, loving obedience to its Creator. Ah. Unlikely.

Hypotheticals are impossible to pursue, but just acknowledging their possibility underscores the compassion of God, who instead chooses to pay the price to fix what humans have broken, submitting Himself to enter into and absorb the suffering of the world.

God's suffering begins with a compassion that shares in the suffering of His creatures.[4]

First, God shares in the sufferings of Adam and Eve by providing clothing to cover their nakedness. God is the first killer, slaying one of His own beloved creatures. This animal becomes the first in creation to experience Collateral Suffering. God sheds its blood in order to provide covering for His beloved first couple on whom He has etched His own image. This act foreshadows His long-term plan of salvation through His Suffering Servant. In compassion He never abandons His own.

* * *

From the beginning, God has allowed suffering, entered suffering, and submitted His entire creation to suffering (Rom. 8:18-20-22). Suffering is a major component of God's "more complex," ultimate good. We have seen that the Creator God exhibits Compassionate Suffering.

We have considered Jesus as the perfect example of the One who suffers with us, humbly carrying our load, suffering for us, taking away our sins.

And we can see the Holy Spirit shares in the suffering also:

"And do not grieve the Holy Spirit of God, by whom you were sealed for the day of redemption" (Ephesians 4:30).

---

4. Genesis 3:21 says, "And the Lord God made garments of skin for Adam and his wife, and clothed them." The skin was animal skin, not from plant life, prefiguring the sacrificial system to come, which would culminate in Christ's all sufficient sacrifice for sin. God "made": this word is from *asah*, a work of constructing from existing material, not an *ex nihilo* act of creation. Human sin exacts negative consequences upon more than mankind.

CHAPTER 5

Grief can be a deep work of suffering for others. Let's chart some key points revealing the grief of the Godhead.

The Holy Grief of God

God the Father	God the Son	God the Holy Spirit	Observations
Genesis 6:6 "And the Lord was sorry that He had made man ... and He was grieved in His heart." Psalm 78:40 "How often they rebelled against Him in the wilderness, and grieved Him in the desert!"	Isaiah 53:3, 4, 10 "He was despised and forsaken of men, a man of sorrows, and acquainted with grief.... Surely our griefs He Himself bore, and our sorrows He carried." "But the LORD was pleased to crush Him, putting Him to grief." Mark 3:5 "And after looking around at them with anger, grieved at their hardness of heart, He said to the man, "Stretch out your hand.: And ...his hand was restored."	Isaiah 63:10 "But they rebelled and grieved His Holy Spirit...." Ephesians 4:30 "And do not grieve the Holy Spirit of God, by whom you were sealed for the day of redemption."	Mark 3:5 places anger and grief together in Jesus. Note that the Father and the Holy Spirit exhibit the same holy quality: Psalm 95:8-11, quoted in Hebrews 3:7-11. God's anger over their hardness of heart involves grief, which begins to explain Isaiah 53:10: "The LORD was pleased to crush Him, putting Him to grief." In Is. 63:10-14, the H. S. grieved because of their rebellion, which placed them as enemies of God. Yet it was the H.S. who gave them rest, "to make for Thyself a glorious name."

Discuss or consider: how does the holy grief of the Godhead illustrate Compassionate Suffering?[5]

Where flows Compassionate Joy?

---

5. Because these passages are imbedded in various narratives, you will be distracted with many questions. Very good. However, we must stick to our purposes in drawing upon these situations, so stick to the main issue of how these verses illustrate Compassionate Suffering by the Godhead.

It flows from passion. While passion is suffering, it is suffering drawn from the deepest of loves—where we find the home of joy. We joy in what and whom we love. Without real love there would be no passion, nothing for which to suffer and to save. People ask, "What is your passion?" People advise, "Follow your passion." In this context, passion is used as the deepest calling of the heart's love. For God, that deepest calling was toward us and toward the creation in which He placed us. Such love called for compassionate action, where we'll travel in our next chapter on Sacrificial Suffering and Joy.

5.3 ADJUSTING THE FOCUS

Adjusting our focus from divine examples to human examples of Compassionate Suffering and Joy, we could spend much time examining the lives of Jeremiah in the Old Testament and the Apostle Paul in the New Testament. Let's just sample a bit of Paul's attitudes and actions.

In Romans 9:1-3, Paul exclaims, *"I am telling the truth in Christ, I am not lying, my conscience bearing me witness in the Holy Spirit, that I have great sorrow and unceasing grief in my heart. For I could wish that I myself were accursed, separated from Christ for the sake of my brethren, my kinsmen according to the flesh."* Amazing! This shows Paul's passionate compassion toward his own people, the Jewish people.

We have read in 2 Corinthians chapter 1 about Paul's compassionate posture toward the Gentiles given to him through the comfort of God Himself to pass on to the believers and for them to pass on to others.

Reread this passage and then read 2 Corinthians chapter 7. At some point you need to study the context, but even a simple reading gives us clues into Compassionate Suffering and joy exhibited here. Verse six through seven explain:

> *But God, who comforts the depressed, comforted us by the coming of Titus; and not only by his coming, but also by the comfort with which he was comforted in you, as he reported to us your longing, your mourning, your zeal for me; so that I rejoiced even more.*

Wow! Don't you want to know more about the situation? Note that Titus is the one who is comforting Paul (and Timothy) now. In chapter one, Paul was comforting/encouraging the Corinthians by pointing them to God who comforts/strengthens us so we can comfort/encourage others. Now, in chapter 7, Paul reports that Titus comforted him, after Titus was comforted/encouraged by the Corinthians, which in turn comforted/strengthened Paul, but now Paul describes his comfort as his increased rejoicing! Yes, comfort/encouragement is a flavor of joy that incites our joy—often a quiet but very deep joy.

- How does the Apostle Paul model the teaching of the Apostle Peter who wrote, *"For you have been called for this purpose, since Christ also suffered for you, leaving you an example for you to follow in His steps"* (1 Peter 2:21)?
- How does compassionate joy grow from the soil of compassionate suffering?

5.4 TREKKING THE TRAIL

Consider the following. Discuss your insight.

- Since God suffers, the Son suffers, the Holy Spirit suffers, all of creation suffers, and every human being suffers, how can my suffering lead me into Compassionate Suffering and Joy with others? How am I being changed?
- How can I specifically practice the principles I see in this chapter's Guidepost passage?

GUIDEPOST

*Blessed be the God and Father of our Lord Jesus Christ,
the Father of mercies and God of all comfort, who comforts us
in all our affliction so that we will be able to comfort those who are
in any affliction with the comfort with which we ourselves
are comforted by God.* (2 Corinthians 1:3-4)

Remember a time when you were dealing with something very hurtful, and then you were really encouraged and comforted by someone (a family member, friend, or acquaintance). Think about what you know about that person. Why was she/he so affective and effective in comforting you? Can you find an element of joy in giving or receiving comfort? Share your story and insight or write about it in your SoJournal. Maybe you would like to write this person a thank you card.

5.5 REST STOP

What I love about Compassionate Suffering and Joy is the mesmerizing dance between passion as deep sorrow and passion as persistently calling joy in which both find their source in the depths of divine love. Passion as love-drenched suffering and passion as joy-drenched love cannot be separated. They are conjoined in one heart. How good!

While the weight of suffering in this world is just too much for any of us to bear, we are not asked to bear it but to share its bearing with our God who bears it and with each other as we are one in the Body of Christ.

Therefore, when Jesus invites us to come to Him, I am consoled, comforted, encouraged, and cheered. *"Come to me, all you who are weary and burdened, and I will give you rest. Take my yoke upon you and learn from me, for I am gentle and humble in heart, and you will find rest for your souls. For my yoke is easy and my burden is light"* (Matt. 11:28-30).

Oh my! How good! And what is the proper human response to God's goodness?

At this rest stop, I come to Jesus. I meditate upon His affirmations. I respond to His imperatives. I accept His comfort—from the God of all comfort.

I offer you the same comfort/encouragement God is giving me. As you are drenched in it, may you splash it on everyone near you (Rom. 5:3-5).

CHAPTER 5

We began this chapter by asking, "What good is my suffering?" What reply would you now give?

Meditate upon the following hymn. What added dimensions of Compassionate Suffering and Joy do you find in these verses?

In Christ There is No East or West[6]

In Christ there is no East or West,
In Him no South or North;
But one great fellowship of love
Throughout the whole wide earth.

In Him shall true hearts everywhere
Their high communion find;
His service is the golden cord,
Close binding humankind.

Join hands, then, members of the faith,
Whatever your race may be!
Who serves My Father as His child
Is surely kin to Me.

In Christ now meet both East and West,
In Him meet North and South;
All Christly souls are one in Him
Throughout the whole wide earth.

* * *

---

6. John Oxenham was a pseudonym for William Arthur Dunkerly (1852-1941), an English journalist, novelist, poet, magazine editor, church deacon, and even a town mayor.

"Lord, help me learn the ministry of simply being present in someone's pain. Teach me to put aside my own discomfort or need to fix things and simply offer silence and coffee."[7]

* * *

This chapter prepares us for the next chapter on Sacrificial Suffering and Joy, which is the center of our theology, our pascharology—the place where the cross of Christ crosses the center of all suffering and joy. You will need more time for the next chapter. Prayerfully ponder while you study.

---

7. Stacy Edwards, *Devotions from the Front Porch* (Nashville, TN: Thomas Nelson, 2016), 207.

CHAPTER 6

"FATHER, WHERE IS THE LAMB?" "LORD, WHAT IS MY SACRIFICE?"

DISCOVERY FIVE

"Father?" asks Isaac on Mount Moriah one chilly morning. "The fire and the wood are here, but where is the lamb for the burnt offering" (Gen. 22:7). The New Testament answers Isaac's question. The Lamb, "chosen before the creation of the world," (1 Pet. 1:20), "the Lamb who was slain from the creation of the world" (Rev. 13:8) is "revealed in these last times for your sake" (1 Pet. 1:20). The ram caught in the thicket, God's provision for Abraham and Isaac, prefigures the "Lamb of God who takes away the sin of the world" (John 1:29).

Notice the *seeming* sleight of hand I've done here. This chapter is about sacrificial suffering and joy, but I lead with the story of Isaac and his father, Abraham, on Mount Moriah. Isaac asks, "Where is the lamb for the burnt offering?" not "Where is the sacrifice?" There it is. The offering (a lamb; where is it?) is a sacrifice (in this case, a "burnt offering") and a sacrifice is an offering. And so it is.

CHAPTER 6

> A sacrifice is an offering.
> But there are different kinds of offerings.
> No matter what kind, the offering or sacrifice is a gift.
> To the giver, the gift is a loss; to the receiver, the gift is a gain.
> To the giver and receiver, the sacrifice draws a circle of love.

6.1 TRAVEL SCOPE

In this chapter we will explore Sacrificial Suffering and Joy:

- We will explore biblical concepts of sacrifice and sacrificial suffering.
- We will then consider the role of sacrificial suffering in our own lives.
- We will also find the connections between sacrifice, satisfaction, and joy.

GUIDEPOST

*But even if I am being poured out as a drink offering
upon the sacrifice and service of your faith,
I rejoice and share my joy with you all.* (Philippians. 2:17)

This is a scripturally dense chapter, so you need to traverse it at a rate which will not overwhelm you but will nourish you. Spread this chapter over a number of days and study sessions. Pray, pace, and savor.

"The measure of all love is its giving," wrote J.I. Packer.[1] Giving is the substance of sacrifice. Christ is the ultimate example of Sacrificial Suffering. But He is much more. Jesus is the fulfillment of the Old Testament sacrificial system, which points to the cross. As God, Christ gave Himself—an infinite, perfect, precious offering, fully suitable

---

1. J.I. Packer, *Redicovering Holiness*, (Grand Rapids, Michigan: Baker Books, 2009),70.

to purchase salvation for every human being. *"But God demonstrates His own love toward us, in that while we were yet sinners, Christ died for us. Much more then, having now been justified by His blood, we shall be saved from the wrath of God through Him"* (Rom. 5:8-9).

After accepting Christ's sacrificial gift for our own salvation (Eph. 2:8-9), we may ask, "Lord, what is my sacrifice?" Ephesians 2:10 show us God is preparing sacrificial opportunities for us. Through them we will experience the blessings of receiving and giving. Write out the verses of Ephesians 2:8-10, and keep them in the back of your mind as you work through this chapter.

6.2 VIEWING THE BIBLICAL MAP

> **Box 1**
>
> What you need to know about "sacrifice":
>
> A sacrifice is an offering. The Old Testament presents five different types of sacrifices or offerings (noted in the following box), but for our purposes, we need to pay attention to three main purposes for sacrifices:
>
> A. To make payment for a debt: propitiation, atonement, necessary to establish a relationship between God and man;
> B. To dedicate or sanctify; to devote something for a purpose;
> C. To offer thanksgiving: a Eucharistic expression.

The first biblical account of a sacrifice was in the story of Cain and Abel (Gen. 4).[2] Their sacrifices were not sacrifices to pay for sin. They were thanksgiving sacrifices, expressions of worship.

---

2. God did not accept Cain's offering. Zodhiates (in his *Key Word Study Bible* notes on Genesis 4) uses the NT to explain the OT: "Cain was not worshipping God in spirit or in truth (John 4:23, 24). When Cain saw that Abel was worshipping God properly (Heb. 11:4), he became angry and jealous. He hated his brother and murdered him (1 John 3:12). God is not unjust,

CHAPTER 6

The story of God, Abraham, Isaac, and the ram in Genesis 22 is an important story of sacrifice prefiguring or foreshadowing the story summarized in John 3:16. *"For God so loved the world that He gave His one and only son, that whoever might believe in Him would be saved."* This type of sacrifice is the giving of life, a payment or atonement.

For the wages of sin is death, but the free gift of God is eternal life in Christ Jesus our Lord. (Romans 6:23)

Approximately 1,400 years before Christ was born, the Lord God spoke to Moses and gave instructions regarding five kinds of sacrifices the Israelites were to practice (Lev. 1-7): 1) Burnt, 2) Grain, 3) Peace, 4) Sin, and 5) Guilt or Trespass Offerings. The last two offerings were required.

Box 2

The five kinds of offerings or sacrifices initiated by God through Moses:

Offering	Purpose	Significance
1. Burnt (Voluntary)	To surrender entirely to God & His will	Shows devotion
2. Grain (Voluntary)	To honor and worship God	Acknowledges God's Lordship & Provision
3. Peace (Voluntary)	To give thanks	Fellowship with God
4. Sin (Required)	To make payment for unintentional sin	Shows seriousness of sin; restores fellowship w/ God
5. Guilt or Trespass (Required)	To make payment for sins against God & others	Provides compensation for injured parties

The first three offerings, "sweet-savor offerings," were voluntary, while the last two were required offerings. Drink offerings (as mentioned in our theme verse) were added to burnt and grain offerings, both voluntary or free will.

---

and sin does not come upon us accidentally." God warned Cain, but he did not listen to God. Zodhiates notes, "Cain's sin began as all others sins begin, with a hostile attitude toward God which leads to disobedience."

To have a relationship with God, our sins must be paid for and forgiven. The first three offerings did not pay for sins, but for Old Testament believers whose sin and guilt were covered, the first three offerings represented godly responses to God's gracious forgiveness and offer of relationship.

Because Jesus Christ fulfilled all the requirements of the Old Testament law and sacrificial system, we don't need to practice these ceremonial offerings, but God does ask us for a sacrifice. According to Romans 12:1, what are we to sacrifice and why?

A. Considering Biblical Statements (Sample Declaratives)

The following are biblical statements declaring Christ's atoning, sacrificial work.[3] By stacking them up, one passage after another, they can create quite an impact on us.

Start with a prayerful heart, a highlighter or colored pencils, and your Bible. Slowly, read a verse and highlight key words or phrases. You may want to check out the context of a text. Talk to God about what He's revealing here. If there are too many references to process right now, choose a few on which to focus.

As you read and highlight, consider:

What insight do you gain, attitude and gratitude do you build, and response can you offer?

> *Genesis 3:15:* "*I will put enmity between you [Satan] and the woman, and between your seed and her seed [Christ]; He shall bruise you on the head, and you shall bruise him on the heal.*"

> *Isaiah 53:4-5:* "*Surely our griefs He Himself bore, and our sorrows He carried... He was pierced through for our transgressions...The chastening for our well-being fell upon Him, and by His scourging we are healed.*" (Note the chapter context.)

---

3. For further reading, try *The Passion of Jesus Christ* by John Piper (Wheaton, Illinois: Crossway Books, 2004). This is a highly recommended book to read while doing this study, especially for this chapter. Piper offers fifty purposes or reasons why Christ suffered and died. The short chapters, drenched in Scripture, totaling 122 pages, are deep yet easy to read. He answers the question, "What did God achieve for sinners like us in sending his Son to die?"

Mark 10:45: "*For even the Son of Man did not come to be served, but to serve, and to give His life a ransom for many.*"

John 3:16: "*For God so loved the world, that He gave His only begotten Son, that whoever believes in Him should not perish, but have eternal life.*"

Romans 3:23-25: "*For all have sinned and fall short of the glory of God, being justified as a gift by His grace through the redemption which is in Christ Jesus, whom God displayed publicly as a propitiation in His blood through faith. . . .*"

Romans 5:6-10: "*For while we were still helpless, at the right time Christ died for the ungodly. For one will hardly die for a righteous man; though perhaps for the good man someone would dare even to die. But God demonstrates His own love toward us, in that while we were yet sinners, Christ died for us. Much more then, having now been justified by His blood, we shall be saved from the wrath of God through Him. For if while we were enemies, we were reconciled to God through the death of His Son, much more, having been reconciled, we shall be saved by His life.*"

1 Corinthians 5:7b: "*For Christ our Passover also has been sacrificed.*"

2 Corinthians 5:21: "*He made Him who knew no sin to be sin on our behalf, that we might become the righteousness of God in Him.*"

Galatians 3:13-14: "*Christ redeemed us from the curse of the Law, having become a curse for us—for it is written, 'Cursed is everyone who hangs on a tree'—in order that in Christ Jesus the blessing of Abraham might come to the Gentiles, so that we might receive the promise of the Spirit through faith.*"

Ephesians 1:7-8a; 5:2: "*In Him we have redemption through His blood, the forgiveness of our trespasses, according to the riches of His grace, which He lavished upon us.*"

"*And walk in love, just as Christ also loved you, and gave Himself up for us, an offering and a sacrifice to God as a fragrant aroma.*"

Philippians 2:8: "*And being found in appearance as a man, He humbled Himself by becoming obedient to the point of death, even death on a cross.*"

Colossians 2:13-15: "*And when you were dead in your transgressions and the uncircumcision of your flesh, He made you alive together with Him, having forgiven us all our transgressions, having canceled out the certificate of debt consisting of decrees against us and which was hostile to us; and He has taken it out of the way, having nailed it to the cross. When He had disarmed the rulers and authorities, He made a public display of them, having triumphed over them through Him.*"

Hebrews 2:10: "*For it was fitting for Him, for whom are all things, and through whom are all things, in bringing many sons to glory, to perfect the author of their salvation through sufferings.*" *Note also chapters 9-10 in relation to Christ's sacrifice.*

1 Peter 3:18: "*For Christ also died for sins once for all, the just for the unjust, in order that He might bring us to God, having been put to death in the flesh, but made alive in the spirit.*"

Consider for thought, discussion, and/or sojournaling:

- What connections or parallels do you see between the five offerings or sacrifices practiced in the Old Testament and the New Testament teachings from the above verses?
- Read again Ephesians 2:8-10 and Romans 12:1-2.
- How may the OT voluntary sacrifices relate to Ephesians 2:10 and Romans 12:1?
- How do these connections inspire you? Influence your attitudes and decisions?

B. Considering Biblical Stories (Sample Narratives):

Now let's focus more directly on the three purposes for sacrifices or offerings and examples of each. Then, we will consider the satisfaction/joy that each produce. Finally, we will consider where and when we can participate in each of these three purposes of sacrificial sufferings and joys.

Box 3 Payment: Dedication: Thanksgiving:

Payment: Atonement, Propitiation	Dedication: Sanctification, Devotion	Thanksgiving: Eucharistic Expression
The One & Only Example: Jesus Christ	Many Examples	Many Examples
	Primary Example: Jesus	Primary Example: Jesus
Propitiation "refers to the removal of God's wrath by providing a substitute."	To devote means to set something apart for a purpose, to dedicate, consecrate, to commit.	The OT grain offering "acknowledged the bounty of God in providing....
The substitute is provided by God Himself. The substitute, Jesus Christ, does not just cancel the wrath; He absorbs it and diverts it from us to Himself. God's wrath is just, and it was spent, not withdrawn.	"On Calvary's altar the Lamb of God was totally consumed by the flames of divine justice"—like a burnt offering, without spot, totally devoted to the Lord.[5]	Symbolically this offering speaks of the moral perfection of the life of our Savior (fine flour), untainted by evil (no leaven), fragrant to God (frankincense), and filled with the Holy Spirit (oil)."[6]
"Let us not trifle with God or trivialize His love. We will never stand in awe of being loved by God until we reckon with the seriousness of our sin and the justice of His wrath against us. But when, by grace, we waken to our unworthiness, then we may look at the suffering and death of Christ and say, 'In this is love, not that we have loved God but that He loved us and sent His Son to be the [wrath-absorbing] propitiation for our sins' (1 John 4:10)."[4]	Secondary Example: Paul: Philippians 2:17	Secondary Example: King David:
	"But even if I am being poured out as a drink offering upon the sacrifice and service of your faith, I rejoice and share my joy with you all."	"The sacrifices of God are a broken spirit; a broken and contrite heart...." (Psalm 51:17).
	How does the Apostle Paul's life exemplify devotion?	In what verses in this psalm of repentance do you see David's gratitude?
	The Apostle Paul explains how we too can be devoted:	_____
Hebrews 12:2 "... who for the joy set before Him endured the cross...."	"Be devoted to one another in brotherly love; give preference to one another in honor; not lagging behind in diligence, fervent in spirit, serving the Lord; rejoicing in hope, persevering in tribulation, devoted to prayer, contributing to the needs of the saints, practicing hospitality" (Rom. 12:10-13).	"Through Him then, let us continually offer up a sacrifice of praise to God, that is, the fruit of lips that give thanks to His name" (Heb. 13:15).
	Consider examples from the lives of: Dietrich Bonhoeffer, Richard Wurmbrand, Jim Elliot, people you know.	Read Jeremiah 33:11 Consider examples from the lives of: John Newton, David Brainard, Elisabeth Elliot, people you know.

---

4. *Ibid*, 21.

5. William MacDonald. *Believer's Bible Commentary*, (Nashville: Thomas Nelson, 1990), 138.

6. *Ibid*. 139.

6.3 ADJUSTING THE FOCUS

We have seen a sacrifice is an offering; that there are required sacrifices to pay for sin and establish a relationship with God; and there are voluntary sacrifices to show sincere surrender, dedication, and gratitude to the Lord. We have seen Jesus Christ's death on the cross is the payment for our sin. *"For by grace are we saved through faith; it is a gift of God, not of works"* (such as ceremonial sacrifices) (Eph. 2:8-9).

What are the three purposes for sacrifices? (Note Box 1 and Box 3.)

A. To make payment for a debt (sin):
   Key words: Pro_____; At_____,
   necessary to establish a _____ with God.
B. To Dedicate or sanctify: to _____.
C. To offer _____: a Eucharistic expression.
D. As listed above, the first purpose, represented in the OT by the Sin and Guilt/Trespass Offerings, required sacrifices. The second and third purposes were represented by the burnt, grain, and peace offerings, which were not _____ but were _____.
E. The introduction noted this:
   To the giver, the gift is a loss; to the receiver, the gift is a gain.
   To the giver and receiver, the sacrifice draws a circle of love.

Because a sacrifice is a loss to the giver, we say the sacrifice is a form of suffering, the highest form of suffering. What did Christ lose in order to offer us the free gift of salvation and an eternal relationship with Him?

Christ has fulfilled the requirements of the sacrificial system: paying our debt and becoming the propitiation (satisfied justice) for us, which has reestablished a relationship between God and us. Under these conditions, we are invited to and enabled by the Holy Spirit to participate in the voluntary sacrificial purposes: to offer sacrifices of devotion and thanksgiving. Not through ceremony but through service.

CHAPTER 6

Our Sacrifices

How are these sacrifices which we can make truly sacrifices, truly suffering?

Our godly, language historian, Noah Webster, provides some fascinating perspective. We've been examining *sacrifice* as both a noun and a verb. In Webster's biblically drenched, original dictionary (1828), he gives a full definition of it as a noun, which you may want to explore, but let's consider his definition of *sacrifice* as a verb:

"To destroy, surrender or suffer to be lost for the sake of obtaining something." The past participle, "sacrificed," Webster defines as "suffered to be lost." He also defines the verb concisely as "to devote with loss."

Do you see something beautiful here? Does the Scripture bear this out? Is this a truly biblical concept?

To sacrifice: "To destroy, surrender or suffer to be lost for the sake of obtaining something."

"For the sake of obtaining something." Hmm. This tells us sacrifice and suffering have a positive purpose or goal. If this is true, then sacrificial suffering should move the sacrificer toward something good, valuable, desirable. Even to obtain joy?

Let's test this idea with Scripture. Read Isaiah 53:10-11. You'll want to look it up and read the chapter.

But the LORD was pleased to crush Him, putting Him to grief; If He would render Himself as a guilt offering.... And the good pleasure of the LORD will prosper in His hand. As a result of the anguish of His soul, He will see it and be satisfied;... My Servant will justify the many, as He will bear their iniquities.

The Sacrificial Suffering of Christ, as predicted by Isaiah, brought both grief and pleasure to the Godhead. Something was obtained by the suffering: the justifying of the many. God's justice and love were satisfied. Joy is the satisfaction of God's nature. Thus, Christ "endured the cross, despising the shame," explains Hebrews 12:2, "for the joy set before Him." Sacrificial Joy originates in God and is then offered to us through Christ and His joy.

God, in His infinite wisdom, determined the suffering was worth the results. Pain and affliction are never gratuitous (purposeless, worthless).

In Numbers 28-29, at least ten times God describes His response to proper offerings as "a sweet aroma" (NKJV) or "a soothing aroma" (NASB).[7] These sacrifices, described through the human sense of smell (anthropomorphic language), reveal God's attitude and posture toward the sacrificer, which brings satisfaction and joy to him/her as well! The sacrifice satisfies God's nature (His holy justice and loving goodness), bringing Him pleasure. This is God's joy, for the appropriate sacrifice (looking forward to Christ's fulfillment of the sacrificial system) has destroyed the barriers between man and God and has reestablished intimacy.

The sacrifice has brought glory to God through this re-alignment of relationship, which was God's eternal intention. Thus, grief produced joy: it pleased the LORD to put Him to grief (Isaiah 53:10); "for the joy set before Him He endured the cross, despising the shame" (Heb. 12:2).

When we accept His sacrifice for us, we walk into His joy. Have you walked into His joy?

There is also the issue of sacrifices that displease the Lord, on which we can only touch here. The book of Hosea presents a clear picture of this. In Hosea 9:4, Hosea claims Israel's "sacrifices will not please Him." It is impossible to please, to satisfy, to bring joy to God through religious practices, even good ones, which belie the state of the hearts of the people trying to reshape God into man's desired images.[8]

Neither Israel's practices nor heart orientation were good. "Since Ephraim has multiplied altars for sin, they have become altars of sinning for him," and therefore, "the LORD has

---

7. Numbers 28:2, 6, 8, 13, 24; 29:2, 6, 8, 13, 36
8. A reference to Cain and his offering may be appropriate here: Genesis 4.

taken no delight in them" (Hosea 8:11, 13). This is a sobering reminder to us that our worship, our sacrifice, cannot come from our own fanciful innovations but through biblical obedience (Rom. 12:1-2).

To sacrifice: "To destroy, surrender or suffer to be lost for the sake of obtaining something."

F. Let's consider the words of Jesus, spoken not long before His crucifixion.

Truly, truly, I say to you, unless a grain of wheat falls into the earth and dies, it remains by itself alone; but if it dies, it bears much fruit (John 12:24).

He who loves his life loses it; and he who hates his life in this world shall keep it to life eternal (John 12:25).

If anyone serves Me, let him follow Me; and where I am, there shall My servant also be; if anyone serves Me, the Father will honor him (John 12:26).

Each of these three verses contains so much nourishment that each can stand alone as a gripping quotation. The accumulative impact is greater. Now, we are considering our own role as sacrificers. Christ has been our sacrifice, and now we sacrifice our lives for Him and for His people and for the people of the world.

Think on all or some of the following questions. Discuss or sojournal your insights.

- What purpose is there for a grain of wheat that is not planted but does not die?
- What satisfaction or joy is there in being alone or solitary and purposeless?
- What is required in order to "bear much fruit?"
- What does this metaphor mean? What does it look like in your life?
- How does verse twenty-five explain verse twenty-four? What new piece of information is added in verse twenty-five?
- How does verse twenty-six explain verse twenty-five?
- What is "suffered to be lost" in these verses, and what is the something of greater value to be obtained?

G. This leads us directly to the little parable of "The Pearl of Great Price."

Again, the kingdom of heaven is like a merchant seeking fine pearls, and upon finding one pearl of great value, he went and sold all that he had and bought it. (Matthew 13:45-46)

- Is the price worth it?

Sacrificial Suffering and Joy have their origins in giving up something of lesser value for something of greater value.

Can it be that to God, the giving up of Himself, of His Son as the Suffering Servant, was a sacrifice for something greater than Himself? No. No. Certainly, humanity and creation are not greater than the Creator. However, the Creator chose to be the Lover. Yes. Yes. What is the relationship between love and joy?

As the Lover, He positioned Himself, willing to empty Himself, "taking the form of a bond-servant, and being made in the likeness of men.... He humbled Himself by becoming obedient to the point of death, even death on a cross" (Philipians 2:7-8). God in His infinite wisdom and love inscrutably ordained that sacrificial suffering was worth the price to secure sacrificial joy—the eternally fresh fruit of His own delight, shared forever with us. Selah!

- The story of "The Pearl of Great Price" is quite the opposite for us. What is there for us to sacrifice?

What do we have to lose that is of greater value than what we have to obtain or gain?

Can it be that to us, the giving up of ourselves (dead in sins as we are by our first nature) is a sacrifice worth making for something greater, for Someone greater than ourselves? Yes! Yes! (Actually, dead as we were, we could not choose, but that's another aspect of this ultimate love story.)

Certainly, we are not greater than our Creator. The Creator chose to be our Lover. Selah. Joy is always the proper response to divine goodness—this divine romance.

- As the Lord's Beloved (we who were made alive in Christ), do we really suffer loss? Ah. We suffer, but what is our loss? Well, what do we have that is our own to claim? (Phil. 1:21; 3:8)

This logic helps us to make sense of Romans 8:18. *"For I consider that the sufferings of this present time are not worthy to be compared with the glory that is to be revealed to us."*

What we suffer is suffering for gain.

This biblical logic led Jim Elliot to write in his journal, "He is no fool who gives up what he cannot keep to gain what he cannot lose."[9]

- What does God pour into our emptied hearts (Rom. 5:3-5)? How do you respond?

6.4 TREKKING THE TRAIL

We've observed three purposes for sacrifices or offerings:

A. To make payment for a debt: propitiation, atonement, necessary to establish a relationship between God and man;
B. To dedicate or sanctify; to devote something for a purpose;
C. To offer thanksgiving: a Eucharistic expression.

We've observed Jesus Christ fulfills the purpose for the required sacrifice, making complete payment for our sin. We cannot pay for our own sins. *"He made Him who knew no sin to be sin on our behalf, that we might become the righteousness of God in Him"* (2 Corinthians 5:21).

---

9. Elisabeth Elliot, *Shadow of the Almighty* (San Francisco: Harper & Row Pub., 1958), 247.

Ephesians 2:8-9 explains our responsibility for our own salvation: *"For by grace you have been saved through faith, and that not of yourselves, it is the gift of God; of as a result of works, that no one should boast."* Our role is to accept God's gift. Jesus did the work on the cross; by faith we accept it thankfully.

"Therefore, if anyone is in Christ, he is a new creation. The old has passed away; behold, the new has come" (2 Corinthians 5:17 NIV).

Accepting Christ's finished work on the cross, we have changed. The change is an inward newness; we are a new creation. Ephesians 2:10 tells us what kind of new creation we are and what our purpose is!

"For we are His workmanship, created in Christ Jesus for good works, which God prepared beforehand, that we should walk in them" (Ephesians. 2:10).

We are new. We are recreated, newly minted, as it were. We are God's workmanship. What is a "workmanship?" A workmanship is the piece of work created by the creator. From the Greek word used here our English word, *poem*, is derived. We are God's poem, speaking in artistic terms. We are God's masterpiece. A poem communicates. A poem has a purpose.

Ephesians 2:10 tells us our purpose: to do _____ works. We are a work of God, created to work for God. What works?

Works that God_____ _____ that we should walk in them.

What a comfort to know that not only has God made us new in Christ but He also has prepared the blessed work we are to do, before we were even born! There's much here that we can study, but let's relate the good works we as His masterpiece are to do to the kinds of sacrifices we are invited to be and to give.

In Romans 12:1, we are urged "to offer ourselves as a sacrifice."

CHAPTER 6

Isn't this fascinating? As freshly minted masterpieces in Christ, we're invited (even urged) to offer ourselves as sacrifices. Living sacrifices! Like burnt sacrifices (the voluntary surrender of the whole gift, not just part of it), but unlike a burnt offering, the offering is alive! It is the offering of oneself and one's entire life.

Like the voluntary sacrifices, burnt, grain, and peace offerings, we are the "sweet-savor" offerings. And the drink offering (mentioned in our theme verse) was poured over the burnt and grain offerings as part of the "sweet-savor." Interesting. These Mosaic, ceremonial offerings become metaphors to picture for us what we are to become: God's newly minted masterpieces, holy and acceptable to Him.

Let's try to track a few parallels between these three, ceremonial, OT voluntary offerings and the NT new creation masterpiece offering (that's us!). You may want to review Boxes 2 and 4 as you pursue the following Box.

Box 4

_____:

(Your Name)

is

A Freshly Minted Masterpiece who is a Living Sacrifice

Like a burnt offering:	Like a grain offering:	Like a peace offering:
Devoted	Honoring God	Expressing gratitude
Consecrated	Worshiping God	Giving thanks
Committed	Acknowledging God's Lordship, authority, and provision	Free to fellowship with God by the peace made on the cross
Set apart for a purpose		
Surrendered entirely to God and His will		
To be consumed (whole body and everything in it) for that purpose		

GUIDEPOST

"But even if I am being poured out as a drink offering upon the sacrifice and service of your faith, I rejoice and share my joy with you all." (Philippians 2:17)

A drink offering is poured over another offering, a burnt or grain offering. What does that mean to us, to be a freshly minted masterpiece who are a living sacrifice?

Amazing. Do you see the offering of ourselves is not singular? It is a "together" offering. We plural, as the body of Christ, are the living sacrifice, as Romans 12:1 says, "present your bodies (plural) a living and holy sacrifice (singular)." We are not to be on our own. Encouraging.

What does the sacrifice of ourselves look like in real terms? Read the rest of Romans 12. In verses ten through thirteen (note Box 3), you see a list of ways (attitudes, qualities, and actions) Paul gives us to stimulate us to serve/worship the Lord through devoted, committed actions—sacrifices, which by the nature of sacrifice involve loss and suffering, but also much joy, as our guidepost reminds us.

Write a few responses below, and then discuss or sojournal about one of them:

- What do I think of the idea of being a living sacrifice-masterpiece?
- In what ways does my life express to God devotion, worship, and thanksgiving?
- What is the relationship between worship and service (Romans 12:1)?
- In what ways does Romans 12:10-13 provide me with ideas for expressing devotion, worship, and thanksgiving (as a living sacrifice) to others?
- In what ways do I work to be a "we" sacrifice rather than a lone "I" sacrifice?

In the last section, let's listen to the wisdom and example from the life of an amazing Christian woman.

CHAPTER 6

6.5 REST STOP

We've reached the summit! This rest stop differs from all the others. I'll let you rest your bones on this bench while I tell you a true story that will help us answer our chapter question, "Lord, what is my sacrifice?" Maybe we should ask, "Lord, what are my daily sacrifices?" Let's listen to the story before we close with a beautiful hymn.

Elisabeth Howard Elliot can show us the way to respond to the invitation of sacrificial suffering and joy. Born four days before Christmas in 1926, she grew up in a missionary-minded home with devout parents and five siblings.[10] With her heart given to God and missions, she attended Wheaton College and prepared to be a Bible translator. There, she met and fell in painful love with a man who for years did not think marriage was God's plan for him, a man also dedicated to the Lord and missions, Jim Elliot. Elisabeth achingly surrendered to God's providence in her life.

Elisabeth and Jim each entered the mission field as single missionaries—in different locations of Ecuador. Each was dedicated to serving God. Elisabeth, so bright, so humbly surrendered, had plenty of questions and plenty of concerns.

She would come to write over thirty books, but one book she wrote that receives little attention is her book *These Strange Ashes* (1975). I read it some years ago, and her descriptive account distressed me. "No wonder I've not seen this book promoted!" I thought. "Reading her experiences makes me not want to be a Christian, and I certainly wouldn't want to be a missionary!" I realized I'm a spoiled lady and a spoiled American. I don't know how to suffer. That is probably one of the reasons God called me to do this research.

The book cover description explains her book as "A deeply personal account of Elisabeth Elliot's first year as a jungle missionary—a year filled with drama, spiritual struggle, and decision—preceding her marriage to Jim Elliot, whose story [she tells] in the best-selling *Through Gates of Splendor*."

---

10. Elisabeth Elliott was born December 21, 1926 and died June 15, 2015.

After the heartbreak of that first year and after suffering five and one half years of unfulfilled longing, she and Jim Elliot are married on October 8, 1953 in a simple service in Quito, Ecuador. She joins Jim in his mission, along with a team of other young couples, and starts on a new adventure to reach an unreached tribe. Their one child, Valerie, is born on February 27, 1955, among the Quichua people of Ecuador. And after twenty-seven months of marriage in the Amazon jungles, on January 8, 1956, their story takes a sharp turn.

In *Through Gates of Splendor*, Elisabeth's own words recount the martyrdom of her husband and his four teammates, Pete Flemming, Ed McCully, Nate Saint, and Roger Youderian. With their wives back at the mission station, waiting for their return, the men attempt to make friendly contact with the Huaorani tribe in eastern Ecuador (also called the "Auca" people, a Quichua word for *savage*). Fearing the five men are cannibals wanting to eat them, the tribesmen spear all five along the beach, leaving them to die there.

Why would God allow such misplaced fear to destroy the lives of these five men who wanted to share the love of God through Christ to this tribe? Elisabeth would ask such questions and come to terms with unanswerable mysteries in time. I recommend you read some of her books.

The news of the missionary deaths in 1956 make headlines around the world, and interest by the secular as well as Christian media continue for years to come. The tragic saga initiates a new focus on missions. In Elisabeth's book *The Savage, My Kinsman*, she continues the story.

Incredibly, Elisabeth does not retreat from the mission work. Her mother-in-law urges her to return to the States. The last words Jim says to Elisabeth were these: "Teach the believers, darling, we've got to teach the believers."[11] Elisabeth and her daughter, Valerie, stay in Ecuador until 1963. Elisabeth continues in language work, helping reduce the oral to a written language. Some of the same natives who killed these five men come to faith in Christ, and the church there grows. Little blond Valerie plays among the Huaorani children and trusts the cradling arms of tribe members who once killed her father but now love her Heavenly Father.

---

11. Valerie Elliot Shepard, "In Memory: Elisabeth Howard Elliot Leitch Gren '48'", *Wheaton Alumni Magazine*, 2016.

CHAPTER 6

Back in the States, Elisabeth's ministry grows through her writing and speaking ministry. After years as a widow, in 1969 she marries again, Addison Lietch, a theology professor, but he dies of cancer a mere four years into their marriage. Again, she is a widow. A third time she marries—Lars Gren, a hospital chaplain who becomes her traveling partner and supports her in her ministries.

I own at least eight of her books, but often when I read them, I hear her voice. Why? I never met her. I hear her saying the printed word because I heard her on the radio for years. She began a daily radio program in 1988, which continued until 2001, called "Gateway to Joy." How amazing! Produced by the Good News Broadcasting Association of Lincoln, Nebraska, you may still be able to find some recordings.

I can hear her say those calming, opening words: "You are loved with an everlasting love. That's what the Bible says, and underneath are the everlasting arms. This is your friend, Elisabeth Elliot." Then she proceeds into her topic, encouraging us always, when we don't know what to do, to trust God and "to do the next thing," which meant: sweep the room, do the dishes.... There's something right there for you to do—for God and others. Elisabeth was a "Titus 2" woman to me, an older woman teaching a younger woman. I'm eight months older than her daughter, Valerie. I've always wanted to meet her.

In the fall of 2000, my health collapsed. I was so weak, and my pain levels were plenary and frightening. A dear friend and colleague lent me her copy of the book *A Path through Suffering* by Elisabeth Elliot, which had been published ten years previously, but I was unaware of it. Concentrating was hard, but I read what I could when I could.

This book, rich in wisdom and Scripture, fed my soul. I said then it was as if it "saved my life." It kept me sane. It held me. It helped me lift my gaze "to acquiesce wholly now in the death sentence of your new birth. Letting new life live at the expense of the old."[12] Her theme verse for the book is John 12:24 ("Unless a grain of wheat falls into the ground and dies....").

---

12. Elisabeth Elliot, *A Path through Suffering*, (Ann Arbor, Michigan: Servant Publications, 1990), 137.

She describes ordinary forms of suffering: menial and repetitious. She describes daily sufferings, physical, spiritual, emotional, relational sufferings; loss of people we love by death, divorce, rebellion, and alienation. There are natural disasters.... She offers biblical and commonsense advice to children, teens, and adults who write to her.

If any human being has the authority, in my books, to speak of what suffering is, it is Elisabeth Elliot. She writes, "The word suffering is much too grand to apply to most of our troubles, but if we don't learn to refer the little things to God how shall we learn to refer the big ones? A definition which covers all sorts of trouble, great or small is this: *having what you don't want, or wanting what you don't have.*"[13] Yes, this fits afflictions, small and great.

We began our chapter with the question "Lord, what is my sacrifice?" Elisabeth Elliot answers this question with a four-step process of what to do with suffering of any kind, from the common to the catastrophic:

1) Recognize it.
2) Accept it.
3) Offer it to God as a sacrifice.
4) Offer yourself with it."[14]

I am amazed that offering myself as a "living sacrifice" (Rom. 12:1) includes offering even my sorrows and messes. Apparently, I cannot offer myself without them.

He who offers a sacrifice of thanksgiving honors Me. (Psalm 50:23a)

Ponder One of These:

How may this four-step process help me to turn my life and a certain suffering I'm facing into offerings of devotion, worship, and thanksgiving to the LORD? How is this a gateway to joy?

---

13. Ibid., 56.
14. Ibid., 141.

CHAPTER 6

> What does it mean to me to view myself as a Freshly Minted Masterpiece who is a Living Sacrifice to the LORD? How is this a gateway to joy?
>
> What does it look like for me to be a "poured out drink offering upon the sacrifice and service of [someone else's] faith" (Philipians 2:17)?
>
> How do shared suffering, sacrifice, and service become gateways to joy?

Take My Life[15]

*Take my life and let it be
consecrated, Lord, to thee.
Take my moments and my days;
let them flow in endless praise,
let them flow in endless praise.*

*Take my hands and let them move
at the impulse of thy love.
Take my feet and let them be
swift and beautiful for thee,
swift and beautiful for thee.*

*Take my voice and let me sing
always, only, for my King.
Take my lips and let them be
filled with messages from thee,
filled with messages from thee.*

We've just traversed the center and heart of our journey. Congratulations!

As pedestrian theologians, we are winding our way up. Let's step around the corner and take a look.

---

15. Frances Ridley Havergall.

CHAPTER 7

WHAT IS THE MESSAGE OF MY WITNESS?

DISCOVERY 6

"Therefore, my beloved brethren whom I long to see, my joy and crown, so stand firm in the Lord, my beloved." (Philippians 4:1)

7.1 TRAVEL SCOPE

In this chapter we will explore Exemplary Suffering and Joy.

- We will explore key characteristics of testimony and witness.
- We will make connections between testimony, witness, and gospel joy.

The heart of Exemplary Suffering and Joy is witness.[1] "What is the message of my witness?"

---

1. Witness means testimony, from the Greek, martus/martur, from which we gain the word, martyr.

CHAPTER 7

GUIDEPOSTS

Follow my example, as I follow the example of Christ.
I Corinthians 11:1 (NIV)

"The things you have learned and received and heard and see in me, practice these things and the God of peace shall be with you."
(Philippians 4:9)

In the last chapter we saw the loving pattern and power of Sacrificial Suffering and Joy. A sacrifice is an offering, a gift, and a loss. It is loss to the giver and gain to the receiver. However, we also observed that the giver, the "sacrificer," gains as well, as was seen in the Parable of the Pearl of Great Price and the joy Jesus envisioned that lay on the other side of His sacrificial death.

Just as Jesus Christ is the ultimate picture of Sacrificial Suffering as the consummation of it through his finished work on the cross, so also Jesus is the ultimate pattern of Exemplary Suffering and Joy. He is a witness to His Father as His Father is a witness to His Son.

As His children, we are called to bear witness. How do saved sinners bear witness? What kind of witness is Exemplary Suffering and Joy? Think of Job. Think of Habakkuk. Think of Peter. Think of Paul and those to whom He ministered. We are going to let their lives illustrate some key characteristics. What are the characteristics of Exemplary Suffering and Joy?

Exemplary Suffering and Joy contains three ideal characteristics in a life worthy of imitation, plus one reality check:

1. Increasingly reflects Christ's character (Philipians 4:9 and 1:6).
2. Increasingly demonstrates fidelity to the gospel of Jesus Christ, the Scriptures, and the kingdom of God (Romans 1:16; 2 Tim. 3:16-17; Matthew 6:33).
3. Increasingly finds satisfaction/joy in the faithfulness of God in spite of opposition or persecution (2 Timothy 4: 3-8).

Plus one Reality Check: Increasingly realizes his/her example is inconsistent (not always Christ-like), modeling at times an "anti-model": what not to imitate (1 Corinthians 10: 6-11; 11:1; 2 Corinthians 13:5). Read all of these references and ponder their significance.

7.2 VIEWING THE BIBLICAL MAP

A sweep of the Scriptures will uncover these characteristics of Exemplary Suffering and Joy through living portraits. Job and Habakkuk offer two Old Testament cases, while Paul and Peter offer two New Testament examples.

Job provides an ancient and foundational picture. Habakkuk offers a troubled and determined picture. Peter presents a surprising yet not surprising picture. Paul offers an athletically joyful picture. We will focus on the last example. Before we do, let's briefly look at the first three to view them as samples of the rich mural preceding the ministry of the Apostle Paul. (I trust that you know their stories or will explore them.)

Job

Both the man and the book provide an ancient and foundational picture. Bible scholar, Walter Kaiser, Jr. insightfully observes, "Job…was a test case to show Satan (and would-be mockers of true religion) that mortals do serve God out of pure love for His person and not because of what they can get out of their obedience."[2] Job was tested with multiple kinds of overwhelming suffering. We observe that God identifies no fault in Job's witness, but honors him at the end of the book. We may say that the reality check of an inconsistent example does not apply to Job. You can debate that. However, his testimony is unusual and can encourage us.[3]

---

2. Walter Kaiser, *A Biblical Approach to Personal Suffering*, (Chicago: Moody Press, 1982), 127. This book walks us through the aching poetry of the book of The Lamentations, which offers an eyewitness response to the destruction of Jerusalem in 586 B.C. Jerusalem's suffering is retributive – Recompensive Suffering. Kaiser's last chapter lists eight kinds suffering in the OT, showing that retributive suffering is not the only kind. His scholarly research provides the basis of my research and categorization of suffering. "Now these things happened as examples for us, that we should not crave evil things, as they also craved:" (I Corinthians 10:6). Rebellious Israel provides an "anti-model."

3. You may want to consider who in Scripture does not leave a mixed record of good and bad modeling.

CHAPTER 7

Job may be the oldest book of the Bible. The man, Job, probably lived during the time of Moses. The five books of Moses and the book of Job lay the biblical foundation on which all the rest of Scripture is built. The Bible is our foundation and heritage, and these six books are the foundation of the foundation on which we build our lives.

Isn't it interesting that in God's providence, He knew that the human race needed the witness of Job and Moses (and all those characters whose lives Moses recorded) early in human civilization in order for us to come to terms with our lives in our times in This Broken Cosmos (Romans 15:4)?

In dealing with his overwhelming grief and sorrow, Job expresses deep lament (in chapter 3 and chapters 29-42). Lament conveys anguish, pain, regret, grief, and sorrow. It is usually expressed through prayer. "My soul is in deep anguish. How long, LORD? How Long?" (Psalm 6:30 NIV). The language of lament consumes at least one third of The Psalms. The book of Job shows that God accepts our expressions of deep grief and sorrow. Lament can strengthen our faith in our God even while we are exposing our brokenness, weakness, emotion, and doubt. Lament is for those in close relationship or seeking it. Job shows us that drawing close to God is possible, no matter how deep the sorrow. While we probably won't get all the answers we want, He draws near to us (James 4:8-10). This is what we most need. When our laments draw us toward deeper intimacy with God, we find that "in His presence is fullness of joy" (Psalm 16:11). Pause and think on this.

Habakkuk

Habakkuk and his book showcase a man of fidelity in a brilliant, three- chapter masterpiece. His oracle begins with lament: *"How Long, O LORD, will I call for help...?"* He dialogues with God, questioning the absence of justice but then acknowledging the holiness of God. *"The just shall live by his faith"* claims Habakkuk (Habakkuk 2:4, KJV), as his people face intimidation and destruction by the Babylonians. He writes, *"But the LORD is in His holy temple. Let all the earth be silent before Him"* (2:20). Then, his prayer shifts as he faces what it means to live by faith in a holy God. With lessons for our time, he declares, "Though the fig tree should not blossom, and there be no fruit on the vines..., yet I will exult in the Lord.... The Lord God is my strength. And He has made my feet like hinds' feet, and makes me walk on my high places" (Habakuk 3:17-19). Habakkuk clearly exemplifies the three ideal qualities.

Consider:

How does the process of lamenting lead both Job and Habakkuk, in extremely different situations, through their dark anguish to the light of hope and joy in their LORD God?

Peter

Peter offers a surprising yet not surprising picture. He shows how a person can recover after losing the integrity of his example. We are drawn to Peter's story because the story of Peter's lost witness parallels our own stories. (Peter's story of loss and recovery: Luke 22:31-32; Matthew 16:23; 26:71-75; Mark 14:69-72: Luke 22: 58-62; John 18:12-27; John chapter 21.) We are not worthy of being examples to others.

I need be open to being used, at times, as a bad example. Wasn't God quite willing to expose Peter and others as bad examples? And by His amazing grace, did Jesus not correct and warn Peter, pray for him, forgive him, and invite him back into His service? Did not Jesus carve Exemplary Suffering and Joy into Peter's story? If we are willing, may He not also do the same in our lives?

"Simon, Simon!" speaks Jesus to Peter. *"Behold, Satan has demanded permission to sift you like wheat, but I have prayed for you, that your faith may not fail; and you, when once you have turned again, strengthen your brothers"* Luke 22:31-32. Note the spiritual warfare involved.[4] Note such love that will call him by name, warn him of danger, encourage him by drawing close to Peter through prayer, predict his repentance, grace him with forgiveness before he fails, and reveal to him that God had work for him yet to do.

---

4. Not enough attention has been given to spiritual warfare in this entire study. It is an element of every genre of suffering. Spiritual warfare is introduced in the Vocab Café under the term Cosmic War. Start there.

Consider:

How does Recompensive Suffering and Repentive Joy impact and relate to Exemplary Suffering and Joy?

How can a recovering or recovered, fallen brother/sister strengthen another brother/sister? How do Peter's experiences witness to you today?

Paul and the Thessalonian believers.

Paul offers an athletically joyful picture. The young, Thessalonian believers follow his leading.

The Apostle Paul wrote about 13 of the 27 books of the New Testament. First and Second Thessalonians are dated as the earliest of Paul's writings (about 51 A.D.).

We are going to explore First Thessalonians, especially chapters one and two.

We discover the backstory for the Thessalonian letters in the book of Acts, written by Dr. Luke. Acts 17 tells us that Paul came to Thessalonica as a missionary (on his second of three missionary journeys) to spread the gospel. If you have a study Bible, read about the background of I Thessalonians and Paul's missionary journeys which are recounted in the book of Acts.

I encourage you to take one study block just to read through this first epistle to the Christians at Thessalonica. It is good to take your colored pencils and to highlight key words and thematic phrases in your Bible. If you choose to study more thoroughly, you may want to answer question 5 and 6 below in your SoJournal.

As you read look for:

1. People: Who is speaking to whom?
2. Key words: repeated words and synonyms which clue you in on themes.
3. Meanings of key words as clarified in the context.
4. Themes: perspectives on topics.
5. Instructions: What are you to know? What are you to do?
6. Observations: Where do you see examples of Exemplary Suffering and Joy in the text?

Let's look at chapter one.

First, we note who is sending the epistle or letter:

I Thessalonians. 1:1 tells us that the letter is from three men: Paul, Silas (Silvanus), and Timothy.
Then we note to whom the epistle is being sent:
To the _____ of the _____.
Next we note whose church this church belongs:
The church of the Thessalonians in _____ the _____ and the Lord _____ _____.

I Thessalonians 1:1b gives the opening greeting: "Grace to you and peace." As William MacDonald so beautifully explains, "Grace is God's undeserved favor in every aspect of our lives. Peace is the unruffled quietness which defies the crashing, crushing circumstances of life. Grace is the cause and peace, the effect."[5]

I Thessalonians 1:2 begins the prayer with thanksgiving: "We give thanks to God always for all of you, making mention of you in our prayers;" This moves into the opening prayer in verses 2-5, which comprise one, long sentence composed of many clauses and phrases.

---

5. William MacDonald, *Believer's Bible Commentary*, (Nashville, TN: Thomas Nelson Pub., 1995), 2023.

CHAPTER 7

Here we see a beautiful relationship between the two parties and a splendid example of Exemplary Suffering and Joy unfolding through this chapter and letter. What makes the example splendid? It is that both parties exhibit the three characteristics, not just one side toward the other. You hear and see it in this passage.

Let's review the three major characteristics plus one reality check of Exemplary Suffering (pages 114-115). The three, ideal characteristics can be summarized in the word *fidelity*. It sets the standard showing us what a consistent and an inconsistent witness looks like.

Fidelity is being true to someone or something:

- Fidelity to Christ
- Fidelity to the gospel and the Word
- Fidelity to one another
- Fidelity amidst opposition or persecution
- Thus, bearing joyful fruit

Now let's read verses 2-5 in I Thessalonians 1, which is a prayer. Highlight key words and phrases.

> *² "We give thanks to God always for all of you, making mention of you in our prayers;*
> *³ constantly bearing in mind your work of faith and labor of love and steadfastness of hope in our Lord Jesus Christ in the presence of our God and Father,*
> *⁴ knowing, brethren beloved by God, His choice of you;*
> *⁵ for our gospel did not come to you in word only, but also in power and in the Holy Spirit and with full conviction; just as you know what kind of men we proved to be among you for your sake."*

Let's observe this passage first.

    A. In verse 3, what characteristics of the believers demonstrate fidelity to Christ? That is, what three phrases describe these Christians?

B. In verse 5, how does Paul describe their relationship with the gospel?

C. What phrases evidence a commitment to fidelity between Paul and the believers and also among the believers?

We – I: First Person Plural and Singular

In writing this letter, Paul uses both first person singular and plural, but he mainly employs first person plural. In verse I Thessalonians 1:2, Paul uses the pronoun "we," as he does through much of the letter. In I Thessalonians 2:18, he says "we" and then states, "I, Paul." But throughout the book, Paul includes his traveling companions, Silas and Timothy, in his "we" – the party sending this letter. In I Thessalonians 5:27, Paul returns to the first-person pronoun and says, "I adjure you by the Lord to have this letter read to all the brethren." We observe interesting team dynamics and fidelity here.

There is so much more to observe, but let's now read verses 6-10, highlighting key words and phrases.

> "⁶ You also became imitators of us and of the Lord, having received the word in much tribulation with the joy of the Holy Spirit,
> ⁷ so that you became an example to all the believers in Macedonia and in Achaia.
> ⁸ For the word of the Lord has sounded forth from you, not only in Macedonia and Achaia, but also in every place your faith toward God has gone forth, so that we have no need to say anything.
> ⁹ For they themselves report about us what kind of a reception we had with you, and how you turned to God from idols to serve a living and true God,
> ¹⁰ and to wait for His Son from heaven, whom He raised from the dead, that is Jesus, who rescues us from the wrath to come."

CHAPTER 7

In this letter Paul is writing to young Christians in Thessalonica whom he had led to the Lord during his previous visit with them and had established a church. Answer these questions regarding this text (within its context).

A. What is the attitude and response of the believers to the gospel/Word presented to them?

B. What is their attitude/response toward the apostle Paul?

C. Who do they imitate? Why does Paul mention "us" first and "the Lord" second? How does this order resonate with your experience?

D. Read Acts 17. What probably were the cause(s) of the "tribulation" mentioned in verse 6?

E. What is the relationship between the tribulation and the "joy in the Holy Spirit"?

F. How did the transformative responses of the believers turn into Exemplary Suffering? To whom did they become examples? How far has their inspirational modeling traveled?

G. How would you describe the fidelity of the Thessalonians to Christ, His gospel/Word, and to other believers including Paul?

7.3 ADJUSTING THE FOCUS

When you read the book of I Thessalonians, you can quickly come to admire these growing, young believers who model Exemplary Suffering and Joy.

The truth is that we live inside a story. The Story. In reality. Within God's Story (human history as it moves through time toward the eternal), we seek to devise our own stories.

Our mini-stories live within the Meta-Story. But God is the introductory, providential, and ultimate Author.

God brought "story" into being during the week of creation. All the elements of story are there and are woven throughout Scripture and throughout our lives. The main elements of story, as you learned in school are these: 1) Setting, 2) Characters, 3) Plot, 4) Conflict, 5) Theme, and 6) Point of View. We easily observe that God sets up all of these by the time you get through Genesis chapter 3.

The Bible characters we've considered and now these Christ-followers in Thessalonica did not have much control over many of their story's elements. They had no choice in their setting: when and where they were born. They had few choices regarding the events and conflicts of their times. They had a limited understanding of the overarching themes in which their lives were working.

It probably never occurred to most of them that they would become examples to show others how to process belief, obedience, and loving service amid opposition. Quite assuredly, none of them ever would have imagined that their collective lives would live through the rest of history and be known and analyzed thousands of years later through the record of the Scriptures.

In reflecting upon their lives, and then our own, we can recognize the powerful influence of a quiet example, like rippling waves, moving, moving, moving outward, from person to person, from generation to generation.

At the beginning of this chapter, we briefly noted the examples of Job, Habakkuk, and Peter. Then through Paul's description, we looked at the Thessalonians. Hebrews 11 lists many biblical personages who have become models for us. Since the closing of the biblical canon, we have two thousand years of Christian examples.

I list a dozen Christ-followers in the next chapter on Communal Suffering who exemplify communion with God in suffering and joy.[6] They belong in this chapter as well as in all of our chapters. Every era offers witnesses.

---

6. The bibliography that follows the appendices closes with a list of people whose biographies are worth your attention. Add more names to the list.

Here are eight Christ-followers from the last five centuries:

1. John Bunyan (1628-1688): English minister imprisoned for 12 years; author of *Pilgrim's Progress*.
2. Fanny Crosby (1820-1915): American, blind hymn writer.
3. Hudson Taylor (1832-1905): Missionary to China.
4. Amy Carmichael (1867-1951): Missionary to China and India.
5. Corrie ten Boom (1892-1983): Imprisoned for hiding Jews from the Nazis.
6. Georgi Vins (1928-1998): Imprisoned in USSR for 8 years.
7. Ajith Fernando (1948): Ministry in Sri Lanka since 1974.
8. Joni Eareckson Tada (1949): Quadriplegic; Sharing Hope through Hardship: Joniandfriends.org.

You can learn about them and the message of their witness through internet searches and by read biographies of them. Add them and many others to our "cloud of witnesses" (Hebrews 11).

Hebrews 12:1-2 explains the purpose for observing their lives: *"Therefore, since we have so great a cloud of witnesses surrounding us, let us also lay aside every encumbrance, and the sin which so easily entangles us, and let us run with endurance the race that is set before us, fixing our eyes on Jesus, the author and perfecter of faith, who for the joy set before Him endured the cross, despising the shame, and has sat down at the right hand of the throne of God"*

Note that the "great cloud of witnesses" leads us to Jesus, on whom our eyes need to be fixed.

- Now read Hebrews 12:3: *"For consider Him who has endured such hostility by sinners against Himself, so that you may not grow weary and lose heart."* Why is observing the example of Christ, as well as that of the great cloud of witnesses important for us today?
- Respond to the following statement: Every test forms a testimony.

The last century was a century of much Christian persecution, and this twenty-first century continues the trend in both familiar and varying ways. We need to be aware of the witnesses of our brothers and sisters in order to support them and in order to be better prepared for what may be in store for us.[7] Their Christian worldview set them in opposition to the worldviews around them. It is the same for us.

Peter admonishes us, "Beloved, do not be surprised at the fiery ordeal among you..." (I Peter 4:12). Ordeals are normal when you choose to follow Christ rather than the world. Romans 12:2 tells us that we must not be conformed to this world. What does this look like in real life?

In This Broken Cosmos, affliction and pain are normal ingredients for everyone. Suffering, especially physical and emotional, is normal for both those who follow Christ and for those who don't follow Him. When giving your suffering that is not caused by following Christ to Jesus, your suffering is folded into Christ and becomes His suffering too, taking on new meaning.[8] In this realization, I recognize His love and comfort.

- When you look over the lives of these people who came before us and think about their responses to suffering, opposition, or persecution, what is one response pattern that you would like to imitate from their examples?

7.4 TREKKING THE TRAIL

We have observed that Exemplary Suffering and Joy contains three ideal characteristics in a life worthy of imitation, plus one reality check:

1. Increasingly reflects Christ's character (Phil. 4:9; Philipians 1:6).

---

7. Persecution.com is the site for The Voice of the Martyrs, which was founded by Richard Wurbrand. They offer prayer guides and maps as well as their magazine, *The Voice of the Martyrs*.
8. We will discuss purpose and meaning in chapter 9.

2. Increasingly demonstrates fidelity to the gospel of Jesus Christ, the Scriptures, and the kingdom of God (Romans 1:16; 2 Tim. 3:16-17; Matthew 6:33).
3. Increasingly finds satisfaction/joy in the faithfulness of God in spite of opposition or persecution (2 Timothy 4: 3-8).

Plus one Reality Check: Increasingly realizes his/her example is inconsistent (not always Christ-like), modeling at times an "anti-model": what not to imitate (1 Corinthians 10: 6-11; 11:1; 2 Corinthians 13:5).

Choose three of the following questions. Reflect on them for discussion, short answer, and/or sojournaling:

A. What is the message of my witness? What are others hearing and seeing in me? What would the world be like if people followed my example?

B. What growth in Christ do you recognize in yourself? Thank God for it. What changes do you need to make to clarify your fidelity to Christ, His gospel, and His kingdom?

C. How can you live an integrated life in which everything is sacred and spiritual? How can you demonstrate love for God and for your neighbor?

D. In our culture today, some Christian beliefs result in actions and lifestyles acceptable to our culture. Other out-workings of our beliefs are not culturally acceptable (and a few may not be legally acceptable). Compare and contrast some of these.

E. In our culture, what could be some situations in which our acceptance of certain biblical teachings would result in "much tribulation"? In I Thessalonians 1:6, what example do the Thessalonians offer that we could follow? What was the nature of their joy (verses 5-6)?

F. Discuss a belief or posture that may conflict with our culture and discuss how you as an individual and as a group can respond now and can also prepare to respond as needed in the future.

Current topics may include:

- Cheating in school or at work, misrepresenting reality: ways of lying
- Sensuality, modesty, sexuality, gender identity, gender care and counsel
- Marriage and divorce, gay marriage
- Temperament, personality, character, and spirituality
- Vocation, calling, business, ministry, evangelism, retirement
- Medical freedom, food freedom, privacy
- Use of time and resources
- Stewardship of physical, mental, emotional, relational, and spiritual health
- Neighborhood, community, and political involvements
- Cancel culture and cancel cooperation
- You can name others

G. How can we love our neighbor and still at times be at odds with our neighbor?

H. When is being disapproved of a good witness for Christ? In situations involving conflict, what are some ways joy may appropriately reveal itself?

I. What roles can lament serve in our personal lives? How can proper expressions of lament in prayer and with those close to us actually strengthen our public as well as our private witness?

J. Our second theme verse, Philippians 4:9, says if we follow the example Paul has set "the God of peace shall be with you." Will your culture be "with you"? What is the relationship between God's peace and God's joy?

CHAPTER 7

7.5 REST STOP

Take a seat and let's rest. Look over the chapter and meditate on the theme verses and other key verses, concepts, or story situations that are speaking to you right now. Talk with God about what He is talking to you about through His Word.

GUIDEPOST

Follow my example, as I follow the example of Christ
(I Corinthians 11:1 NIV).

The things you have learned and received and heard and see in me, practice these things and the God of peace shall be with you"
(Philippians 4:9).

We will close with the special song that was played at my father's funeral in 2004. This music meant so much to my sister, me, and our whole family. John Mohr wrote the lyrics, and Steve Green is known for his musical presentation of it, first published in 1988.

Find Us Faithful[9]

We're pilgrims on the journey
Of the narrow road,
And those who've gone before us line the way
Cheering on the faithful, encouraging the weary;
Their lives a stirring testament to God's sustaining grace.

Surrounded by so great a cloud of witnesses
Let us run the race not only for the prize,
But as those who've gone before us.
Let us leave to those behind us
The heritage of faithfulness passed on through godly lives.

---

9. John Mohr

CHORUS:
Oh may all who come behind us find us faithful.
May the fire of our devotion light their way.
May the footprints that we leave
Lead them to believe,
And the lives we live inspire them to obey.

Oh, may all who come behind us find us faithful.

After all our hopes and dreams have come and gone
And our children sift through all we've left behind,
May the clues that they discover and the memories they uncover
Become the light that leads them to the road we each must find.

* * *

"Forgive me, Lord, for the times when I have chosen the route
of self-pity instead of praise. Remind me, even in my pain,
that the world is watching and they need to see You.
Don't let me waste my pain."[10]

A Traveler's Review

Our travels through suffering began with a sampling of the soil under our feet in This Broken Cosmos. There we recognized the pain of our own causation, **Recompensive Suffering** which was answered by **Repentive Joy** (Rom. 6:23; 1 John 1:9). Our sin is greater than we want to face, but our joy is that God's mercy and grace are still greater.

We knew that there is more to suffering than personal causation. In this same soil we discovered the pain of outside causes inflicting Collateral Suffering. There we mingled our grief with the consolation of God's wise and loving skill at taking abuse, accidents, and violence, redeeming something good from the damage. We have come to see a more

---

10. Stacy Edwards, *Devotions from the Front Porch* (Nashville, Tennessee: Thomas Nelson Pub., 2016), 47.

complex good emerging from it, or in mystery, we may not, yet we have met a new lifelong friend, **Redemptive Joy**.

These first two ingredients in the soil of suffering and joy introduced us to the third discovery—transformations: microbial changes of substance and quality that suffering works within us and around us. Our third discovery presented a response and reaction to the mix of the first two ingredients. Mix vinegar and soda, and you make a foaming volcano, a response. Mix Recompensive and Collateral Sufferings and the change-response will be both substantive and qualitative. We have the choice to become hard and bitter or deaf and blind, to live in defeat and discouragement, deforming us. Or we can choose Repentive and Redemptive Joy, through which the Holy Spirit performs productive heart change (James 1:2-4). God has invited us to travel the path of **Transformative Suffering and Joy.** The soil under our feet is still uneven, rocky, and sometimes dangerous, but the chemical (spiritual) reactions within the soil of our hearts now produce resilient beauty. What the enemy has meant for evil, God is using for good, a more complex kind of good than the straightforward good experienced before the Fall.

Breaking open to us on the winding trail of Transformative Suffering and Joy is a new vision, not of less suffering but of more meaningful kinds, saved for those willing to be shaped by the person and attributes of Christ Himself. Stunningly, we see the exquisite perfections of Christ who has no strengths because He has no weaknesses is the reflective vision God has in mind for us, Christ's bride. We paused, and we pause again in wonder.

We turned the corner to new breezes along a wide horizon. We discovered coves and refuges of safety. Here, we met the life-nurturing struggles of **Compassionate Suffering and Joy** as we learned comfort, a flavor of joy, is God's gift to us, which increases as we pass it on. On up the hill we climbed to the ultimate affliction, **Sacrificial Suffering and Joy**, where we witnessed Christ on the cross, enduring our shame because of the joy He would receive for purchasing our salvation. There, we met our own crosses to carry, learning how to become living sacrifices, wholly acceptable to God and the joy of being acceptable, servant-worshipers (Rom. 12:1).

Finally, we entered the region of **Exemplary Suffering and Joy** where we learned our participation in the Body of Christ invites us into meaning-filled positions of modeling for others how they too can flourish in the Lord. Now it is time for some unexpected views along the trail of the final tier. Here, we will explore the depths and peaks of **Communal, Eschatological, and Doxological Suffering and Joy**.

Part III

Exploring the Depths and Peaks: THE UNEXPECTED VIEWS

CHAPTER 8

IF I'M NEVER ALONE, HOW DO I LIVE THAT WAY?

DISCOVERY 7

We've traveled a long way. Jesus reassures us, "Lo, I am *with* you always, even unto the end of the age" (Matt. 28:20). While we may doubt His presence, we've been told we are never traveling alone. He is *with* us. That's what this chapter is about: "withing."

8.1 TRAVEL SCOPE

In the third and final tier of pascharology we will explore Communal Suffering and Joy.

GUIDEPOSTS

That I may know Him, and the power of His resurrection and the fellowship of His sufferings, being conformed to His death; in order that I may attain to the resurrection from the dead.
(Philippians 3:10-11)

Rejoice in the Lord always; again I will say, rejoice! (Philippians 4:4)

CHAPTER 8

Why do the theme verses of Philippians 3:10-11 feel awkward? It is because these two verses do not compose a complete sentence. We're jumping in in the middle of a train of thought. The sentence begins in verse eight! Oh, the Apostle Paul loved to shape long sentences, digging deep dimensions of meaning expressed through phrases and clauses! Read the context. Note the book's context. Ironies run behind and through this call for joy—written from a prison in Rome—joy in the all-sufficient Lord Jesus Christ—no matter one's circumstances (Phil. 4:11-13).

Where are we? Maybe we're where we really never expected to be. As we grow in Christ, we expect life should become smoother because, after all, isn't that consistent with the sow-reap principle? If we obey, we prosper; if we disobey, we suffer.

Just as the first two tiers of suffering have shown the incompleteness and danger of such a myopic perspective, Communal Suffering continues to teach us godliness is not a recipe for a smooth path. Not in This Broken Cosmos. Suffering has more good purposes, and joy in the Lord is always available. Communal Suffering and Joy address the question, "If I am never alone, how do I live that way?"

So what do we mean by Communal Suffering and Joy?

Communal Suffering and Joy begins with shared experience. The adjective *communal* is from this word family: common, communicate, communion, and community. The Greek *koinonia* contains the idea of fellowship, the sharing of life, of selves.

Communal Suffering and Joy is "the fellowship of His sufferings": God's sufferings for humanity and our sufferings with God within the fuller context of persistent joy.

We can recognize at least two categories of "His sufferings":

1. God's suffering *for* the sins of humanity;
2. God's suffering *with* the sufferings of sinners whom He loves with an everlasting love.

We can recognize numerous kinds of undergirding and overriding joy within affliction:

1. Joy in the Lord (Nehamiah 8:10); 2) Joy as optimism and courage (John 16:33);
3. Joy as blessedness (Matthew 5:3,10,11); 4) Joy in sharing (Luke 1:58).

Divine suffering becomes communal (shared), amazingly, when He joins His creatures in suffering, lovingly and providentially, and when His own creatures enter into His affliction with Him, lovingly and worshipfully—the "in Christ" life.[1] This divine-human community engenders an intimate joy of its own. How can such suffering and joy be?

We come to realize that godliness will actually increase our trouble and pain in This Broken Cosmos. Godliness draws us near to God, while escalating our conflict with the world, the flesh (our own and other's fallen natures), and the devil (1 John 2:15; James 3:15; Ephesians 2:2-3). Within this battle, we are drawn deeper into God, experiencing the sprouting of various and determined joys—beyond logical explanation.

Who models for us Communal Suffering and Joy? Consider examples from biblical and post-biblical history. A few biblical examples would be the lives of Daniel, Jeremiah, and Mary, Christ's mother. In the post-biblical, historical chain, we could explore examples from every century. Here are a few beginning a millennium and a half after the first century:

Thomas Case (1598-1682), Samuel Rutherford (1600-1661), John Bunyan (1628-1688), David Brainerd (1718-1747), Fanny Crosby (1820-1915), Hudson Taylor (1832-1905), Amy Carmichael (1867-1951), Aiden Wilson Tozer (1897-1963), Corrie ten Boom (1892-1983), Richard Wurmbrand (1909-2001).

If you know something of their lives, think about how these historical figures portray the concepts of these chapters. If you aren't familiar with some of them, make it a goal to read biographies of these and other Christians. (We'll return to this list near the end of the chapter.)

Communal Suffering and Joy begins with shared experience: sharing in God's experience of suffering and joy. Consider your own experiences. Have you participated in something like this?

---

1. David K. Spurbeck Sr., *The Christian "In Christ"*, (Forest Grove, Oregon: Know to Grow "In Christ" Pub., 1999). This thick volume explores the New Testament's teaching about our position and possessions "in Christ."

CHAPTER 8

8.2 VIEWING THE BIBLICAL MAP

A. The Historical Narrative:

Let's intrude, so quietly and carefully, upon a scene late in the short life of Christ: Christ's agony in the garden of Gethsemane. The synoptic gospels (Matthew, Mark, and Luke) describe the scene in the garden, while the gospel of John references it in one verse and moves right into Judas's betrayal.

While the fourth gospel does not describe the Gethsemane scene, chapters 13-17 prepare us for Christ's final days. These chapters describe the Passover that was our Lord's Last Supper and provide "the upper room discourse" of Christ in which Christ predicts His betrayal (13:21-38), comforts His disciples (14:1-15), declares the coming Holy Spirit (13:16-31, 16:5-15), explains the relationship between the Vine and the branches (15:1-11), exhorts his followers to love one another (15:12-17), warns them of their conflict, as His witnesses, with the world (15:18 - 16:4), foretells His death and resurrection (16:16-33), and offers His "High Priestly Prayer" which includes His prayer for us (chapter 17). By reading John 13-17 before reading the synoptic accounts of His Gethsemane experience, your understanding and insight will be heightened and your heart will be tenderized.

The Garden of Gethsemane

Read at least the Matthew and Luke accounts listed below. Add summary notes and comments in the right column.

The Texts	My Summary Notes
1. Matthew 26:36-46	
2. Mark 14:32-42	
3. Luke 22:39-46	
4. John 18:1-12	

This Gethsemane scene offers a profound example of Christ's suffering preceding His ultimate suffering on the cross for our atonement. This scene also presents the potential of divine-human Communal Suffering as Christ invites His three close disciples, Peter and the two sons of Zebedee (James and John), into His most intimate and intense communion with God: "My soul is deeply grieved, to the point of death; remain here and keep watch with Me" (Matt. 26:38). *"Watch with Me."* He doesn't ask them to do anything but to be *with* Him. He offers a sharing of suffering only in the sense of close, observable vulnerability in presence and in prayer. Jesus would do the suffering, but they could pray too (he told them what to pray about) and could share in the experience as loving witnesses. To share *with* Christ. "Withing."

However, they, as we would have, squander the prime opportunity. Their lack of prayer, their inability to observe and taste His suffering became a lost opportunity. We know that in time other opportunities would emerge in which they will be able to participate in His sufferings, after Pentecost. The Holy Spirit will enable them to "fill up" what is yet to be filled in the continued affliction in Christ and for the growth of His Body, the church, and the salvation of the world.

B. The Biblical Declaratives:

So what do we make of God's suffering in Christ? What do we make of His followers participating in His suffering and filling up Christ's suffering? Read the following verses or passages and explain the communal nature of Christ's and our suffering and joy.

1. 1 Corinthians 12:27: *"Now you are the body of Christ, and each of you is a member of it."*
2. Act 5:41: *"And they departed from the presence of the council, rejoicing that they were counted worthy to suffer shame for his name."*
3. Acts 9:4: *"Saul, Saul, why are you persecuting me?"*
4. 2 Corinthians 1:5 in context of verses three through eleven:

    "For just as the sufferings of Christ overflow to us, so also through Christ our comfort overflows."

CHAPTER 8

5. Romans 8:16-17: *"The Spirit Himself testifies with our spirit that we are children of God, and if children, heirs also heirs of God and fellow heirs with Christ, if indeed we suffer with Him in order that we may also be glorified with Him."*

6. Colossians 1:24: *"Now I rejoice in my sufferings for your sake, and in my flesh I do my share on behalf of His body, which is the church, in filling up what is lacking in Christ's afflictions."*

8.3 ADJUSTING THE FOCUS

Let's think about this concept of filling up what is lacking in Christ's sufferings (Colossians 1:24).

Is the Apostle Paul implying Christ's death on the cross is not sufficient as a payment for our sin, so we have to add to Christ's work to complete it?

No. Just look at the next chapter in Colossians and you'll read Paul's great declaration of the blatant and open triumph of Christ over sin through his death.

> *When you were dead in your transgressions and the uncircumcision of your flesh, He made you alive together with Him, having forgiven us all our transgressions, having canceled out the certificate of debt consisting of decrees against us, which was hostile to us; and He has taken it out of the way, having nailed it to the cross. When He had disarmed the rulers and authorities, He made a public display of them, having triumphed over them through Him* (Col. 2:13-15).

Christ cried from the cross, "It is finished," and His resurrection proved it. In Colossians 1:24 Paul is not speaking of the suffering of Christ that paid our sin debt but the affliction of Christ in and for the body of Christ, as it is formed and matured, in an environment of hostility from Satan and God-rejecters, until the return of Christ when suffering will be no more.

Paul, once named Saul, will never forget his introduction to Jesus Christ when he was traveling to Damascus.

Read Acts 9:1. What is Saul doing?

Yes, he is enraged by the disciples of the Lord, threatening them with murder! He thought he was a God lover, but instead he was a Messiah hater!

Excitedly, he supports of the stoning of Stephen (Acts 8).

What is Saul doing in Acts 8:3?

So when a light from heaven flashes around him on the road to Damascus and a voice cries out to him, "Saul, Saul, why are you persecuting Me?" whose voice is it?

Is it the voice of Stephen or another martyr? No.

When Saul asks who he is, what is the answer? Acts 9:5

Here we learn that when people persecute Christ-followers, they are persecuting the body of Christ and thus are persecuting Jesus Himself. As church history has continued for 2000 years, opposition to the Bible, Jesus Christ, and Christ's church has continued, even as Christ's church has grown—"filling up" or completing the afflictions necessary until Christ returns and culminates "This Broken Cosmos" by bringing in His Kingdom, "The Cosmos to Come."

Jesus declared, "In the world you will have tribulation, but be of good courage. I have overcome the world" (John 16:33).

"Good courage," you remember, is one flavor of joy. Joy expresses itself as "good courage." Courage is only needed when there are challenges, obstacles, opposition, or conflict. "Good courage" is a brand of joy necessary and available in This Broken Cosmos.

CHAPTER 8

Reflect upon a time or situation in which you participated in or witnessed affliction that contributed to the filling up of Christ's passion: an example of injustice, undeserved suffering for the gospel or Christian beliefs. Write about it here or in your sojournal or discuss it within your group.

8.4 TREKKING THE TRAIL

Communal. Shared. Suffering. Joy.

Remember we closed chapter 6, which is about Sacrificial Suffering and Joy, with advice from Elisabeth Elliot. She gave us four steps to take when we don't know what do to with our suffering, no matter what kind of suffering it is.

She said: 1) recognize it (face it; it's real.); 2) accept it; 3) offer it to God as a sacrifice; 4) offer yourself with it.[2]

Here is a woman who has experienced Communal Suffering. She has suffered with and for Christ. She has suffered righteously. She has loved the Lord loyally, even when her trials did not make sense, humanly speaking. Yet, she wrote that sometimes she questioned whether she suffered for Christ or the gospel, or just suffered. She concluded that all (or at least most) suffering can be suffering for Christ, if it is given to Christ.

Elisabeth Elliot's four steps sanctify suffering. I have not suffered on the mission field. I have not been persecuted for my faith. I have not been imprisoned for biblical positions I hold. So how possibly could my trials qualify as Communal Suffering? They only can if I give myself along with them to the Lord. "Withing."

Look back at section 1 of this chapter and the list of post-biblical examples I provided: Thomas Case, Samuel Rutherford, John Bunyan, David Brainerd, Fanny Crosby, Hudson Taylor, Amy Carmichael, A.W. Tozer, Corrie ten Boom, and Richard Wurmbrand. Wow. What lives!

---

2. Elisabeth Elliot, *A Path through Suffering*, (Ann Arbor, Michigan: Servant Publications, 1990), 137.

Of these ten, four were imprisoned for their faith beliefs and or practices (Case, Bunyan, ten Boom and Wurmbrand). At least six of them experienced serious health issues (Rutherford, Brainerd, Crosby, Taylor, and Carmichael, and Wurmbrand's torture produced lifelong affects). To me, each of them exhibit all nine of these genres of suffering and joy. Oh, I hope you explore their lives!

Then there's me. Then there's you. Here's my experience trekking the trail.

While I have not been imprisoned for my faith (or for anything, praise God!), I have lived in a prison for over fifty years. (Apparently, that's what drew me, against my will, to do this research.) My prison is a health prison limiting my participation across the board in things I love and limiting my contributions to others. I too wonder what part of my suffering is righteous or at least not selfish or self-inflicted (Recompensive Suffering). I take courage (and courage is a flavor of joy) in Elisabeth Elliot's sane, biblical counsel. I have discovered Communal Suffering and Joy within my own prison.[3] No matter how isolated I feel at times, at home alone or in public, I am never alone. Awaking in pain or sitting in the invisible anger of my body, my mind nearly always goes right to God, and my thoughts whisper one of His names. "God of the universe." His majesty calms me. "Lord Jesus." My Lord is my friend. "Lord, have mercy," I pray simply. "Jesus, sweet Jesus." His name softens my heart. His comfort strengthens me. And my heart keeps beating.

The main question at the beginning of this chapter was this:

"If I am never alone, how do I live the 'never alone' life?"

Christ's incarnational life answers with the irony of His own seeming alienation. "He came to His own and His own received Him not" (John 1:11). Pause and think on this. Yet, He was never alone (John 17), except for that hellish crisis on the cross when He cried out to his father, "My God, My God, why hast thou forsaken Me?" quoting Psalm 22:1.

---

3. My "prison" of course is a palace compared to the real prisons of Wurmbrand and others. I don't mean to diminish real prison life. Yet, I tell others we should not compare our sufferings with others, rating them. We respect each other's afflictions, so I should respect my own as well and not be embarrassed (but I am embarrassed). "Look to Jesus!" I counsel myself and you.

CHAPTER 8

While John 1:11 says Christ's own people did not receive Him, verse twelve continues, "But as many as receive Him to them He gave the power or right to become the children of God." "Yes!" we say. "We receive You!" In receiving Him, we are *with* Him. "Lo, I am *with* you always," Jesus claimed, ironically, right before ascending to the Father. Not ironically, for then He sent the Holy Spirit to be *in* and *with* us. To commune *with* us no matter our situation. "Withing."

I live the "never alone" life by receiving Him, daily listening to Him, communing with Him quietly in my heart, and openly living for Him. Each of us lives in some kind of a "prison" where probably no one else but the Lord understands us and knows our brokenness. It is here in our inner person that our spirit communes with His Spirit (Rom. 8:16), and lo, we come to realize we are never alone.

The enmity in This Broken Cosmos against Him becomes enmity against us, for we are "in Christ." Thus, you and I share in His sufferings, doing our part in filling up His sufferings. Communal Suffering. In such a battle, suffering stimulates our receptivity to His grace. We are encouraged: joy-couraged. Communal joy.

So what do you think? How do you trek the trail of Communal Suffering and Joy? How do you pursue living the "never alone" life? How does "withing" increase your joy-courage?

8.5 REST STOP

It's time to be quiet. To meditate on meanings arising from this chapter.

GUIDEPOST

*That I may know Him, and the power of His resurrection
and the fellowship of His sufferings, being conformed to His death;
in order that I may attain to the resurrection from the dead.* (Philippians 3:10-11)

Rejoice in the Lord always; again I will say, rejoice! (Philippians 4:4)

It's time to sit quietly, pray, and maybe sing. Here is verse four from the rich hymn "The Sands of Time are Sinking" by A.R. Cousin (1857). She composed it based upon writings by Samuel Rutherford. You may want to look up the other verses.

> *The bride eyes not her garment,*
> *But her dear bride-groom's face;*
> *I will not gaze at glory,*
> *But on my King of grace;*
> *Not at the crown he giveth,*
> *But on his pierced hand;*
> *The Lamb is all the glory*
> *Of Emmanuel's land*

I have the extant letters of Samuel Rutherford. He is such a fascinating Scottish Presbyterian figure (1600-1661). His letters, written when he was removed from his church and not allowed to pastor his people, were communications between him and his flock.

His life shows such contrasts. He contributed to the writing of the Westminster Confession of Faith and the shorter catechism. He wrote *Rex Lex,* his major political contribution, which advocates for limited government. Yet he also composed tender replies to young people and old people and hurting people. His letters, wise and articulate, employing a rich grasp of the English language, exude a tenderness drawn from affliction and his closeness to the Lord.

True theology is applied theology—for Pedestrian Theologians. It is the life of Christ being formed in us—through the engrafted Word, engraved via the effectual sword of sorrow and balm of joy—if we cooperate. Let's not resist. As Moses reminds us, we dwell in the Lord.

> *O, Lord, You have been our dwelling place through all generations.*
> *The wisdom of Moses in Psalm 90:1*

CHAPTER 9

HOW DOES MY TOMORROW CHANGE MY TODAY?

DISCOVERY EIGHT

I have suffered too much in this world not to <u>hope</u> for another.[1]

*Rejoice in glorious <u>hope</u>! Our Lord the Judge shall come and take
His servants up to their eternal home: Lift up your heart; Lift up your voice!
Rejoice, again I say, rejoice.*[2]

9.1 TRAVEL SCOPE

How does my tomorrow change my today? What is the practical impact of the eternal future on our lives now?

In this chapter, we continue in the third and top tier of discoveries.

---

1. Jean Jacques Rousseau (1712-1778). (Underline added.) How ironic. How sad. How logical. Ironic, because Rousseau's philosophical and political views fed the French Revolution. Sad, because his hope was not in the Lord. Logical, because God has created us with a conscious awareness we were created for much more than what this life holds.
2. Charles Wesley (1707-1788). (Underline added.) How beautiful.

We travel from the interior terrain of Communal Suffering and Joy to the wide horizons of Eschatological Suffering and Joy to see what we can see.

GUIDEPOST

For I consider that the sufferings of this present time are not worthy to be compared with the glory that is to be revealed to us. (Romans 8:18)

Eschatology is all about hope. It is about the relationship of the future to the present and the present to the future. It provides context for our lives. We live in history, a continuum of time moving toward eternity.

Eschatology, a branch of systematic theology, is the study of "last things."[3] It addresses many topics about the future. It deals with how This Broken Cosmos ends, to the fascination of many, but also with what can be known about The Cosmos to Come. Much has been written and debated. The broad scope of eschatology explores what the Bible teaches about "death, the believer's immediate presence with the Lord, the hope of Christ's return, the resurrection, judgment, and the eternal state," about which traditional, orthodox Christianity has found much agreement.[4]

Eschatology looks to the end or the future to explain life's purpose and meaning. That's why this is an essential exploration. God's Word gives us eschatological vision.

The book of Ecclesiastes shows us the benefit of an eschatological view of reality. Often seen as a pessimistic book about the vanity of life lived "under the sun" (that is, the era of This Broken Cosmos), Ecclesiastes clearly brings sanity to life and meaning to vanity (the passing breath of life) by viewing life through eschatological eyes (keeping the end in sight).

---

3. Eschatos: (Strong's #2078) in regards to time and order, it means *last*; a synonym: telos (Strong's #5056) *end* or *goal*.
4. Paul Enns, *The Moody Handbook of Theology*, (Chicago: Moody Publishers, 2008), 383. This volume provides an excellent beginning point and foundation for understanding Bible study through the analytical tools of theological study. This text provides a good introduction to theological vocabulary, theological approaches and systems, and theological movements through church history.

CHAPTER 9

> *Remember also your Creator in the days of your youth. . . .*
> (Ecclesiastes 12:1)

Why?

> *The conclusion, when all has been heard, is:*
> *fear God and keep His commandments because this applies to every person.*
> *For God will bring every act to judgment, everything which is hidden,*
> *whether it is good or evil.* (Ecclesiastes 12:13-14)

Each breath holds eternal significance. Within that significance God gifts us with opportunity for joy.

When we wear eschatological lenses, our afflictions of all sorts take on meaning or new meaning and a tender yet resilient hope and joy.

- Our troubles that have appeared insignificant to others ("What's your problem?") but are significant to us (so we feel isolated) are recognized with an eschatological vision.
- Then there are times when we have the choice to suffer or not to suffer, depending upon our perspective and goal. Is the suffering of delayed gratification or of undeviating loyalty worth the end goal? Often, suffering is the godly choice.
- Toward those deep sorrows appearing to be gratuitous, meaningless, mocking us in despair, we grow composure, a patient peace passing human explanation. No matter how elusive, we know meaning is there and justice will come.

An eschatological vantage point, keeping the end in sight, can nurture, motivate, and encourage Pedestrian Theologians.

9.2 VIEWING THE BIBLICAL MAP

By the time we finish our excursion through this section, we will have discovered three characteristics governing Eschatological Suffering and Joy we can classify as three biblical principles or laws.

Key Biblical Narratives Showcasing Biblical Declaratives

Let's begin with *story* (biblical, historical accounts). Our stories in this chapter come from the lives of Jesus, King Hezekiah, the Apostle Paul, and Abel, the son of Adam and Eve. We'll start with an illustration from the life of Jesus.

Jesus

Through all our travels thus far we have seen Jesus is the ultimate sufferer of all the genres of suffering except deserved suffering, Recompensive Suffering. His earthly life was filled with Collateral, Transformational, Compassionate, Sacrificial, Exemplary, and Communal Suffering.

How can it be, we ask, that Christ, the second person of the Trinity, experienced Transformational Suffering? God does not change. But God incarnate willingly experienced human restraints. "And Jesus kept increasing in wisdom and stature, and in favor with God and men" (Luke 2:52). Christ intentionally "learned obedience from the things which He suffered" (Heb. 5:8). We are stunned at the unfathomable humiliation of Christ (Phil. 2:5-11). The trajectory of His earthly life was purposeful—that is, eschatological. He held the end (goal/purpose) in sight. He experienced Eschatological Suffering and Joy.

In one broad sweep Hebrews 12:2 encompasses the journey of Christ. Highlight key words or words that strike you in this verse:

> *. . . Jesus, the author [archegos] and perfecter [teleiotes] of faith,*
> *who for the joy set before Him endured the cross, despising the shame,*
> *and has sat down at the right hand of the throne of God.*

CHAPTER 9

The first characteristic of Eschatological Suffering and Joy is a clear gem, ready for us to pick up and grasp from this verse.

- Jesus is the "archegos" or cause. The originator, author, and founder.
- Jesus is the "teleiotes" or completer, finisher, bringing the goal to its fulfillment.

In this text (as well as elsewhere) we see Jesus views life through eschatological eyes. Like an architect, He created the design, the plan, the goal, the **telos**—the end.[5] As the perfecter of our faith, He completes our faith, His plan, and brings it to fulfillment or end.

1. Read Hebrews 12:2 again. Then read John 19:28-30. According to Hebrews 12:2, what did Jesus do after enduring the cross and despising its shame?
2. According to Hebrews 12:2, what purpose, stated in just five or six words, motivates Jesus to endure the convergence of all evil upon Himself?
3. What was that joy set before Him, that *telos*, purpose, or end? John 4:34; Hebrews 1:1-4; Philippians 2:5-11
4. What power does JOY have over shame?

End, purpose, goal—this is the key to Jesus' perspective. In John 4:34, He said, *"My food is to do the will of Him who sent Me and to accomplish His work."* That word *accomplish* is translated as *finish* in the KJV and NIV. Jesus, within the Trinity, is the Architect, Contractor, and Construction Worker. What He planned, He executed and finished.

Biblical Declaratives: The Three Principles or Laws

The key to interpreting biblical stories (and our lives) eschatologically is to view the entire arc of the story from the *telos*— the end or the goal.

An eschatological interpretation, seeing the present in light of the end which is currently the future, is based upon the belief in God's sovereignty: He has a plan, a decreed

---

5. Zodhiates, Spiros. *The Complete Word Study Dictionary*, (Chattanooga, TN: AMG Pub., 1992). The Greek term telos (Strong's, #5056), in which numerous words find their roots, denotes "end, term, termination, completion. Particularly only in respect to time." It takes on multiple figurative meanings such as "final purpose, that to which all the parts tend and in which they terminate, the sum total (1 Tim. 1:5)."

will working its way from eternity "past," through time-space history, and into eternity "future." Thus, there is a *telos*, an end or goal. Note the double meaning of *end*: *end* as conclusion and *end* as purpose. When the purpose (end) is completed, the conclusion (end) has arrived.

Hebrews 12:2, a powerful passage, illustrates all three principles or laws of Eschatological Suffering and Joy. (Many other passages demonstrate and expand these truths, which you will traverse on your own explorations.) The second law interrupts the first and third laws. It does not belong at the end. Actually, the first and third can be viewed as one law viewed from two angles. Hold on to your questions. For now, let's state laws #1 and #3.

Law # 1: The Law of Telos

*When the purpose (end) is completed, the conclusion (end)] will arrive. Eschatological Suffering is the endurance of current affliction in light of a good and godly outcome (the **telos**) that is yet to come.*

In Hebrews 12:2 we see another principle. We see the goal in mind in Eschatological Suffering is a *good* goal. *Good* produces *joy*. Remember joy is always the proper response to goodness. In this verse, the *telos* is "the joy." The purpose causes joy.

Read Nehemiah 8:10b (and then note the context): *"Do not be grieved, for the joy of the LORD is your strength."* Joy makes you strong. This may seem like an odd idea, but it is a biblical one which experience corroborates.

- Discuss the relationship between disappointment and grief (as the Jews were experiencing, described in Nehemiah 8) and gratitude and rejoicing.

One definition of joy is satisfaction.[6] When you attain your goal (purpose or end), you feel satisfied, and that satisfaction expresses itself through joy—rejoicing, pleased relief,

---

6. Note the charts in the appendices listing over a dozen kinds of joy in the Bible. This is a source of encouragement. It is also a springboard for your own research.

gladness. When the purpose (end) is fulfilled, the conclusion (end) has arrived so that joy bursts forth. But there is also a joy available before you reach the conclusion.

Law # 3: The Law of Joy

A focus on the telos (end/purpose) will produce both joy as anticipation and joy as consummation.

Anticipatory joy strengthens. Consummate joy features the achievement of the goal (the end).

Joy is a resilient force (process) and eternal reward (product and state of being).

1. Meditate upon Hebrews 12:2 and Nehemiah 8:10b (and contexts). Pray your gratitude. In these contexts, what relationship do you see between suffering and joy?
2. In your own story, how have you observed Laws #1 and #3 working?

Inserting itself between God's *telos* and joy is man's Fall-causing wish to be first. To be his/her own god. God's world becomes an upside-down world, this Broken Cosmos, which is the middle cosmos awaiting The Cosmos to Come. Between the *telos* and the joy comes Christ's cross.

- What separated Jesus from the throne of God? Hebrews 12:2; Philippians 2:5-11

Predicting and explaining His own death, Jesus said, *"Truly, truly, I say to you, unless a grain of wheat falls into the earth and dies, it remains by itself alone; but if it dies, it bears much fruit. He who loves his life loses it; and he who hates his life in this world shall keep it to life eternal"* (John 12:24-26).

Jesus *"... endured the cross, despising the shame..."* (Hebrews 12:2).

- Jesus is the rejected cornerstone. Read Matthew 21:42 or Mark 12:10 in context. Also note Ephesians 2:20, 1 Peter 2:4, and Psalm 118:22.

What happens to the rejected cornerstone?

- After His death, resurrection, and ascension, Peter preached to those in Jerusalem, claiming *"This Man, delivered up by the predetermined plan and foreknowledge of God, you nailed to a cross by the hands of godless men and put Him to death"* (Acts 2:23).

What does Peter say next? Acts 2:24

When we see Jesus as the chosen one rejected by man but exulted by God, the middle law comes into sight. So what is the middle law?

Law # 2: The Law of Reversal

*The last shall be first. The **telos** trumps and guides everything.
That is, the last (eschaton) is determined by the purpose/goal (**telos**).*

*God's goodness always governs God's **telos**.
Since this Broken Cosmos is an upside-down world,
our desires are naturally the inverse of God's good **telos**.*

In John 12:24-26, Jesus explains the necessity of loss and death in order that we may experience gain and resurrection as God's happy conclusion (end).

"But many who are first will be last; and the last, first" (Matthew 19:30).

"For whoever wishes to save his life shall lose it; but whoever loses his life for My sake shall find it" (Matthew 16:25; Luke 9:24).

1. Meditate on the above passages and then summarize the meaning in your own words. Consider how this Kingdom principle can express itself in your life or in certain decisions you have to make. Discuss or sojournal your response.
2. We see the laws of God's Kingdom are the inverse of the laws of This Broken Cosmos. We can call this the Kingdom principle of reversal. Jesus also teaches this principle in The Sermon on the Mount (Matthew 5-7).

3. The Apostle Paul also teaches the law of reversal:

> *"If we suffer, we shall also reign with him..."* (2 Timothy 2:2, KJV);

> *"If we endure, we will also reign with Him..."* (2 Timothy 2:2, NASB, ESV, and NIV).

In the above translations of 2 Timothy 2:2, what are the two words that mean affliction? What are some other synonyms that could be used?

In the above translations, what is the one joy/reward word?

Let's review all three laws which are biblical principles seen in the narratives and declaratives. Then let's observe the relationships between the three.

Law # 1: The Law of *Telos*

When the purpose (end) is completed, the conclusion (end) will arrive. "For what will a man be profited if he gains the whole world, and forfeits his soul? Or what will a man give in exchange for his soul? For the Son of Man is going to come in the glory of His Father with His angels; and will then recompense every man according to his deeds" (Matt. 16:26-27).

Eschatological suffering is the endurance of current affliction in light of a good and godly outcome (the *telos*) yet to come.

Law # 2: The Law of Reversal

The last shall be first. The telos trumps and guides all else. "Truly, truly, I say to you, unless a grain of wheat falls into the earth and dies, it remains by itself alone; but if it dies, it bears much fruit. He who loves his life loses it; and he who hates his life in this world shall keep it to life eternal" (John 12:24-26).

The last (*eschaton*) is determined by the purpose/goal (*telos*).

God's goodness always governs God's *telos*. Since This Broken Cosmos is an upside-down world, our desires are naturally the inverse of God's good *telos*.

Law # 3: The Law of Joy

A focus on the telos (end/purpose) will produce joy as anticipation and joy as consummation.

"... Jesus, the author [archegos] and perfecter [teleiotes] of faith, who for the joy set before Him endured the cross, despising the shame, and has sat down at the right hand of the throne of God" (Heb. 12:2).

Anticipatory joy strengthens. Consummate joy features the achievement of the goal (the end).

Joy is a resilient force (process) and eternal reward (product or state of being).

Consider for discussion and/or sojournaling:

- What relationship do you see between The Law of *Telos* and The Law of Reversal?
- How do these first two laws strengthen your endurance and activate within you the third law, The Law of Joy?

No matter which one you start with, all three laws weave together.

Learning from a Bad Example[7]

Let's move to an Old Testament account illustrating the opposite of an eschatological perspective toward suffering and joy. We will also consider the consequences.

Reading the text, you will not see this negative turn coming. Who is our negative example? A "bad" man? No. Actually, he is listed as one of the few, good kings of Judah. Turn to 2 Kings 18.

---

7. 1 Corinthians 10 encourages us to use the examples found in the Old Testament as instruction so that we will be wise and not foolish, "that we should not crave evil things as they craved" (10:6), and so on. God uses people as both bad and good examples. Romans 15:4 says, "For whatever was written in earlier times was written for our instruction that through perseverance and the encouragement of the Scriptures we might have hope."

CHAPTER 9

Hezekiah, the twelfth king of Judah, is described as a man who *"did right in the sight of the LORD, according to all that his father David has done"* (2 Kings 18:3). Hezekiah did good by removing high places, breaking down the Asherah, destroying the bronze serpent that Moses had made which the people turned into an idol (verse four). The text goes on to say that Hezekiah *"trusted in the LORD ... so that after him there was none like him among all the kings of Judah, nor among those who were before him. For he clung to the LORD; he did not depart from following Him"* (verses five through six). What accolades! Wouldn't you love to have it said of you that you clung to the LORD and did not depart from following him?

Yet, strikingly, after an illness which almost takes his life, so that God grants him fifteen more years in answer to his pleading prayers, Hezekiah's vision blurs as his eyes turn inward. What does he do that undermines his clear record of following the LORD?

1. Read 2 Kings 20:12-15. What is his focus? What does he do?

2. The prophet Isaiah, who has encouraged and advised him in the past, now returns to the king with a chiding rebuke, informing him that because of his prideful foolishness, *"all that your fathers have laid up in store to this day shall be carried to Babylon"* including some of his sons. Read 2 Kings 20:16-19. How does Hezekiah respond?

3. Hezekiah is relieved judgment will not happen in his days but will occur after he is gone. Does this sound like the Hezekiah we've read about in previous chapters? How has his heart turned? How has he changed (not for the better—transformation, but for the worse—deformation)? What is now important to him?

Hezekiah exposes his self-centered myopia. He rejects Law # 1: The Law of *Telos*. He has his own *telos* in mind. Thus, he rejects Law #2: The Law of Reversal. The king hungers for present tense comfort and the adulation of men, forgetting the approval and pleasure of God and His purposes for the kingdom of God. Therefore, he forfeits Law #3: The Law of Joy.

All his life he has clung to the LORD, trusting Him, following Him, but after his miraculous recovery from his illness, he rejects the grace to be humble, which is a deferred gratification, an eschatological suffering.

4. Read James 4:10. How is humility an act of Eschatological Suffering and Joy? When does the joy come? Or we could ask, what kind of joy is available now, and what kind comes later?

5. How can an anticipation of future joy actually nurture joy in the present tense, even during difficulty?

6. What warning or lesson do we gain from Hezekiah's failure?

We have traveled through two biblical scenarios: 1) Jesus' fulfillment of the divine goal of substitutionary, sacrificial atonement through his death on the cross, resurrection, and His subsequent majesty and 2) Hezekiah's choice to pursue his own, present tense glory at the expense of the future. These biblical accounts are two of many biblical narratives illustrating the three laws of Eschatological Suffering and Joy.

Let's explore these ideas in the next section.

9.3 ADJUSTING THE FOCUS

We have contrasted the eschatological approach of Jesus (Heb. 12:2) against the myopic, small man approach of King Hezekiah (2 Kings 18-20). We have extracted three biblical laws Jesus both taught and demonstrated. Praise Him!

How can we apply these laws to our lives? We all live in mortal bodies, so an immediate application is to our health. From babies to the aged, we experience injuries and illnesses. How can an "eschatological" view transform us?

CHAPTER 9

Contrasting Responses to Physical Suffering:
Apostle Paul and King Hezekiah

When the Apostle Paul experienced physical afflictions, "a thorn in the flesh, a messenger of Satan to torment me" (2 Corinthians 12:7), he prayed. Paul wrote, *"Concerning this I implored the Lord three times that it might leave me"* (verse eight). In all Paul's writings, we see he was a praying man.

Compare this to Hezekiah's response to physical illness. He too prayed! Let's also remember Hezekiah's history of seeking the Lord and following him (chapters 18-19). We are so impressed with the way the king turned to God, praying, and leaning on Him. So God gave the victory. Both King Hezekiah and the Apostle Paul were praying men, God-dependent men.

After great dependence on God accompanied by great public victory, the king became mortally ill (2 Kings 20). The prophet Isaiah informed the king he was going to die. How did Hezekiah respond?

"Then he turned his face to the wall and prayed to the Lord, saying, 'Remember now, O Lord, I beseech You, how I have walked before You in truth and with a whole heart and have done what is good in Your sight.' And Hezekiah wept bitterly" (2 Kings 20:2- 3).

Is this a good prayer?

While we don't know the words of Paul's prayer, we do know he implored the Lord three times in prayer. To implore in prayer certainly means fervent prayer. But notice God's differing responses.

To Paul, God answers this way:

"My grace is sufficient for you, for power is perfected in weakness"
(2 Corinthians 12:9).

To Hezekiah, God answers this way:

"I have heard your prayer, I have seen your tears; behold, I will heal you. On the third day you shall go up to the house of the Lord. I will add fifteen years to your life, and I will deliver you and this city from the hand of the king of Assyria; and I will defend this city for My own sake and for My servant David's sake"
(1 Kings 20:5-6).

Why would God agree to heal Hezekiah but refuse to heal Paul? While we have no explicit answer per situation, we do have our biblical principles to apply, our three eschatological laws. We know God governs through His *telos* which is always good.

What else do we know? We know each man's illness follows great achievement. King Hezekiah has won great victories (but notice it was God who fought for Judah and gave the people victory). The king's success built him up and up and tempted him with great pride.

Now Paul's greatness was in unrivaled, divine revelations given to him (2 Corinthians 12:7). Look at how much of the New Testament Paul penned! Yes, he was insightful and wise beyond human understanding. Not only this, according to 2 Corinthians 12:4, some years previously, Paul had been *"caught up into Paradise and heard inexpressible words, which a man is not permitted to speak."* Paul has experienced visions and revelations that would greatly impress his audiences.

So both men were situated to be tempted by pride and self-adulation.

However, Paul records that *"Because of the surpassing greatness of the revelations, for this reason, to keep me from exalting myself, there was given me a thorn in the flesh, a messenger of Satan to torment me—to keep me from exalting myself!"* (2 Corinthians 12:7).

What is going on here?

CHAPTER 9

God tested each man. Each test was unique to the person, though there were similarities.

God tested Paul through illness and Hezekiah through healing. God tested Paul with restriction and Hezekiah with greater freedom.

While the plotline varied, the theme of testing was the same for each man: will you see through eschatological eyes, viewing My divine end and accepting the joy of anticipation now along with the accompanied hardships and humility, while waiting for the glory that is assured for later?

We should study in their contexts Isaiah 48:10-11 along with Romans 8:18-21. Condensed, here are the ideas. In Isaiah 48, "I have tested you in the furnace of affliction.... My glory I will not give to another." In Romans 8, our suffering can't be compared to the coming glory; "...the creation will be set free...into the freedom of the glory of the children of God." We have lights from two ends of the field to lead us.

- Read Paul's response to God's denial in 2 Corinthians 12:8-10:

Concerning this I implored the Lord three times that it might leave me. And He has said to me, 'My grace is sufficient for you, for power is perfected in weakness.' Most gladly, therefore, I will rather boast about my weaknesses, so that the power of Christ may dwell in me. Therefore, I am well content with weaknesses, with insults, with distresses, with persecutions, with difficulties, for Christ's sake; for when I am weak, then I am strong.

- Compare and contrast Hezekiah's response to God's answer (2 Kings 20) with Paul's response to God's answer.

Consider for discussion:

- How do you apply The Law of *Telos*, The Law of Reversal, and the Law of Joy to each man?
- This is a test.

Ironically, God's willingness to heal King Hezekiah presents the king with a humility and loyalty test which he fails, whereas God's refusal to heal the Apostle Paul protects him from exalting himself, yet presents him with the test of trusting God's grace in living with chronic pain or illness, with persecution, and with various trials. Paul passes this test.

Since all tests coordinate within God's good *telos*, even when we don't understand our circumstances, we can know our tests are purposeful and not arbitrary. This is comforting. How does Paul encourage us in 2 Timothy 4:7-8?

Consider for discussion or sojournaling:

- Whatever you are experiencing along the trail of life, this is a test. Whatever God's answers to your prayer, the answer (yes, no, wait . . .) presents a test of your loyalty, humility, endurance, grace, and growing character. It is a test to see if you and I will wear the eschatological lenses His Word provides for us and will focus on the *telos*, "fixing our eyes on Jesus" (Heb. 12:2).

Describe a current challenge you are in and ways you can employ the Three Laws of Eschatological Suffering and Joy to your current turn in the road.

9.4 TREKKING THE TRAIL

We began this chapter in the book of Ecclesiastes. We also found Ecclesiastes helpful when we traversed Collateral Suffering and Joy back in chapter 3. All portions of Scripture speak to the various themes of pascharology. One particular word in Ecclesiastes strikes at the heart of Eschatological Suffering and Joy: vanity.

Translated as "vanity" in the KJV, NASB, and ESV and "meaningless" in the NIV, this word, *"hebel" or "hevel"* means vapor, mist, or breath.

> *The words of the Preacher, the son of David, king in Jerusalem.*
> *"Vanity of vanities! All is vanity." What advantage does man have*
> *in all his work which he does under the sun? (Ecclesiastes 1:1-2)*

CHAPTER 9

"Vanity" is the translation of the Hebrew word *hebel* or *hevel*.[8] Old Testament Bible scholar, Walter C. Kaiser Jr. asks, "But is [vanity] the correct meaning of *hebel*?" or is it "a fair way to render *hebel*?"[9]

Hebel is employed as a metaphor comparing something material (a mist) to something experiential (the quick passing of time and life). When translating to another language, Jews and Christians alike have tended to jump right to descriptive, interpretive terms such as vanity, meaninglessness, futility, and even absurdity.[10]

Kaiser presents his case for retaining the metaphorical term, such as vapor, mist, or breath. He unpacks Ecclesiastes as a book written by one author, and shows the closing theme is not just tacked on later but is found within the text. This is important in order to see the *telos* (purpose) within the text and in the conclusion. If the author[11] meant vanity and meaningless, Kaiser asks then "why go on reading the book? It was all meaningless anyway!"[12] Kaiser notes a change in tone when "the translation of *hebel* is changed from 'vanity, emptiness,' or 'meaninglessness' to the more accurate sense of 'mist, change, transience,' or 'puzzling.' "[13]

Look together at Ecclesiastes 1:2 and 12:13-14. When we see our lives as a vapor or mist, and then pair this truth with the preacher's conclusion, what can we conclude?

---

8. Translators have struggled with how best to translate this word, going all the way back to the Septuagint, the Greek translation of the Hebrew texts over 280 years before Christ.

9. Walter C. Kaiser, Jr., *Coping with Change Ecclesiastes*, (Ross-shire, Scotland: Christian Focus Publications, Ltd, 2013), 58. This is an undated edition of his 1978 edition entitled *Ecclesiastes Total Life*.

10. Michael V. Fox, *The JPS Bible Commentary: Ecclesiastes*, (Philadelphia: The Jewish Publication Society, 2004), xix. Fox gives us a good example of a Jewish interpretation of the book. Fox translates *hevel* as senselessness or absurdity. The commentary's renderings: "futility… amounts to nothing, fleeting, illusory, brief span, frustration, nothingness." It is the "central motif of the book." "Hevel literally means 'breath' or vapor.' Ecclesiastes uses it metaphorically. The different translations reflect the ways the metaphor has been understood." Then he lists five ways: as vain, futile, ephemeral, incomprehensible, and absurd.

11. "The Preacher," transliterated: Koheleth or Qoheleth (which is the basis for the Hebrew name of the book). Although Solomon's name never occurs in the book, he is traditionally considered to be Koheleth.

12. Kaiser, 29.

13. Kaiser, 67. I agree with Kaiser, although adding "puzzling" as an "accurate sense" of *hebel* moves us back to that interpretive track that led to "vanity" and "meaninglessness."

> *"Vapor of vapors. All is vapor"* (1:2).[14]
>
> *"...Fear God and keep His commandments...for God will bring every act to judgment, everything which is hidden, whether it is good or evil"* (12:13-14).

We conclude that our vapor has eternal value. Not one single breath is vanity, meaningless, or absurd. Selah.

■ Consider for discussion or sojournaling:

Compare the above insight to our three laws: The Law of *Telos*, The Law of Reversal, and The Law of Joy. How do these laws undermine a vain, meaningless, nihilistic worldview? How do the three laws reinforce the eternal value of our vaporous lives?

For the Christian, the book of Ecclesiastes is not an "under the sun" (without God, materialistic) worldview. Some may say vanity and meaninglessness is a reasonable worldview for secular people who view life "under the sun" (an expression used twenty-nine times in this book).

1. However, if God will bring "every act to judgment, including everything hidden, good or evil (v. 14), which applies to every person (v. 13), can there be such a thing as vanity or meaninglessness even for the unbeliever?

2. How do 2 Peter 3:11-13 and Ecclesiastes 12:13-14 work together and challenge us?

3. Ecclesiastes 11:8-10 instructs us to enjoy our lives. If all is vanity/meaninglessness, then this advice creates mere cognitive dissonance. But if we view our misty lives as God's gift infused with meaning (*telos*), how can we humbly learn to enjoy the misty present?

---

14. https://biblehub.com/ecclesiastes/1-2.htm. This provides you with various translations. This is a good site for research. I hope you study the whole book of Ecclesiastes after completing this journey.

CHAPTER 9

Abel illustrates these realities. *Abel's* name is *hebel*! Abel's life was vaporously short, but its *telos* is eternal. His life has the commendation of God, and his prophetic message still speaks.

1. Review the record of Abel: Genesis 4:10; Luke 11:50-51; Hebrews 11:4. What testimony does his short life continue to give?

2. What are your limitations and vaporous changes that cause you to suffer? How do *hebel*, Ecclesiastes, and Abel challenge and encourage you?

The *telos* of Ecclesiastes 12:13-14 transforms the message of the book, extending to us in all of our challenges eschatological meaning, hope, and joy.

9.5 REST STOP

Let's sit on this knoll on the top of this hill and scan the scenes ahead and behind us.

Deep breath. Let your muscles relax. Having considered the lives of Jesus, Hezekiah, Paul, and Abel, let's now meditate upon our Guidepost.

GUIDEPOST

> *For I consider that the sufferings of this present time are not worthy to be compared with the glory that is to be revealed to us.* (Romans 8:18)

After traveling this chapter, how do you answer our chapter question:

How does my tomorrow change my today?

Here is a Latin hymn from the eighth century. We do not know the author, but we know that it was translated by John Chandler in 1837.

O Christ, Our Hope, Our Heart's Desire[15]

O Christ, our <u>hope</u>, our heart's desire, redemption's only spring!
Creator of the world art Thou, its Savior and its King.
How vast the mercy and the love which laid our sins on Thee,
And led Thee to a cruel death, to set Thy people free.
But now the bands of death are burst, the ransom has been paid;
And Thou art on Thy Father's throne, in glorious robes arrayed.
O Christ, be Thou our lasting joy, our ever great reward!
Our only glory may it be to glory in the Lord.

Finally, our eschatological vision transforms into doxology! Now, we enter our summative discovery in chapter 10.

---

15. *Trinity Psalter Hymnal* (Willow Grove, PA: Trinity Psalter Hymnal Joint Venture, 2018), 267.

CHAPTER 10

HOW CAN MY MESSY LIFE GLORIFY GOD?

DISCOVERY NINE

"Gloria in excelsis Deo." "Glory to God in the Highest."

Glory? Glorify? Doxology??

We approach our ninth and last discovery on this adventure under this framework, but you and I will continue to discover! In this last of three tiers, we've explored the depths of Communal Suffering and Joy which led us upward to view suffering from eschatological horizons and to accept its anticipatory joys. From these heights we reach the peak where we ask, "How can my messy life glorify God?" Here we directly confront Doxological Suffering and Joy.

You probably know the hymn called the Doxology: "Praise God from whom all blessings flow. Praise Him all creatures here below. Praise Him above, ye heavenly hosts. Praise Father, Son, and Holy Ghost."

- From this context, what would you assume the word *doxology* means?

Of course! You'd think *doxology* means "praise." Certainly, *doxology* becomes praise, but the core meaning is disarmingly more basic.

The word is built on two Greek roots: *Doxa + logos*. *Doxa* is from *dokeo* which means "to think, recognize, glory"[1] *Logos* means word, discourse, intelligence, from which we get our word, logic.[2] At the root of doxology is the thinking, reasoning process, one of mankind's greatest, divine gifts, a unique gift, especially designed for God's image bearers—human beings. Through our thinking, which directs our attitudes and activities, we are designed to reflect specific characteristics of our Creator-God. Before you can praise God, you must think on God, think rightly about Him (John 4:24), and come to know God (Ps. 46:10). *Doxa + logos* = glory-word.[3] True thoughts about God are glory. True thoughts about God will cause praise and wonder and fear and all that is the profusely proper response.

Amazing! I am so delighted to know that just to think about Him, to meditate upon who He is and what He does, initiates doxology—to glorify Him, to praise Him. "Bless the Lord, oh my soul" (Ps. 103:1). To bless God by thinking about Him stirs joy within me. How encouraging for when we are sick or physically limited. Doxology expresses true thoughts about God, resulting in praise. Oh, my! Christianity is something quite other than a mindless, irrational, superstitious religion. We are offered a deep and rich, reasoning faith that works.

So we ask in this chapter, "How can my messy life glorify God?"

10.1 TRAVEL SCOPE

Now, we reach the pinnacle of our third tier, the ninth and final discovery in our explorations. Here, the ultimate meaning of interwoven suffering and joy within God's providential plan is clarified through Doxological Suffering and Joy.

---

1. Zodhiates, Spiros. *The Complete Word Study Dictionary.* Chattanooga, TN: AMG Pub., 1992. Doxa (Strong's #1391) from dokeo (Strong's # 1380).

2. Logos, as you probably remember is the word translated "word" in John 1:1 and 1:14.

3. Etymology does not determine meaning but presents origins. Context shapes meaning. Both should be considered in understanding meaning, range of meanings, and meaning narrowed by usage.

CHAPTER 10

> **GUIDEPOST**
>
> *But if anyone suffers as a Christian, let him not feel ashamed,
> but in that name let him glorify God.* (1 Peter 4:16)

Let's put these concepts of doxology into a story recounted by Richard Wurmbrand in his classic, *Tortured for Christ*.[4]

The Crude Russian Officer

After World War II when Russian communism has come to power in Romania, Wurmbrand meets a Russian officer in Romania. To share Christ with Russians is "heaven on earth" to him, a Jewish believer in Jesus as the Messiah and a Christian pastor who has spent time in prison under the Nazis and will spend many years in prison under the communists. But while free, he is introduced to a Russian officer by an Orthodox priest because Wurmbrand speaks Russian and the priest does not.

Providentially, Wurmbrand's hunger to preach to Russians meets this particular Russian officer's hunger for God. Yet this officer has not "the slightest knowledge of [God]" and had never even seen a Bible.[5] He visits Richard Wurmbrand's home, and Richard reads from the Bible to the man. Wurmbrand must tell you the story.

> I read to him the Sermon on the Mount and the parables of Jesus. After hearing them, he danced around the room in rapturous joy proclaiming, 'What a wonderful beauty! How could I live without knowing this Christ!' It was the first time that I saw someone so joyful in Christ.
>
> Then I made a mistake. I read to him the passion and crucifixion of Christ, without having prepared him for this. He had not expected it and, when he heard how Christ was beaten, how He was crucified and that in the end He

---

4. Richard Wurmbrand, *Tortured for Christ* (Bartlesville, Oklahoma: Living Sacrifice Book Company, 1967, 1998).
5. Ibid., 17.

died, he fell into an armchair and began to weep bitterly. He had believed in a Savior and now his Savior was dead!

I looked at him and was ashamed.... I had never shared the sufferings of Christ as this Russian officer now shared them. Looking at him, it was like seeing Mary Magdalene weeping at the foot of the cross, faithfully weeping when Jesus was a corpse in the tomb.

Then I read to him the story of the resurrection and watched his expression change. He had not known that his Savior arose from the tomb. When he heard this wonderful news, he beat his knees and swore—using very dirty, but very "holy" profanity. This was his crude manner of speech. Again he rejoiced, shouting for joy, "He's alive! He's alive!" He danced around the room once more, overwhelmed with happiness![6]

A holy hush, a *selah* is required here. This account not only illustrates Doxological Suffering and Joy; it instructs seasoned Pedestrian Theologians.

What lesson(s) can you derive from Wurmbrand's story?

As the Russian soldier takes in an accurate picture of the Son of God through the Word of God, he rejoices with a joy unspeakable and full of glory. Crude exclamations have never been so lovely. But the story does not end here.

Wurmbrand invites him to pray. He has never prayed! Wurmbrand recounts his first prayer—doxological expressions.

"Oh God, what a fine chap you are! If I were You and You were me, I would never have forgiven You of Your sins. But You are really a very nice chap! I love You with all my heart."

Wurmbrand showcases God to the Russian officer simply by reading the Scriptures to him while kindly offering home hospitality to this stranger. Up to now God has been obfuscated, indeed, hidden from the man. This officer has had no control over many

---

6. *Ibid.*, 18.

elements of his own story: when and where he was born, as well as the government, family, and education under which his life was shaped. Yet he had some choices.

Deep within his spirit stirred a craving for the "numinous" (as C.S. Lewis and some others would call that mysterious recognition of and longing for the divine). He could have buried it. He could have refused to give it attention. As Romans 1:18 explains, he could have "suppress[ed] the truth in unrighteousness." However, God had set in motion the revelation of His glory from before time when He designed a creation through which He would make Himself evident within His image bearers and throughout His creation, which would manifest His "invisible attributes, His eternal power and divine nature."[7]

This Russian officer did not know God. Before Wurmbrand, he had no exposure to the Scriptures. He did not even know himself very well. Yet his story powerfully illustrates the reality of this Romans 1 discourse in reverse—through his positive, doxological posture, rather than through the negative, judgment-inducing posture described in the biblical text toward the ungodly.

Rather than accepting the suppressive, dishonest teaching of his government and education, he listened to the teaching of his longing: "that which is known about God is evident within them for God made it evident to them" (Rom. 1:19). By seeking the God he wishes to exist but has been taught does not exist, the officer honors the God he wants to know. By exchanging depraved suppression and futile speculations for the light of the Word which Wurmbrand reads to him, his dark heart is illuminated. He enters into faith.

1. According to Romans 10:17, from where does faith come?

2. What characteristics of conversion, belief, and faith do you hear in the Russian officer's unorthodox and awkward but enthusiastic prayer?

The light of the Word of God that enters this officer expresses itself in joyous glory to God. Crude as he presently is, he glorifies God by gratefully showcasing his agreement

---

7. Romans 1: 18-21.

with who God reveals Himself to be from the Scriptures he has heard (and how different God is from himself!). He recognizes God's goodness and his own sinfulness and neediness. His Doxological Joy is rooted in his own suffering, for he has been spiritually abused. The degree of his starvation enriches the potency of his joy.[8]

Let's go back to the word *doxology*. We learned it is based upon two Greek roots: *doxa* + *logos*. Condensing the meaning to make a working definition, doxology is the expression of true and logical thought about God.

Doxology is more than true and logical thought. It is thought that must be exposed, communicated, revealed, showcased, lived, and shared. Because doxology is the expression of what is real, what is true, who God truly is, as He has made Himself known, then doxology becomes praise. God is good, God does good (Ps. 119:68), and God works all things together for good to those who love Him (Rom. 8:28). Doxology pulls back the curtain to show His glory.

To *glorify God* is to showcase what is real about God.

3. Write a working definition of *doxology*?

4. Write a working definition of *glorify*?

Doxology pulls back the curtain to show His glory. What is the opposite of doxology? It is to keep the curtain down, to try to cover up God or make a substitute god, to suppress the truth of God (Rom. 1:18). This is to *obfuscate* God. This word, *obfuscate*, provides us with a clarifying antonym (opposite concept) for *glorify*. To obfuscate is "to darken, obscure... to deprive of light... to eclipse."[9] Wow! How can puny mankind eclipse the infinite God?

5. To obfuscate is to make something intelligible seem unintelligible. Returning to Dr. Hodge's description of the change in human nature at the Fall of man, we see that by the change in the human mind, emotion, and will, God was obfuscated from our

---

8. In America we witness a similar spiritual abuse and resultant spiritual starvation as generations of citizens have been denied biblical education through our public education system and secular institutions. Near starvation cultivates deep hunger and longing, which can be satisfied. "Lord, give us Wurmbrands and hungry soldiers. Amen."

9. *The Oxford English Dictionary.*

CHAPTER 10

vision and hearing. We spiritually died. Our wisdom became fleshly. What does 1 Corinthians 1:25 call the wisdom of mankind? Why does human wisdom consider God's wisdom to be foolishness?

Because sin darkens, deprives, distorts, suppresses, and does not recognize reality—that is, truth and goodness for what it is—sinfulness disqualifies people from glorifying God. Our glorifying God was and is His creative intention for us (Rom. 3:23). We, by our natural, sinful nature, are opposed to God, evoking a loving God's wrath (Rom. 1:18). It is the gift of God (Rom. 6:23) that places a new heart within us so that, whereas previously, we obfuscated the glory of God, now in the righteousness of Christ, we become glory to Him and can glorify God (2 Cor. 5:17; 1 Cor. 6:20; Ezek.11:19-20).

To glorify God is to showcase God through the narrative of one's life. All human stories involve characters, settings, plots (life situations), themes, conflict, and some kind of change for the characters—to be transformed or deformed. All life stories involve the interaction of God with us and us with others. Constant opportunities exist to glorify God, showcasing His person and providence. Yet, equal opportunities exist to obfuscate God, to distort or suppress His presence and involvement in our lives. These are choices that Pedestrian Theologians make daily and hourly.

Like the rough Russian officer, we do not choose our lifetimes, place of origin, and many of our circumstances or opportunities. God sets up the elements of our stories, but doxology as a responsive lifestyle is always our choice to make.

6. Reflect upon your life and identify some situations when you really did glorify God. A simple time. A quiet time. And a public time. Doxology flowing from you. You may want to sojournal and then share some thoughts with your group.

7. Reflect upon your life and identify some times when you chose, intentionally or inadvertently, to obfuscate God and His involvement in your life.

8. Take some time to meditate on the concept of doxology and its integration into your life as a theme that others can truly notice in your life.

10.2 VIEWING THE BIBLICAL MAP

We've defined doxology, we've peered into the experience of a Russian officer's first exposure to God as revealed in Scripture, and we've reflected upon our own experiences of offering doxology to God or obfuscating God through our choices. Now, let's observe two biblical examples, one from the Old Testament and one from the New Testament of people who chose doxology over obfuscation.

The narrative lens: let's look at doxology in the midst of Joseph's suffering.

The life of Joseph illustrates the power of the doxological option. Indeed, Joseph did not get to choose his family, his nation, his location, and the nature of his situational conflicts. His opportunity to showcase God is unique in history in his role in saving his people, the Israelites, from whom the Messiah would come, and his life as a type or foreshadowing pattern of the Messiah Himself. "Joseph's thirteen-year separation from his family at the hands of his heartless brothers,"[10] and his grotesquely unfair imprisonments in Egypt (Collateral Suffering) showcase Doxological Suffering. From this torment emerges God's providential plan to save His covenant people.

Joseph's story is told in Genesis 37-50. Spend some study time reading these chapters. It's an engaging story. Jacob is the father of Joseph and his eleven brothers and at least one sister. Note family dynamics: patterns that would unite family members and patterns that would upset relationships. Note dysfunctional patterns. Note characteristics that would complicate family life. Certainly, polygamy would intensify conflict.

Note environmental, geographical, and finally, political challenges. How would any young person deal with the kind of abuse Joseph encountered, and how would that shape a person's mindset for future attitudes and responses? You may want to take some notes in your sojournal.

---

10. Walter Kaiser, "Eight Kinds of Suffering in the Old Testament," in *Suffering and the Goodness of God*, 76.

CHAPTER 10

Just think. Joseph lived almost 3,800 years ago, and we still have his story which includes some dialogue. His words, recorded at the conclusion of the Genesis record, have gifted the world with his legacy, showing us how to respond well to conflict and to enter into all the genres of suffering and joy.

From your reading of Joseph's story, jot some notes in the following chart.

Genres of Suffering and Joy	Joseph's Demonstration of these Genres:
Foundational Tier with Genres:1-3: 1. Recompensive Suffering and Repentive Joy 2. Collateral Suffering and Redemptive Joy 3. Transformational S & J Next Tier of S & J w. 4-6: 4. Compassionate S & J 5. Sacrificial S & J 6. Exemplary S & J Top Tier of S & J w. 7-9: 7. Communal S & J 8. Eschatological S & J 9. Doxological S & J	References and Notes

The declarative lens:

Joseph's statement to his brothers who hatefully sold him into slavery decades earlier: *"You meant evil against me, but God meant it for good"* (Gen. 50:20). This statement is a biblical principle we should all memorize and utilize.

"Here suffering serves a good end and purpose under the guiding hand of God."[11]

---

11. Walter Kaiser, *A Biblical Approach to Personal Suffering*, 126.

Through the life of Joseph, we see the amazing impact of suffering well, trusting the wise and caring hand of God. We see all the kinds or genres of suffering expressed in his life. We may not see all the kinds of joy, but the record does reveal his endurance, his hope, and his final joy in being reunited with his family and in providing welfare for millions of people.

Next, let's look doxology in the life of an obscure, New Testament person.

Read John 9. Before you start reading, look over the content of chapter 8 and the content of chapter 10. In the back of your mind, consider the order and placement of these scenes.

This New Testament incident involves obscure characters but consumes an entire chapter (forty-one verses) in the book of John, and illustrates the doxological principle behind this kind of suffering. The location is in Jerusalem. The main characters are Jesus, his disciples, a man born blind, his parents, some neighbors, and the Pharisees. The account is ensconced between the dramatic and forceful claims of Christ in chapter 8 and the reassuring and comforting claims of Christ in chapter 10. One must wonder if the location of the incident is nearly as instructive as the story itself. This story clearly illustrates Doxological Suffering and Joy.

The disciples ask an odd question which evokes an answer from Jesus that reframes the life of this obscure fellow, setting him on a new path. Does the Spirit of God direct the curiosities of people so that God may be glorified in a decided way? Apparently.

"Rabbi, who sinned, this man or his parents, that he should be born blind?"

Why would the disciples take notice of this beggar? The supposition of a retributive cause is as natural as breathing, but since he was born blind, his personal sin could not have been a cause, unless his blindness was a divine protection against some possible future sin—worth a thought, but not knowable. The fact the disciples know the blind man was born blind may indicate this is not the first time that they have seen this beggar. They are familiar with his situation. Apparently, his disadvantages trouble them. So they ask an odd question which opens up some deeply held and conflicting attitudes evidenced by the various characters in this account.

Stephen F. Saint, the son of Nate Saint, one of the five slain missionaries in Ecuador in 1956, articulates a gutsy insight concerning this biblical story. From my perspective, Saint's own deep experiences of suffering which began in childhood qualify him to state what many people may be too timid to articulate. He writes, "I was perplexed to realize that the poor blind man who begged outside the temple in John 9 had been blind his whole life just so Jesus could prove God's power. That was a lot of suffering in a society without 'Americans with Disabilities Act' laws."[12] Nonetheless, Saint projects that "God also uses suffering to *demonstrate his power*."[13]

Jesus pointedly answers his disciples' misdirected question.

"It was neither that this man sinned, nor his parents; but it was in order that the works of God might be displayed in him" (John 9:3).

1. If you were this man's parents, how might these words comfort and encourage you?

The works of God to be displayed in him, the doxology from suffering, are unfolded through the forty-one verses as the man learns who his healer is. The Jewish leaders have the opportunity to believe and display God's works, but they reject the opportunity. Jesus's gift of physical sight to the man born blind blatantly displays God's power over the physical world. He now has physical vision and is poised to receive spiritual vision. Later, probably that same day, after the beggar has been put out of the temple and is rejected by the Jewish leaders, Jesus questions him.

"Do you believe in the Son of Man?" (Verse 35)
"And who is He, Lord, that I may believe in Him?" (Verse 36)

---

12. Stephen F. Saint, "Sovereignty, Suffering, and the Work of Missions," in *Suffering and the Sovereignty of God*, eds. John Piper and Justin Taylor (Wheaton, Illinois: Crossway Books, 2006), 112. Stephen was five years old when his father was killed by Waodani Indians in Ecuador, along with four other missionaries including Jim Elliot as they were trying to befriend them. Thus, Stephen was initiated early into suffering for Christ. Later he would suffer the loss of a young adult daughter, and would suffer an accident that would break his back. Through "various trials" he has been a faithful Pedestrian Theologian.
13. *Ibid.*, Italics in the original text.

"You have both seen Him and He is the one who is talking with you." (Verse 37)

Ah. The beggar man, once the man born blind (and a beggar because he was blind), learns through two senses: sight and sound.

Powerful words pour from of the humble beggar who has just heard powerful words from his Healer.
"Lord, I believe!" (Verse 38a).
These are doxological words, but the text does not end there.
"And he worshiped Him" (Verse 38b). This is doxological action.

Ah! Another appropriate place for holy pause. The beggar man's doxological suffering bursts into joy.

2. Have you ever noticed that when you believe and trust the Lord, you are actually worshiping Him? Do you see how points of trust and obedience showcase God in your life?

God's power is being displayed in this man. However, his display of doxology will not end his suffering. Neither physical sight nor spiritual sight offers closure to his suffering. Even before he knows who Jesus is and worships Him, his association with Christ strikes fresh wounds of rejection as he is expelled from the temple by the Jewish leaders. The beggar has responsively displayed the works of God—on the Sabbath—and God's work is totally offensive to the religious leaders. The beggar's new suffering provides the opportunity to reveal his spiritual transformation.

3. What other genres or categories of suffering does the once blind beggar display?

4. What choices of response does the beggar have toward Jesus, the Pharisees, and his parents?

B. Let's map doxology through biblical statement.

CHAPTER 10

1. How does our chapter Guidepost, 1 Peter 4:16, guide us into a lifestyle of Doxological Suffering and Joy?

2. How does our chapter Guidepost comfort you?

3. Where is the joy in doxology?

10.3 ADJUSTING THE FOCUS

Consider some wisdom from J. I. Packer:

> The triune God of the plan [of salvation] is great—transcendent and immutable is His omnipotence, omniscience, and omnipresence. He is eternal in His truthfulness and faithfulness, wisdom and justice, severity and goodness—and He must be praised and adored as such. Praise of this kind is the doxological foundation of human holiness, which always starts here. Just as there could be for Jesus no crown without the cross so there can be for us no holiness without praise.[14]

Doxology showcases God to others through our faithful, truthful words and lifestyle, in all times—through sickness and health, through natural disaster and pandemic, through economic comfort and deprivation, through blessing and persecution. We don't control circumstances, but through the Holy Spirit, we can produce doxological fruit.

We've witnessed the touchingly sacred response of a rugged Russian officer, deprived of knowledge of God but longing for this God denied to him, who discovered God through the sacred text of Scripture finally poured into his heart. His famine over, he jumps and shouts for joy. (Notice he has no bitterness for abuses against him.)

---

14. J.I. Packer, *Rediscovering Holiness* (Grand Rapids, MI: Baker Books, 2009), 65-66.

1. John 10:17 tells us that faith comes by hearing God's Word. How does this Russian soldier's delight in the hearing the Gospel account impact your attitude toward hearing and reading the Bible with fresh eyes of faith?

We've witnessed the doxological responses of Joseph. With such a dysfunctional family, he does not complain of their various abuses and personality deficiencies. He focuses on providing for them and takes great joy in doing so. He does not forget or ignore their cruelty toward him, but his eyes do have eschatological sight, seeing far beyond the pain to God's purposes, which walks him right into Doxological Suffering and Joy. He has suffered faithfully for God and reaps rewards.

2. Joseph's story piles one agonizing saga upon another: his destructive, toxic, and abusive family experiences, his faithfulness in the house of Potiphar from which he is "rewarded" with prison, his forgotten service for others which left him rotting years longer in prison, and finally his rise to fame in which he saves a people, but not his own, the Egyptian people. Ah. But then God weaves the family threads together and reunites Joseph with his own so that he may save and preserve them. Such sorrow but such redemption.

Joseph exemplifies Collateral Suffering at multiple turns in his life. But he lets God use unjust suffering to transform him into a sterling man of integrity, worthy of leading, like a king. We can connect the dots from the foundational genres of suffering up to the top tier genres.

How can Joseph's epic story instruct and inspire you in your own journey of suffering?

We've witnessed the doxological responses of the beggar man born blind. He too did not become bitter about his life-long trials and disadvantages. He did not expect Jesus to correct all the wrongs in his circumstance. Instead, he accepted Christ's healing and Lordship in his life. He worshiped the one the religious leaders denigrated. His was graced with a doxological focus. God poured out doxological joy on him even as his life took on new difficulties. This humble beggar's story preserved in Scripture has for millennia consoled and strengthened believers.

3. We don't know the blind man's name. If this person lived in your neighborhood today, maybe with other health and financial needs, how might you engage with this person? Expressing what you know of your Savior? Comforting the neighbor rather than ignoring him or her? What if you are the needy one, dependent on others to get along? What do you learn from this man born blind?

10.4 TREKKING THE TRAIL

Just as in the last chapter, we see the law of reversal at work in Doxological Suffering and Joy.

Apparently, in This Present Cosmos, the glory of God revealed and communicated through us requires a human reversal: from proud to humble, from rebellious to obedient, from going astray to returning to the Shepherd of our souls. This human reversal is actually plural—reversals. Based upon daily repentance—a daily dying of the old self.

We must daily remind ourselves of this unchangeable order: He is God and we are not. God will share His divine glory with no other, a law for all three cosmos, past, present, and future. And this should relieve us. We are created to be His creatures, so what a relief to be just what He intended us to be. As His creatures, created in His image, He does have a glory to show us, for us to show others, and for us to share with Him. Note Romans 8:28-29; Romans 1:16; 11:33-36.

As we trek along the trail God has prepared for us (Col. 2:6), let's ponder some steps can that we can take to turn any genre of suffering we endure into Doxological Suffering and Joy.

Doxological Joy exists in both our contexts of suffering and of blessing. Doxological Joy is delight in God, stemming from an accurate though finite understanding of who God is and what He does—through our lives, within our messy situations.

Remember suffering cannot separate a Christ-follower from joy, unless a believer chooses to turn from a fixed gaze upon God to a fixation on self, one's situation, or this broken world. Cultures, societies, and governments have obfuscated a vision and understanding of God, thus subverting their people from an orientation to glorify God. To "praise God from whom all blessings flow," people must first believe that God exists, blesses, judges, and rewards.

What steps do the following verses guide us into in order to turn suffering into doxology and joy?

- Romans 10:17
- 1 Peter 4:12
- Psalm 9:10

Consider the lives of the crude Russian soldier, Joseph in the book of Genesis, and the blind beggar in the book of John. In what ways do you see them glorifying God through their messy lives? Even when the picture is not pretty, we can see God lifted up and honored in their lives.

What about your messy life? How do you orient your life so that even in the messiness of your story God is truthfully lifted up and honored?

10.5 REST STOP

Time to rest from our travels and think about where we've traveled. Let's start by reviewing our Guidepost.

GUIDEPOST

But if anyone suffers as a Christian, let him not feel ashamed, but in that name let him glorify God. (1 Peter 4:16)

CHAPTER 10

Let's close with doxology expressed in lyrical loveliness:

May Jesus Christ be Praised[15]

When morning guilds the skies, my heart awaking cries,
May Jesus Christ be praised!
Alike at work and prayer to Jesus I repair,
May Jesus Christ be praised."
"Does sadness fill my mind, a solace here I find;
May Jesus Christ be praised;
Or fades my earthly bliss, the loveliest strain is this:
May Jesus Christ be praised.

---

15. The authorship of this hymn, one of my favorites, is unknown, but the German lyrics were translated by Edward Caswall in 1836.

CHAPTER 11

O JOY, WHY DO YOU SEEK ME THROUGH PAIN?

GUIDEPOSTS

*As you therefore have received Christ Jesus the Lord,
so walk in Him. (Colossians 2:6)*

*Beloved, do not be surprised at the fiery ordeal among you,
which comes upon you for your testing, as though some strange thing
were happening to you; but to the degree that you share the sufferings of Christ,
keep on rejoicing; so that also at the revelation of His glory,
you may rejoice with exultation. (1 Peter 4:12-13)*

* * *

Tracing Rainbows through the Rain

*O Love that will not let me go,
I rest my weary soul in thee;
I give thee back the life I owe,
That in thine ocean depths its flow
May richer, fuller be.*[1]

---

1. George Matheson. "O Love that Will Not Let Me Go." You can find this hymn in many hymnbooks and online at such sites as Hymnary.org. Matheson (1842-1906) was a Scottish theologian, pastor, and poet.

CHAPTER 11

These words poured from George Matheson's pen one lonely evening. This forty-year-old pastor, single and blind, was emotionally torn with happiness and sadness. He was happy for his dear sister who was to start a new life the next day when she was to be married. How wonderful! She had been his eyes, pen, and close friend for decades. Quietly, personally, he was sad for the loss of his sister's closeness.

His mind traveled back twenty years to when his heart, filled with joy, contemplated his own marriage to his sweetheart. In love, they wanted to marry. However, their dreams were dashed as she faced the reality George was going totally blind. Not wanting to support a blind man, she broke the relationship. That was all so long ago. Erupting with quiet emotion, the poem formed fully in his mind and then gushed onto the page. She let him go. But another Love would not let him go. "I rest my weary soul in Thee." And the words kept coming.

> *O Light that follows all my way,*
> *I yield my flickering torch to thee;*
> *My heart restores its borrowed ray,*
> *That in thy sunshine's blaze its day*
> *May brighter, fairer be.*

Like the blind man in John 9, the darkness of Matheson's night could not be accounted for by some rebellion in his own heart, by some sin for which his blindness and personal rejection were a just repayment. His darkness represented layers of Collateral Suffering but, ultimately, of Doxological Suffering. From that suffering he recognized an inner light from Love which restored his flickering light. More words flowed as another image formed in his mind.

> *O Joy that seeks me through pain,*
> *I cannot close my heart to thee;*
> *I trace the rainbow through the rain,*
> *And feel the promise is not vain,*
> *That morn shall tearless be.*

Pursued by Love—You will not let me go! Guided by Love's Light—Thy Word is a light unto my path. Sought by Joy—hounded through pain, he traced each hurt's hue to its final, tearless end. And through his rainbowed tears, his vision cleared.

> *O Cross that lifts up my head,*
> *I dare not ask to fly from thee;*
> *I lay in dust life's glory dead,*
> *And from the ground there blossoms red*
> *Life that shall endless be.*

On and on, his pen flowed, from one vision to another, until Matheson was brought to Christ's cross, and his head was lifted up. From the lonely dust blossomed an eternal joy—discovered at the cross. Had not Jesus claimed, "The Spirit of the Lord God is upon me, because the LORD has anointed me to bring good news to the afflicted; He has sent me to bind up the brokenhearted . . . to comfort all who mourn" (Isaiah 61:1-2)? A fresh grace in grief assuaged his soul.

Here we see, feel, taste, and touch the wooing of the Lover toward His beloved. Jesus saved Matheson not only from his sin but also from his brokenness in a broken world.

1. Reread these hymn lyrics in light of your own journey, in light of each chapter of your life.

- How has Love held on to you ("O Love that will not let me go")?
- How has Jesus' Light led you, reigniting your flickering flame?
- How has Joy sought you through pain?
- How has the Cross lifted your head?

So we have asked, *"O Joy, why do you seek me through pain?"* And Joy answers back. We turn, just as Mary Magdalene turned and raised her eyes to the man she thought was a gardener that early Sunday morn (John 20). He speaks her name. As sorrow flees, she sees Joy whom she thought she had lost. "Rabboni!" For the joy set before him, Jesus had endured the cross. Why through pain? "That they may have My joy made full in themselves," Jesus had prayed, "that they may all be one, even as Thou, Father are in Me and I in Thee, that they also may be in Us," prayed the Son (John 17:13,21). Why? Because that is what Love does.[2]

Retracing Our Trail

Remember God's first question to Adam? "Adam, where are you?"

This is still a good question. Where are you?

Look around you. Look straight ahead. Look back and trace where we've traveled. Do you see where you are and from where you have come?

Returning to The Original Cosmos, that era of exceeding goodness, we see, as Charles Hodge so perceptively describes, humanity "was originally created in a state of maturity [non-infancy] and perfection."[3] God's image shaped into the human race was not a physical but a moral/spiritual/personal image, in which, as Charles Hodge describes, humankind's

"Reason was subject to God;
his will was subject to his reason;
his affections and appetites to his will;
the body was the obedient organ of the soul.
There was neither rebellion of the sensuous part
of his nature against the rational,
nor was there any disproportion between them
needing to be controlled or balanced by ab extra gifts or influence."[4]

Such inward harmony produced outward harmony! Such peace! No "ab extra"—that is, "from outside" control or influence—was needed! Human thought, attitude, desire, and

---

2. "How deep the Father's love for us, how vast beyond all measure," pens Stuart Townsend in his hymn by this title. Explore this hymn on Townsend's own site: https://www.stuarttownsend.co.uk/song/how-deep-the-fathers-love-for-us.

3. Charles Hodge, *Systematic Theology*, Vol. II, 92.

4. Ibid., 99. Line divisions are mine, added to help us "eat" the sentences in cumulative "thought bites."

action were a symphony of goodness, agreement, beneficence, and beauty. Ahh. This lovely thought is not fantasy but history and prophecy.

Sadly, the lovely thought is not current reality, not in This Broken Cosmos. Graciously, God did give us a sighting of such in the life of Jesus Christ. The gospels picture this perfect man in the Son of God. J. Oswald Sanders describes Christ in his wonderful volume, *The Incomparable Christ*, in which he pens:

> The character of our Lord was wonderfully balanced, with neither excess nor deficiency.... It stands out faultlessly perfect, so symmetrical in all its proportions that its strength and greatness are not immediately obvious to the casual observer. It has been said that in Jesus' character no strong points were obvious because there were no weak ones. Strong points necessarily presuppose weak ones, but no weaknesses can be alleged of Him.... He was without flaw or contradictions.[5]

This is the LORD we worship! This is God's Son who is our friend and bridegroom as well as our saving Sovereign. This is the one to whom we are being shaped into His likeness to fit us to be His bride, made worthy.

We look at Jesus, our Savior, and we discover that in the looking we are gaining His looks.

1. What does 2 Corinthians 3:18 tell you?

Gratefully, we can look back and trace our travels. "All we like sheep have gone astray," Isaiah declares in Isaiah 53:6a. Nothing is more natural than to travel. We need no guide. Where have we turned? Isaiah 53:6b tells us that "each of us has turned to his own way." Our hearts' GPS will take us anywhere (there are so many choices) but where we need to travel.

The Psalmist admits, "Before I was afflicted, I went astray." Follow your first-born heart, and away you go! Astray we go. "Before I was afflicted"—no matter the kind of affliction,

---

5. J. Oswald Sanders, *The Incomparable Christ* (Chicago: Moody Press, 1971), 2.

CHAPTER 11

deserved or undeserved, just or unjust—I was afflicted variously. In various ways, "I went astray."

My first-born mind was not subject to God;
My first-born will did not desire His Will;
My first-born affections and appetites were but idol-makers, and
My first-born body is subject to corruption.
Sigh.
But then I was given
a new heart—a new mind, will, and affection!
Follow your twice-born heart,
tuned by God's Spirit and Word,
goaded by suffering and wooed by joy,
and your path leads to the place where
"the LORD has caused the iniquity of us all to fall on Him" (Isaiah 53:6c).
Humbled and relieved, in this fresh beginning I begin anew,
knowing that nothing in all creation can separate me
from the love of God, which is in Christ Jesus our Lord (Romans 8:38-39).

2. Read 1 Cor. 15:1-4 which explains the gospel foretold in Isaiah 53.

3. According to Isaiah 53:4, He (Christ) bore and carried *what* and *whose* what?

4. According to Isaiah 53:5, not only did he bear our grief and carry our sorrows, He also was pierced through for our _____.

5. Not only was He pierced through for our transgressions; he was crushed for our iniquities. The chastening for our _____ fell upon Jesus. We are healed by His _____.

6. Our grief and our sorrows include all of our Collateral Suffering, but our transgressions are composed completely of our _____ suffering. He bore both kinds of our suffering.

7. According to Isaiah 53:7, it is foretold the Messiah would be oppressed and afflicted, "Yet He did not open His mouth; Like a lamb that is led to slaughter, and like a sheep that is silent before its shearers, so He did not open His mouth."

What portion of Christ's suffering was Collateral Suffering?

For whose Recompensive Suffering did Christ atone?

"Before I was afflicted, I went astray, but now I keep your word" (Ps. 119:67). Now, I follow after You. I've turned in my old, stony heart, hardened by my own inclinations, and I've been given a new heart, a soft heart hearing what I had never heard before, seeing what I had never seen, and is carefully shaped by the Holy Spirit.

8. Review and summarize these verses:
   A. Ezekiel 11:19-21

   B. 2 Corinthians 5:17

   C. 1 Corinthians 2:14-16

   D. Ephesians 5:22-23

Now I recognize the goodness of God woven through the fabric of my sorrows, as I admit with the Psalmist what is truly true: "It is good for me that I was afflicted that I might learn your statutes" (Ps. 119:70). This nears the bottom line. All of our troubles, no matter the kind, present rich value because they hold a spiritual power to shape and train us for a high and holy goal—that we might be well transformed—by the life of Christ dwelling within us, conforming us to His image. Then Christ's priestly prayer in John 17 will be fulfilled.

9. What does Psalm 119:68 tell us about God's nature and behavior?

You will remember that C.S. Lewis explained:

... God saw the crucifixion in the act of creating the first nebula. The world is a dance in which good, descending from God, is disturbed by evil arising from the creatures, and the resulting conflict is resolved by God's own assumption of the suffering nature which evil produces. The doctrine of the free Fall asserts that the evil which thus makes the fuel or raw material for second and *more complex kind of good* is not God's contribution but man's (italics added).[6]

10. What biblical truths do you observe that are stuffed within this quotation? Note, for one example, Romans 8:28 and 29. Verse twenty-nine gives the reason for verse twenty-eight.

(Note God's sovereignty, providence, wisdom, goodness, ownership, love, determination, condescension, humility, involvement, victory, power, and majesty implied or expressed in the above quotation.)

When the Scriptures declare it is good for me to be afflicted, we recognize the good is what Lewis describes as "a more complex good" which is educational and re-formational. A simple good is what we see in The Original Cosmos: everything was directly and consistently good and blessed. A more complex good includes "evil" as a factor working through the equation to a good end (Rom. 8:28-29).

The fruit of the Tree of the Knowledge of Good and Evil is always a mixed fruit. In The Cosmos to Come, good and evil will be permanently divorced, separated eternally in Heaven and Hell. By God's grace through faith in Christ, I am traveling to Heaven.

Traveling is what humans do: astray or God's way. I desire to travel together with you, you, and you, following Christ our Savior and Guide—a pilgrimage of Pedestrian Theologians, traveling to that celestial city.

---

6. C.S. Lewis, *The Problem of Pain*, (San Francisco: HarperCollins Publishers, 1940), 80.

Reviewing this *Traveler's Guide* Journey

Our study began by locating the three cosmos of reality.

The Original Cosmos	This Broken Cosmos	The Cosmos to Come
The Era of Exceeding Goodness	The Era of Enmity and Grace	The Era of Eternal Goodness
Genesis chapters 1-3	Genesis chapters 3 through most of the Scriptures	Focus Tree
Focus Tree	Focus Tree	Tree of Life
The Tree of the Knowledge of Good and Evil	The Cross of Christ	Genesis 2:9; 3:22-24
Genesis 2:9, 16-17; 3:3	1 Peter 2:24	Revelation 2:7; 22:2, 14,19
	Isaiah 53	
	Romans 8:19-22	

Recognizing our lives in This Broken Cosmos, we have discovered nine kinds of suffering and joy.

The Nine Discoveries or Genres of Suffering & Joy

Tier 3 The Unexpected Views (Chapters 8,9,10)	7 Communal Suffering and Joy	8 Eschatological Suffering and Joy	9 Doxological Suffering and Joy
Tier 2 The Winding Way Up (Chapters 5,6, 7)	4 Compassionate Suffering and Joy	+ 5 Sacrificial Suffering and Joy	6 Exemplary Suffering and Joy
Tier 1 The Ground Under Our Feet (Chapters 2, 3, 4)	1 Recompensive Suffering and Repentive Joy	2 Collateral Suffering and Redemptive Joy	3 Transformative Suffering and Joy

Note the chart on pages 206-207.

CHAPTER 11

We've surveyed biblical narratives and declaratives and imperatives: stories, propositions and principles, and commands or instructions. We've been taught by Adam, Eve, Cain, Abel, Abraham, Isaac, Joseph, Moses, David, Hezekiah and such OT examples. We have listened to our Savior in the Gospels. We've watched Peter and Paul be transformed. Every biblical story and statement can shed light upon our developing pascharology and personal lives—to feed and lead us.

Elisabeth Elliot encouraged us to offer our sorrows as sacrifices to God and then to offer ourselves to Him as living sacrifices (Rom. 12:1-2). I will never forget the story of the man born blind in John 9 or Richard Wurmbrand's report of the Crude Russian Soldier. Both stories present broken men who do not succumb to victimhood and bitterness but who discover glory and joy in worshipping a Savior whom they need and who turns out to be real!

Do you see yourself as a Pedestrian Theologian? Do you see how every chapter of your "story" or life-experience can be interpreted through the lenses of these nine biblical discoveries or genres of suffering and joy? Do you see how you can pull into your life every biblical concept to help you interpret not just the meaning of the passage but the meaning of your life?

Our purpose in this Traveler's Guide is to chart out a biblically tethered pascharology or theology of suffering and joy so that we will "not be surprised at the fiery ordeals" coming in life "for [our] testing" (1 Peter 4:12). Peter instructs us to be prepared for such things and to know they are not something strange happening to us.

This is counterintuitive to our Western thought in which we've felt that we should be rewarded (recompensed, compensated) with a pleasant life for obeying the Lord, for following His ways. So to varying degrees we've been surprised. Any upset or outrage we feel at injustices toward us or others is evidence we are surprised and unprepared. We naively want to reap only from the good seeds, while the bad but forgiven seeds, and other people's cross-pollinating of harmful seeds, we hope and pray won't grow, nor be reaped. However, we are called to suffer, and simultaneously, we are called to joy.

This study helps us correct our vision and expectations in order to strengthen our faith. We are learning to live a simple glory (thinking God's way) leading us to glorify Him (walking God's way) and finally to the glory of The Cosmos to Come.

This framework organizes the nine kinds of suffering and joy into three sets of three, building from the ground up, so that we can observe and study them. However, in life the nine mix and mingle. Naming the pain and the joy assists us in recognizing God's loving providence in our lives. Providence is evidence of divine purpose.

I hope you can improve this study as you apply your gained wisdom long after you are done traveling with me. So much more can be done with this framework. Share this with others, helping them to make better sense of their lives.

All of these concepts must grow in the soft, watered, nourished soils of our hearts. As we have received Christ Jesus our Lord, so we walk in Him, constantly nourished on the word of the faith, not surprised at the fiery ordeal among us, fed daily on the joys set before us. Richly, we are graced as Christ's pedestrian theologians and coming bride.

> *'Let us rejoice and be glad and give the glory to Him,*
> *For the marriage of the Lamb has come and His bride has made herself ready.'*
> *And it was given to her*
> *To clothe herself in fine linen, bright and clean;*
> *For the fine linen is the righteous acts of the saints.*
> *And he said to me,*
> *'Write, 'Blessed are those who are invited to the*
> *Marriage supper of the Lamb.'*
> *And he said to me, 'These are true words of God.'*
> Revelation 19:7-9

* * *

Prayer:
Father God of the Universe,
We acknowledge that this is Your universe, and we are Yours.
You are responsible for us and we are responsible to You.
Holy is Your Name:
Your Kingdom come,
Your will be done in our lives as it is in Heaven.
All we have is from you: You give and you take.
Blessed be the good name of our Blesser.
Daily, You grace us with more than we need.
Thoroughly thankful may we be.
In our journey, deliver us from evil.
In our affliction, fortify us with endurance.
In each day, fill us with joy-touched faith.
Ever keep our eyes on You.
In this Broken Cosmos,
Touch others through your transforming work in us,
That increasingly, we may be Christ-shaped gracers.
Amazingly, may we even be joy to Your Heart.[7]
Glory to the Father, Son, and Holy Spirit,
Now and forever,
Your Cosmos to Come.
Amen.

---

7. 2 Corinthians 5:9-10.

APPENDIX

1: Vocab Café

2. Charts

3. Travel Guidelines:

- Travel Directions and Options
- What Kind of Pedestrian Theologian Am I?

Recommended Tours:

- Tour 1: Additional Resources for Personal Study
- Tour 2: Additional Resources for Extended Study

VOCAB CAFÉ

Welcome, travelers, to the Vocab Café, serving up satisfying quenches of meaning for particular terms you encounter in this Traveler's Guide. All key terms when first or early encountered in the text will be printed in bold print. Thus, you know you can travel to the Vocab Café for some defining sips of nutritious explanation.

You may find it enlightening to explore this Café before attempting the chapters. As you pursue the chapters, return to this spot for refresher sips whenever your mind feels a bit fuzzy about the material you are studying.

* * *

Collateral. Being side by side, not in a direct line. Collateral suffering is suffering that does not follow directly in line from the cause. It is the fall out of another source/cause. Thus, the suffering is indirect, unjust, and sometimes mysterious.

Conflict. The collision of opposing forces; struggle. An element of "story" added at the Fall of mankind (Genesis 3), existing in all stories until This Broken Cosmos concludes and The Cosmos to Come fully commences.

Cosmos. Order: how reality works within a particular world, the governing laws or principles of a system. *Cosmos* is both singular and plural, determined by usage. Taking the wide lens view of history, we see three cosmos.

The Original Cosmos: *The Era of Exceeding Goodness* with Adam and Eve in the Garden of Eden (Genesis 1 and 2).

This Broken Cosmos: The Era off Enmity and Grace with the fallen sons and daughters of Adam and Eve scattered around the world whom God loves and for whom Christ died, living in a creation temporarily subject to corruption (Romans chapters 3 through 8).

The Cosmos to Come: The Era of Eternal Goodness in which The New Heaven and Earth will be the Kingdom of God in its eternal state (Isaiah 66:22-23; Revelation 21-22).

Cosmic War. Conflict between God and Satan involving creation and humankind, first declared in Genesis 3:15 when God said to the serpent, "I will put enmity between your seed and her seed...." This conflict involves invisible, spiritual forces of good and evil (Eph. 6:10-20; Rom. 8:18-39; 2 Thes. 2:3; Col. 1:13; 2:13-15) as well as visible results evident in nature and throughout human history.

Elohim. First word in Old Testament translated *God* (Gen. 1:1) and the most commonly used word for God in the O.T. It is masculine and plural yet has both singular and plural usages (used for pagan gods, angels; for God with a singular verb consistent with a monotheistic view of God). Christians see it as foreshadowing the Trinity.

Enmity. The posture of an enemy; hostility, malevolence. "I will put enmity between you (Satan) and the woman..." (Genesis 3:15). "The carnal mind is enmity against God..." (Romans 8:7).

Evil. The privation or perversion of good; also a power and principality at enmity with God. According to Girdlestone, evil is the breaking of harmony; it is injury or destruction, touching all mankind and all creation.[1] John Frames writes, "Natural evil is God's curse, the pains brought into the world by the fall. Moral evil is sin, the transgression of God's law (1 John 3:4)."[2] D.A. Carson writes that "evil is evil because it is rebellion against God.... The dimensions of evil are thus established by the dimensions of God; the ugliness of evil is established by the beauty of God; the filth of evil is established by the purity of God; the selfishness of evil is established by the love of God."[3]

---

1. Robert B. Girdlestone, *Synonyms of the Old Testament*, (Grand Rapids, Michigan: W. B. Eerdmans Publishing Company, 1897).
2. John Frame, "The Problem of Evil", in *Suffering and the Goodness of God,* ed. Christopher W. Morgan and Robert A. Peterson (Wheaton, Illinois: Crossway Books, 2008), p 151. Frame also argues against the Augustinian view of evil as deprivation of good. His chapter in this book deals with theodicy and various views of the nature of evil.
3. D.A. Carson, *How Long, O Lord?*, (Grand Rapids, Michigan: Baker Academic, 2006), 42.

The Fall. A term naming the point at which another force (sin via Satan's influence) entered earth's original and pristine cosmos, spoiling the original design and order, introducing a parenthetical rule/order within time and space, described in Genesis 2-3. The Fall is the door into This Broken Cosmos.

Genre. A category, a kind, or a class composed of things similar in nature or function. In literature, we have such genres as fiction, nonfiction, poetry, prose, drama, essays, and so on. In music, we have such genres as baroque, classical, romantic, jazz, and pop. The Scriptures list "songs, hymns, and spiritual songs" (Eph. 5:19). In pascharology, we have the nine kinds or discoveries of suffering and joy.

Good. God's storehouse of blessing; beneficence, that which is beneficial (Psalm 31:19). Scripture's first main adjective describing the result of a good God's work (Genesis 1-2; James 1:17): synonyms include "pleasant, beautiful, excellent, lovely, delightful, convenient, joyful, fruitful, precious, sound, cheerful, kind, correct, righteous," virtuous, and happy.[4]

Simple good and complex good:

A. During the Original Cosmos all reality was good—blessing and benefitting all creation and glorifying the Creator. *Good was simple*, composed of a single substance—goodness.

B. During This Broken Cosmos, *good* is still God's storehouse of blessing, but it is no longer simple, composed of only one substance, goodness. Now, *good* becomes *complex*. *Complex:* a composite of differing substances, both good and bad woven together.

C. In The Cosmos to Come, good will again be composed of the singular substance of goodness. Hell (separate from The Cosmos to Come) will be composed singularly of evil. (One could say that Hell is not a cosmos [order] but is an "anti-cosmos" because order is good and no goodness is there. The Lake of Fire as the ultimate anti-cosmos could be called The Chaos to Come.)

C.S. Lewis writes: "The doctrine of the free Fall asserts that the evil which thus makes the fuel or raw material for the second and *more complex kind of good* is not God's contribution but man's."[5] Study Romans 8:28-29.

---

4. Girdlestone.
5. C.S. Lewis, *The Problem of Pain*, (San Francisco: HarperCollins Publishers, 1940), 80.

Heart. The Old and New Testaments' assimilated picture equals the eternal, immaterial, inner person, the seat of the inner person: the mind, emotion, will, affections, desires, and conscience. Gen. 6:5; Ex. 14:4; Ps. 14:1; 28:7; 51:10, 17; Prov. 15:28; Matt. 13:15; Jms. 4:8.

Heaven. The place and throne of God (Isaiah 66:1; Matt.5:34-35). Jesus is there, interceding on our behalf (Heb. 8:1-2; 9:24; 10:19-22). Heaven is the believer's future home (John 14:1-4); The coming kingdom or the Cosmos to Come is described in Isaiah 66 and Revelation 21-22 as the New Heaven and Earth in which heaven comes down from above and joins a renovated earth. Death is swallowed up in victory.

Hell. The place or state of the lost and condemned. Gehenna (Strong's # 1067). The Greek, Gehenna, transliterates the Hebrew, "the valley of Hinnom" where children were sacrificially burned (2 Chron. 28:3, 33:6; Jer. 7:31, 19:1-6). At the time of Jesus, Gehenna was the burning trash dump outside of Jerusalem, which Jesus used to illustrate hell. In the O.T., *sheol*, *hades*, and *paradise* are names used for the abode of the dead. Jesus presented heaven and hell as real places.[6]

Human Nature. The qualities and constitution of humanity. Human nature, as originally designed by God, was a nature in harmony with God and His nature. Dr. Charles Hodge describes that nature in which man's "reason was subject to God; his will was subject to his reason; his affections and appetites to his will; and the body was the obedient organ of the soul."[7] No influence was needed to keep the human being harmonized within the self or with God. In man's fallen nature, man's reason, will, emotions, and body are not naturally aligned to God or each other. Outside influences are necessary to change the human heart. (Also note "sin nature.")

Ineffable. Unspeakable, beyond words; God's infinite attributes are ineffable—beyond our ability to put into words, beyond our human comprehension. Yet, paradoxically, He has condescended to us, by making us in His image so that we, the finite creature, can comprehend a cup full of the infinite sea of His revealed thus speakable glory.

Joy. The divine response and proper human response to goodness: God is good; God does good; God's works are good. Synonyms or kinds: exaltation, sacred rapture

---

6. Erwin W. Lutzer, *The Truth about Heaven and the Afterlife: The Truth about Tomorrow and What it Means for Today*, (Chicago: Moody Publishers, 2016).

7. Charles Hodge, *Systematic Theology*, Vol. II (Peabody, Maine: Hendrickson Pub., 2003), 99.

(magnifying God for His wonderful deeds), optimism, cheerfulness, hopeful mindset, courage and encouragement, delight, gratification, confidence, boasting, glory, satisfaction, having the "kingdom within"—indwelt by the Holy Spirit via faith in Christ; leaping for joy, pleasing/pleasure, shared joy, laughter, gladness, happiness, related to *charis* (grace).[8] Makarios (Strong's 3107): "The believer is indwelt by the Holy Spirit because of Christ and as a result should be fully *satisfied* no matter the circumstances."[9]

Kingdom. A reigning order or cosmos imposing its laws upon that which it rules. Because God is purely good, His kingdom is purely benevolent.

Lament. An expression of anguish, grief, regret, or sorrow. Lament is a genre of poetry and prose found in Scripture and other literature. The book of Lamentations by Jeremiah is the Bible's most significant example. At least one third of the Psalms are laments. Job, Habakkuk, and Ecclesiastes also contain lament. Lament presents an expressive language Christ-followers need to learn in order to unlock the doors of their suffering leading to various comforting joys.

Law. As in "the law of suffering" and "the law of joy": a statement explaining the underlying design producing obligatory order and rule; a functional system of operations; how something works; an operative principle creating patterns.

Pascharology. *Pronounced "pass'-car-o'-logy"; pascho* (Greek root meaning suffering) plus *chara* (Greek meaning *joy*, related to *charis* meaning *grace*); the study of suffering and joy and their interrelation. As a category in Systematic Theology, Pascharology fits within Biblical Anthropology, Soteriology, and Hamartiology. This term is coined by this author and will not be found in theological literature.

Pedestrian Theologian. One who walks with God. A Christ-follower who follows Christ. A Professional Theologian studies and promotes theology. Every Christ-follower, professional or layman is called to be a Pedestrian Theologian. *A Christian Pedestrian Theologian is one who aims to apply the Scriptures to all avenues of life.* People of every religion and non-religious persuasion are also "Pedestrian Theologians," following their

---

8. William Morrice, *Joy in the New Testament*, (Grand Rapids, Michigan: Eerdmans Publishing Company, 1984). Morrice explains eleven kinds of joy in the New Testament based upon eleven Greek roots and their clusters.

9. Spiros Zodhiates, *The Complete Word Study Dictionary New Testament*, (Chattanooga, TN, 1992). Italics added. Note chart #1 in the following appendix.

own gods, idols, or worldviews. People may not be consistent with their gods/beliefs, but humans follow what they believe. This term is coined by this author.

Recompense/Recompensive. A wage, a compensation; that which is earned; the consequence of a cause; the outworking of the sow-reap principle. The wage can be reward or punishment. "The wages of sin is death" (Rom. 6:23a).

Redeem/Redemption/Redemptive. To purchase back; to deliver or ransom. In Redemptive Joy, God buys back our sorrows by investing them with meaning and new purpose. Thus, even with undeserved, mysterious sufferings, God weaves into them meaningful, complex good.

Repentance. Greek: *metanoeo*. A change in the mind including regret resulting in "a true change of heart toward God. The word means to know *noeo* (3539) after *meta* (3326)."[10] After knowledge. To know after sinning, which Zodhiates says results "in regret for the course pursued and in a wiser view of the past and future." It is not regret merely because of the consequences (note Esau: Heb. 12:15-17). It is a deeper comprehension, related to one's relationship with God. The eating of the Tree of the Knowledge of Good and Evil produced an "after knowledge," ironically, from which we are all still learning. Faith is a "before knowledge" that believes what God says and acts accordingly (Heb. 11:3).

Selah. Pause, ponder, and praise. A notation found over seventy times in the Psalms which probably was originally a musical notation, but the original meaning is lost. The Septuagint (LXX, the Greek translation of the OT from the second century BC) translates it as "intermission." We see it as a musical and thought pause. Selah reminds us to meditate in wonder on God, His Word, and His ways.

Sin. Noun: offense and trespass against God; error, transgression; Verb: to transgress is to miss the mark: to fall short of the glory of God, the original design He made for us, whom He created in His own image. To trespass is to leave the path: to go one's own way rather than God's way (Isaiah 53:6), which equals allegiance to self rather than to God. Sin is idolatry.

Sin Nature. The self-reliant, God-defiant natural propensity of mankind since the Fall of the race. This nature is our "default setting" or innate orientation of mind (reason,

---

10. Spiros Zodhiates, "Lexical Aids to the New Testament" in *The Hebrew-Greek Key Word Study Bible*, (Chattanooga TN: AMG Publishers, 1990), 1856.

thought, and conscience), emotion (affections, desires, and attitudes), and will (desires, lusts, and choices). Our sin nature is our fallen heritage, a self-directed nature.

Sojournal. In this traveler's guide, a sojournal (noun) is a journal in which you record your special thoughts and responses to any of the given prompts. Sojournal (verb) combines the verb, *to sojourn* (to stay somewhere temporarily) with the verb *to journal* (to write in a journal). You see the connection between journey, journal, and sojourn in the French word for day, *jour*. Originally, a journey was a day's travel, a sojourn was a day's stay, and a journal was a daily writing. Writing in your sojournal is sojournaling, whether daily or not. It is a place to ponder, explore, express, lament and praise. Create your own *My SoJournal.*

Suffering. The divine response and proper human response to evil, sin, brokenness, and destruction. Synonyms: affliction, anguish, trials, tribulation, trauma, pain, sorrow; results of the Fall involving God, creation (the material world), the spirit world, and all mankind. (Note the definition and explanation of the wrath of God below.)

Taxonomy. A framework or an orderly system of categories in which to place collected data. The inspiration for this framework of pascharology was Bloom's *Taxonomy of Educational Objectives* (1956) and Walter Kaiser's classification of suffering (1982; note his text and article listed in the bibliography).[11]

Telos. The end goal. (Strong's, #5056). Denotes "end, term, termination, completion. Particularly only in respect to time." It takes on multiple figurative meanings such as "final purpose, that to which all the parts tend and in which they terminate, the sum total (1 Tim. 1:5)."[12]

---

11. Benjamin Bloom led a team of educational psychologists from the University of Chicago in constructing an educational taxonomy, first published in 1956, and since used by educators in designing courses and curriculum. It is entitled *Taxonomy of Educational Objectives: The Classification of Educational Goals*. The six tiers are divided into lower and upper levels of cognitive processing (thinking): from lower to upper tiers: 1) Knowledge (rote learning), 2) Comprehension (demonstration of understanding), 3) Application (problem-solving), 4) Analysis (breaking apart information into components), 5) Synthesis (re-arranging parts into wholes, often new creations), and 6) Evaluation (critique/judgment based upon criteria). In 2000, the last two categories were reversed. With Synthesis at the top, it is often now called Creation. (Creativity is considered more complex than critique. Creativity has been promoted and critical thinking has been demoted.) Upper level or critical thinking is not possible without lower level thinking. You must know something (lower levels) in order to analyze, evaluate, or create (upper levels). Similarly, my framework for Pascharology takes foundational levels of suffering and joy from which upper levels become possible. Taking Dr. Kaiser's eight kinds of suffering, I arranged my version of them in three ascending tiers of three each, showing more than categories. This framework shows flow, relationship, and integrated meaning.

12. Zodhiates, Spiros. *The Complete Word Study Dictionary*, (Chattanooga, TN: AMG Pub., 1992).

Theodicy. An explanation attempting to support the belief in a good and sovereign God who rules over a world exhibiting both order and disorder, both goodness and evil, both pleasure and pain. It addresses the question, "If God is good and all powerful, why is there evil and suffering in the world?"[13]

Theology. Many definitions are available. From the Greek: "*theos*" (God) + "*logos*" (word, discourse, logic, intelligence) = God talk or discourse about God. A "God word" pointing Godward.

Theology Proper studies the divine, God Himself. Theology in general is the broad scope and detail of all biblical teaching/doctrine. For Pedestrian Theologians, we employ Dr. John Frame's definition: "the application of God's Word by persons to all areas of life."[14]

FURTHER EXPLANATION, IN CASE YOU'RE INTERESTED:

Theology. Categories of usage: Theology: broad scope term for Christian doctrine (teaching); Types of theology:

1) Biblical Theology (textual-historical, specific view).
2) Systematic Theology (plenary view; what the Bible teaches from Genesis to Revelation divided topically into about ten categories: Bibliology (doctrine of the Bible), Theology Proper (doctrine of God), Christology (doctrine of Christ), Pneumatology (doctrine of the Holy Spirit), Anthropology (doctrine of humanity), Angelology (doctrine of angelic beings), Soteriology (doctrine of salvation), Hamartiology (doctrine of sin), Ecclesiology (doctrine of the church), and Eschatology (doctrine of last things); <u>this study adds Pascharology (doctrine of suffering and joy)</u>.
3) Exegetical Theology (Textual Interpretation: knowledge of ancient languages, linguistics, history, and archaeology).
4) Historical Theology (Ancient, Medieval, Reformed, Modern, Post-Modern).

---

13. For further reading, consider starting with *The Problem of Pain*, by C.S. Lewis; *Suffering and the Goodness of God* editors Christopher W. Morgan and Robert A. Peterson; *How Long, O Lord?* by D.A. Carson; and *If God is Good* by Randy Alcorn.
14. John Frame, *The Doctrine of the Knowledge of God*, (Phillipsburg, New Jersey: P & R Publishing, 1987), 76.

5) Dogmatic Theology (Calvinistic, Arminian, Covenant, Dispensational, Roman Catholic, Eastern Orthodox).
6) Contemporary (Liberal, Fundamental, Neo-Orthodox, Liberation, Catholic, Conservative, Evangelical, Feminist, Charismatic, Emergent, Analytic....).[15]

Transform/Transformation/Transformative: To transform is to change forms.

Transformation is the process of metamorphosis. The butterfly passes through four transformative stages: larva, pupa, cocoon, and then the adult—the butterfly.

Transformative suffering is suffering that changes us (the process involving a "more complex good") by the power of the Holy Spirit and His Word! It is the opposite of deformation, that harmful, carnal, destructive process of change. Transformative suffering is the process of spiritual sanctification, which leads us in Christ to greater Christ-likeness and thus into transformative joy. In us it is Christ-formative.

Walk. To follow. A biblical metaphor for a person's conduct which reveals a person's worldview, loyalty or allegiance, and who the person really is. Genesis 17:1 ("walk before Me and be blameless"); Ex. 16:4 ("walk in My instruction"); 2 Corinthians 5:7 ("we walk by faith"); Galatians 5:16 ("walk in the Spirit"); Ephesians 5:2 ("walk in love"); Ephesians 5:8 ("walk as children of the light"); Colossians 2:6 ("so walk in Him"). In your concordance you will find many more instructive passages employing this metaphor.

Witness. A testimony. One who testifies to the truth of what he or she has seen, heard, or experienced. In Rev. 1:5, Jesus is called "the faithful witness." Heb. 12:1 calls the biblical figures listed in Heb. 11 "the cloud of witnesses." Greek: martus, marturos (Strong's 3141, 3142, 3144), from which we derive the word, martyr.

Wrath: God's wrath is His irreconcilable opposition to evil rooted in His goodness, holiness, and love, requiring justice in order to reconcile the creation to the Creator (Genesis 3:15). The cross of Christ, where God suffered, is the place where love and judging justice kissed in reconciling harmony. Study in their contexts Romans 1:18-20; 3:23-24; 5:1-11; 8:1, 38-39.

---

15. Most of these categories are referenced or explored in *The Moody Handbook of Theology*, by Paul Enns.

CHARTS

CHART 1

Nine Discoveries or Genres of Suffering & Joy with Guidepost Verses

Overarching Guideposts: "As you therefore have received Christ Jesus the Lord, so walk in Him" (Colossians 2: 6). "Beloved, do not be surprised at the fiery ordeal among you, which comes upon you for your testing, as though some strange thing were happening to you; but to the degree that you share the sufferings of Christ, keep on rejoicing...." (I Peter 4:12-13).

Three Cosmos Guidepost: "...Train yourself to be godly. For physical training is of some value, but godliness has value for all things, holding promise for both the present life and the life to come" (I Timothy 4: 7b-8 NIV).

Read the following chart from the bottom tier to the top: 1) The ground under our feet, 2) The winding way up, and 3) The unexpected views.

Unless otherwise indicated, Scriptures are from the NASB.

#7 Communal Suffering & Joy	#8 Eschatological Suffering & Joy	#9 Doxological Suffering & Joy
Vertical relationship: In Christ: fellowship of S & J "That I may know Him, and the power of His resurrection and the fellowship of His sufferings, being conformed to His death; in order that I may attain to the resurrection from the dead." "Rejoice in the Lord always; again I will say, rejoice!" Philippians 3:10-11; 4:4	Future-focused tenacity, Eschatological eyes, Delayed gratification "For I consider that the sufferings of this present time are not worthy to be compared with the glory that is to be revealed to us." Romans 8:18	Showcasing God accurately, Aligning my life to His design, Glorifying God "But if anyone suffers as a Christian, let him not feel ashamed, but in that name let him glorify God." 1 Peter 4:16
#4 Compassionate Suffering & Joy	**#5 Sacrificial Suffering & Joy +**	**#6 Exemplary Suffering & Joy**
Horizontal relationship: Fellowship of suffering, Mercy-grief, collective pain "Blessed be the God and Father of our Lord Jesus Christ, the Father of mercies and God of all comfort, who comforts us in all our affliction so that we will be able to comfort those who are in any affliction." 2 Corinthians 1:3-4	Generous and gracious giving, Sacred offering, voluntary "But even if I am being poured out as a drink offering upon the sacrifice and service of your faith, I rejoice and share my joy with you all." Philippians 2:17	Gospel-driven witness, A testimony and model "The things you have learned and received and heard and see in me, practice these things and the God of peace shall be with you." Philippians 4:9 "Follow my example, as I follow the example of Christ." (I Corinthians 11:1 NIV).
#1 Recompensive Suffering & Repentive Joy	**#2 Collateral Suffering & Redemptive Joy**	**#3 Transformative Suffering & Joy**
Deserved, retributive, Sow-reap principle "For the wages of sin is death, but the free gift of God is eternal life in Christ Jesus our Lord." Romans 6:23	Undeserved, unjust, Sometimes mysterious "And they that know Thy name will put their trust in Thee." Psalm 9:10a (extended option: Ps. 9: 9-10)	Mix of #1 and #2 producing Christ-transformations "Consider it all joy, my brethren when you encounter various trials, knowing that the testing of your faith produces endurance...." James 1: 2-4

CHART 2 WORDS FOR JOY IN THE NEW TESTAMENT

English Term   Greek Term(s)   Semantic Range   Sample References   Sample Narrative

English Term	Greek Term(s)	Semantic Range	Sample References	Sample Narrative
1) Exultant Joy	Agallian, Agalliasis	Exuberant joy in God; Spiritual exaltation, sacred rapture; magnifies God for His wonderful deeds.	Sept: Psalms 30:5; 45:15; 65:12; Luke 1:14,44,46; Acts 2:46; Hebrews 1:9	Luke1:46 Mary says, "My spirit has *rejoiced* in God my Savior."
2) Optimism	Euthumein, Euthumos	Of a good mind, a benign, positive, hopeful mindset or temperament, a good, cheerful attitude.** Encourage, courage The mood of faith.	Acts 24:10; 27:22,25,36; James 5:13	Shipwreck on the way to Rome: Paul stirred them to a trusting, courageous mindset.
3) Gladness, Good cheer	Euphrainein, Euphrosune	Good spirits, well mind, cheerful, joyful in mind, in a spiritual sense; Faith gives assurance that all will be well.	Acts 2:26,28; 2 Corinthians 2:2; Luke 12:19;15:23, 24,29,32	Luke 15—Prodigal Son: Father calls all to *be merry*.
4) Pleasure	Hedone, Hedus, Hedeos	A. Delight, enjoyment; Sensual pleasure, gratification, enjoyment, in NT only used of physical pleasure**; Worldly passions; B. Best use: superficial gladness in hearing the Word.	A. Luke 8:14; Titus 3:3; James 4:1,3; 2 Pet. 2:13; 2 Corinthians 11:12; B. Mark 6:20, 12:37; Luke 8:13	Luke 8—Parable of the Sower: 8:13- received word with rootless *joy*; 8:14- choked by *pleasures*.
5) Courage	Tharsein, Tharrein, Tharsos	To be of good cheer, have courage, be full of hope & confidence**Confidence connected with faith.	Acts 28:15; 2 Corinthians 5:6,8; Hebrews 13:6; Matthew 9:2, 22; 14:27; Mark 6:50; 10:49; Luke 8:48; John 16:33	Acts 28:11-In Rome, Paul took *courage* from the brethren there.
6) Hilarity	Hilaros, Hilarotes	Cheerfulness associated with generous giving and serving as outpourings of love.	Romans 12:8; 2 Corinthians 9:7	Romans 12:8- Spiritual gift of mercy to be given cheerfully. 2 Corinthians 9:7- God loves a cheerful giver.
7) Boasting	Kauchasthai, Kauchema, Kauchesis	"To boast, glory, exult both in a good and bad sense."** Strong element of joy, glory; Element of God's character in joy & glory.	Jeremiah 9:23; 1 Corinthians 1:31; 2 Corinthians 10:15; Galatians 6:4,13; Philippians 2:16	Man has nothing to *boast* of (Eph. 2:8) but should *boast* in God (Rom. 5:11).

8) Blessedness, Happiness	Makarios, Makarizein, Makarismos	Fully satisfied; satisfaction coming from God and not from favorable circumstances. Having God's kingdom within. Indwelt by Holy Spirit because of faith in Christ.**	Matthew 5:3,10,11; Luke1:45; Acts 20:35; John 13:17, 20:29; Romans 4:7-8;14:22; 1 Corinthians7:40	Matthew 5 Beatitudes John13:17—the obedient are blessed
9) Leaping for Joy	Skirtan	To spring, leap, or bound, used of animals and humans. Natural movement expressing joy in living.	Sept: Psalms 114:4; Luke 1:45; 6:23	Psalms 114:4—Mountains skipped like rams; Luke6:23- Leap for joy when persecuted.
10) Inward Joy	Chairein, Chara	Rejoice, joy, gladness, joy in the Holy Spirit, joy of faith.** Related to charis—grace; an attitude of joy or delight.	Rom 14:17;Philippians 1:25; 1 Thessalonians 1:6; 3:9; 2 Timothy 1:4; Jms.4:9; 1 Pet.1:8	1 Thessalonians 1:6—They imitated Paul…and received the word in tribulation and joy of the Holy Spirit.
11) Shared Joy	Sunchairein	To rejoice with; to laugh with	Sept: Gen 21:6; Luke 1:58; 15:6; 1 Corinthians 13:6; 2 Corinthians 12:26; Philippians 2:17	Genesis 21:6—After birth of Isaac, Sarah declares that everyone can laugh with her.

The above chart is based upon *Joy in the New Testament* by William Morrice and *The Complete Word Study Dictionary* by Spiros Zodhiates. Items marked with a double asterisk are specifically from Zodhiates. Some Old Testament references for comparison are from the Septuagint. The key terms do not list or clarify the endings the root word can take as nouns, verbs (and tense forms), adjectives, and adverbs. The goal is simply to gather a range of meaning per root word. The grammatical forms presented follow Morrice's text. Morrice presents a short chapter per term and then writes a series of chapters that follow these various words of joy in the New Testament.

One aspect of joy is missing from the above. Let's add the following.

CHART 3 PLEASE, PLEASING, AND PLEASURE AS CHARACTERISTICS OF VOLITIONAL JOY

English Term	Hebrew or Greek Term	Semantic Range	Sample References	Sample Narrative
1) Please, Delight,	Chaphets	To have delight, to please, to will	Psalm 115:3; 135:6; Ecc. 8:3; Song 2:7; 3:5; Is. 53:10; 55:11	Whatever the LORD pleases, He does. Psalms 135:6
2) Please, Good benefit	Tob al	To be good as regards to something	Nehemiah 2:5; Esth. 1:19; 3:9; 5:8; 7:3; 9:13; 18:5	If it please the king, let it be granted.... Esth. 9:13
3) Please	Aresko	To please	Romans 8:8; 15:1-3; 1 Corinthians 7:32-34; 1 Thessalonians 2:4, 15; 4:1	In the flesh cannot please God. R. 8:8; Please the Lord or wife. 1 Corinthians 7:32-34
4) Well pleased	Euaresteo	Eu- good, well, plus aresteo— pleasing	Hebrews 13:16	For with such sacrifices God is well pleased
5) Pleasure, Delight	Chaphets	Delight, pleasure, will	Job 21:21; 22:3; Eccles. 4:5; 12:1; Is. 44:28; 46:10	Pleasure in his house. Job 21:21; Cyrus will perform God's pleasure. Is. 44:28
6) Pleasure	Ratson	Good will or good pleasure	Ezra 10:11; Nehemiah 9:37; Esth. 1:8; Psalms 51:18; 103:21	Those who serve God do His will or His pleasure. Psalms 103:21
7) Good pleasure	Eudokia/eo	Good thought, thinking well, kind intention	Ephesians 1:5, 9; Phil 2:13; 2 Thessalonians 1:11-12; 2 Corinthians 12:10; Hebrews 10:6,8,38	Paul takes pleasure in his infirmities. 2 Corinthians 12:10. Predestined according to His volitional, kind intention. Ephesians 1:5
8) Will, pleasure	Thelema	Will, inclination of pleasure creating joy	Revelation 4:11; Matthew 26:42; Acts 21:14; Ephesians 5:17; 1 Pet. 2:15; 4:2,3,19	Worthy art Thou... He created for His pleasure or will. Revelation 4:11

CHART 4 MAJOR KEY WORDS FOR SUFFERING IN THE NEW TESTAMENT[1]

English Term	Hebrew or Greek Term	Semantic Range	Sample References	Sample Narrative
Afflicted/Affliction	Kakoucheo Kakopatheia	Kakos = evil plus echo = to have; maltreated; Kako = evil plus patheia/pascho = suffering, torment	Romans 8:18; 7:5; 1 Pet. 1:11; 4:13; 5:1; Hebrews 2:9; 11:25,37; Galatians 5:24;	"For I consider that the *sufferings* (pathema/pascho) are not worthy to be compared to the glory..." Romans 8:18
Conflict	Agon, athlesis	To lead, agonize, struggle; where Greeks assembled for Olympic games—a metaphor for conflict, race, contest against spiritual enemies; to stand against, to strive	Ephesians 6:12; Philippians 4:3; 1 Timothy 6:12; 2 Timothy 4:7; Hebrews 12:1; 1 Thessalonians 2:2; Colossians 2:1; Hebrews 10:32	Put on the armor of God to stand against evil. Ephesians 6:11-12.
Endure	Hupomeno	To remain under, "to sustain a load of miseries, adversities, persecutions...in faith"	Matthew 10:22; 24:13; Romans 12:2; 1 Corinthians 13:7; Hebrews 12:2	"You will be hated by all on account of My name but it is the one who has *endured* to the end who will be saved." Matthew 10:22
Grief/Grieve	Lupe Sunlupeo	Pain in body or mind; sorrow; heaviness with grief, to be grieved	1 Pet. 2:19; Hebrews 12:11; Mark 3:5	"After looking around them with anger, *grieved* at their hardness of heart..." Mark 3:5

---

1. Spiros Zodhiates, *The Complete Word Study Dictionary New Testament*, (Chattanooga, TN, 1992). This chart presents concise summaries of key meanings or usage of words to provide you with a starting point to deepen your understanding and a jumping off point to initiate further research. Online resources such as Logos.com may take you further.

Longsuffering	Makrothumia	Long passion, Forbearance, "The person who has power to avenge himself, yet refrains from the exercise of this power." Patience.	Romans 2:4; 9:22; Galatians 5:22; Ephesians 4:2; Colossians 1:11; 3:12; 1 Pet. 3:20; 2 Pet. 3:15	"Or do you think lightly of the riches of His kind-ness and for-bearance and *patience* (makrothumia)… the kindness of God leads you to repentance. Romans 2:4
Passion	Pathos	To suffer, wound. Passion, lust. Occurs 3 times in NT. "…the soul's diseased condition out of which the various lusts spring."	Colossians 3:5; 1 Thessalonians 4:5; Romans 1:26	"Therefore, consider the members of your earthly body as dead to immorality, impu-rity, *passion*, evil desire, and greed…" Colossians 3:5.
Persecution	Dioko	To pursue, pros-ecute, persecute. "To pursue with repeated acts of enmity".	Luke 21:12; John 5:16; 15:20; Acts of the Apostles 7:52; 22:4, 7 8; 26:11,14,15; Rom 12:14; 2 Timothy 3:12; Revelation 12:13.	"Blessed are those who have been *per-secuted* for the sake of righteous-ness." Matthew 5:10
Sorrow	Lupe	Grief, sorrow	Luke 22:45; John 16:6, 20-22; Romans 9:2; 2 Corinthians 2:1; Phil 2:27	"…You will be sor-rowful, but your *sorrow* will be turned to joy." John 16:20
Suffer/suffering	Pascho	To experience some evil	Galatians 3:4; Matthew 16:21; Acts of the Apostles 28:5; 2 Corinthians 1:6; 1 Pet. 5:10; Philippians 1:29	God has granted that we believe on Christ and suffer for His sake. Philippians 1:29
Trial	Purosis Dokime Dokimion	A burning; set on fire; as refin-ing gold. Experience Proof	1 Pet. 4:12; 1:7 2 Corinthians 8:2 1 Pet. 1:7	"Do not be surprised at the fiery ordeal among you…" 1 Pet. 4:12
Tribulation	Thlipsis Thlibo 2346-2347	Affliction, anguish, pressure from evil, burdens the spirit. To press, com-press, crush	Mark 4:17; 1 Thessalonians 3:3; 2 Thessalonians 1:4; Acts 14:22, 2 Corinthians 1:4; 4:17; 7:4,6; Revelation 7:14	"Rejoicing in hope, per-severing in tribulation, devoted to prayer." Romans 12:12 (& 14).

TRAVEL GUIDELINES

PART I:
DIRECTIONS AND OPTIONS

Welcome to this traveling Bible study, traveling through the Word of God and through our lives as we explore the themes of suffering and joy and their dance together. I have named this framework of biblical study *pascharology* (Greek: "pascho" = suffering plus "chara" = joy). This study explores the global landscape of biblical teaching on these themes, gathering content together within a framework of categories that help us to analyze, synthesize, and utilize God's Word, as we ask the Holy Spirit to feed, lead, and transform us in Christ.

Every Bible study must have a personal element to it, no matter how occupied the study is with the message of the Word. All Scripture is inspired by God and is profitable in multiple ways (2 Tim. 3:16-17).

In this study we are particularly aware that the personal element precedes the study of the Word. Before we know anything of the Bible's teaching, we know our experience: our delights and desires, our hurts and trials, our disillusionments and hopes. To the Scripture, we bring our wounds, questions, and longings. From there, we learn to be shaped by the Holy Spirit through His Word!

While study cannot be merely academic, it cannot be anti-academic. God teaches us through language (revelation and instruction) in the context of relationship (the body of Christ) and our circumstances.

"As you therefore have received Christ Jesus the Lord, so walk in Him," Colossians 2:6 admonishes us. This is the overarching Guidepost verse for our travels through this study. Walk through this study with the Lord, knowing you are never alone. In the introduction I encourage you to do this study with a partner or in a group, if possible. However, you can approach the study on your own, knowing that the Lord is walking with you! Talk with Him continuously (John 16:13).

If you are not a Christian, I invite you to travel along. If so, I pray you will discover you are not alone! The Lord is nearer to you than you have ever realized. May you reach out to Him, to receive the Lord and walk with Him. Traveling with others doing this study will be your most effective approach. God bless your walk!

If you are approaching this as a group: Leaders, your role as a travel guide through this Bible study may differ somewhat from your role in other Bible studies. You need to be particularly alert and sensitive not only to the texts of Scripture but also to the heart of each participant, as each person brings her/his own sorrows and joys to the study.

I encourage every traveler to do the following:

1. Overview the material and pray about what you see. Read and pray over the table of contents. Browse through the appendices. Keep them in mind as reference sources to check out during your chapter studies. The vocabulary and charts will shed light upon your path as you travel. Flip through the pages of the entire book in order to pick up a first acquaintance view. Note some of the visuals, enlarged quotations, boxes, and charts. You are making a friendship with the book. Such an overview will give you the big picture of your coming adventure so that you will be more comfortable traveling through each chapter, because you are aware of the direction.
2. Ask questions about this study:
a. What is the study about?
b. What does it have to do with me?
c. What might it mean to me?
d. What would I like to get out of it?

e. What are my first three questions about this study?

    1.

    2.

    3.

3. Get organized.

    - Gather your Bible, writing tools, maybe a journal or notecards, and you may want to choose a place to study in your house. I like to have a canvas bag in which I keep all my study material for the particular study I'm currently doing. By keeping things in the bag, I'm organized and set.

    - Gather writing and marking tools: pens (one color or multiple colors), pencil, highlighters or a few colored pencils. (I prefer colored pencils so I can color code. Colored pencils don't bleed through the page.) I encourage highlighting and making marginal notes in both the text of your Bible and the Bible study book. Look up references and write answers as much as you can.

4. Journal or notecards.

    - The book suggests journaling in a "sojournal," your journal of your journey. You will find a few blank pages called *My SoJournal* in the back of this book to get you started. However, a separate journal will be needed if you choose to participate. You will find sojournaling prompts in each chapter. Pursue the ones of your choice.

    - You may want to create a section in your sojournal for chapter remembrance cues.

    - Record key insights, passages, and quotations per chapter. This can become like a chapter by chapter summary of the book for your future reference. Include book page numbers so you can quickly locate your source points. Or you may prefer to integrate your chapter prompt reflections and your chapter remembrance points. Whatever makes sense to you.

- If sojournaling is too much for you, you could use 3 x 5 cards to copy favorite quotations or ideas you want to remember. You may want to place cards in strategic locations.

5. Traveling through one chapter a week is a good pace, so you have reflection and process time and won't be overwhelmed by too much material. You can do this in one quarter of the year. Groups may want longer.

6. While each chapter has five sections, the sections are not even. I suggest you plan on three study sessions a week. Begin with prayer and ask God to speak to you through His Word.

    - *Session one*: overview the chapter with a highlighter in hand. Read part 1, the Guidepost verse, and maybe get into part 2. Skim the chapter and highlight interesting things that grab your attention. Talk with the Lord about the Guidepost verse, what you have read, and what you anticipate.

    - *Session two:* Travel through section two and three, looking up references and highlighting in your Bible and in this traveler's guide. Write in the guide and attempt a journal response. Always pray through your studies. God is speaking to you through His Word.

    - *Session three:* Travel through sections four and five. Engage with the biblical texts and the travel guide, highlighting, writing, and doing some sojournaling.

    - If you need longer (chapters may very), adjust your plan. When you are struck by a biblical truth, you may need to stop for a while and do other things so you can process and ponder. If you are participating in a group study, do not miss a meeting because you haven't finished a chapter. Come anyway!

7. If your Bible study group reads the chapters aloud, working through the text during each session (thereby not expecting travelers to have studied at home), then probably two quarters will be needed. You may need to skim over some places in the

meetings. Try to do some study on your own during the week. Pray and do what you can!

PART II:
WHAT KIND OF PEDESTRIAN THEOLOGIAN AM I?

Our first Guidepost, Colossians 2:6, encourages us, "As you therefore have received Christ Jesus the Lord, so walk in Him." As Christ-followers, walking with Christ, we see ourselves as Pedestrian Theologians. (This is explained in the introduction.)

We are preparing to tour the broad terrain of Scripture in order to discover a biblical theology of suffering and joy that will feed us and lead us through our own journeys of life.

One thing I know is that everyone suffers. The degree, load, and timing vary. Suffering is not optional. Joy need not be either. As travelers or *Pedestrian Theologians*, we ask, "What shape am I in for this journey?"

I envision a number of types of readers/participants. We all are Pedestrian Theologians. However, we are all in different stages of growth and maturity. So I've developed some categories of Pedestrian Theologians to help us evaluate what shape we are in for the journey or where we are in our maturing process. These categories are generalities. You don't fit any of them absolutely, but you'll find something of yourself in several of them. Here are five possibilities:

Five General Categories of Pedestrian Theologians

1. **New and Young Pedestrian Theologian:** You are new to spiritual walking. New to watching where and how you walk. Ah. You are a beginner in life: young, wide-eyed, *maybe* blessed with a good childhood and foundation. You haven't run you into suffering beyond the levels of inconveniences, irritations, learning to share, and natural challenges to reaching your goals. I was there for years but needed this material for

what was to come. *The goal here is to prepare you for hardships to come.* For you, this is the classroom of your Spiritual Bootcamp as well as an adventurous walk. *"Let no one despise you for your youth, but set the believers an example in speech, in conduct, in love, in faith, in purity"* (1 Tim. 4:12 ESV).

2. **The Journeyman Pedestrian Theologian:** You are in the thick of life. You've been faithful at church, are reading your Bible, praying, taking care of your family, and fulfilling your responsibilities. Maybe you participate in a small group, so you have a good support system. But you have experienced some problems, setbacks, relational conflict, health challenges, work struggles, death of some dear ones. You are aware you are in a spiritual battle as you walk through life. *"Be on the alert, stand firm in the faith, act like men [or women], be strong"* (1 Cor. 16:13).

3. **The Elder Pedestrian Theologian:** In terms of the ancient progression of skill acumen from *apprentice* to *journeyman*, the next level is m*aster*. We'll use the biblical term, *elder*. He/she is the Christ-following docent, the older/experienced person who comes alongside the younger and middle aged in order to lead them along the narrow path, shining biblical light in the right direction, carrying some of the load, and providing a shoulder for support at times. The apostle Paul audaciously advised, *"The things you have learned and received and heard and seen in me, practice these things, and the God of peace will be with you"* (Phil. 4:9).

4. **The Non-Christian Pedestrian Theologian:** You don't claim Christianity. You don't "know" Jesus Christ. But you do have some views on life, God/god, and yourself, so you are a theologian of your own theology, walking through your life following your worldview. How did you get this book or end up in some book club or study group? Hmm. Hang in there and travel along. I'm praying for God's grace to be poured into your heart and life. *"For whoever will call upon the name of the Lord will be saved"* (Rom. 10:13).

5. **The PTSD Pedestrian Theologian:** You may have been in one of the above categories, but injuries along the journey have changed your life. Indeed, they have changed you. The diagnosis is clear enough: PTSD: Post Traumatic Stress Disorder. Oh, maybe it's MTSD: Mid-Traumatic Stress Disorder. There's nothing "post" about it. It continues. Maybe you were surprised by the blows against you or by the depravity that has spilled out of you. Maybe not, but here you are. Wounded.

Paralyzed. Shamed. Playing with anger, resentment, and all those horrid responses. Maybe PTSD is too strong of a term for you. Still, you are wounded, broken, looking for healing. What's going on?

"Blessed be the God and Father of our Lord Jesus Christ, the Father of mercies and God of all comfort, who comforts us in all our affliction so that we will be able to comfort those who are in any affliction with the comfort with which we ourselves are comforted by God" (2 Cor. 1:3-4).

Whatever your category or variation thereof, you realize that you can't get through life in this world without coming to terms with hardship, difficulty, challenges, inconveniences, irritations, difficult people, natural disasters, illness or disease, relational conflict, and death. Your death and the death of everyone you know. Many people have to face some manifestation of violence and malevolence, far beyond the general afflictions of life. I am deeply sorry!

Ironically or so it seems, the more straightforwardly we face life, the more peace and joy open to us.

How you personally deal with your own suffering varies, most likely, moving like the waves of the sea. Sometimes you handle difficulty well, you think, and sometimes it seems to drown you. Sometimes in the midst of distress you gratefully waft the scent of the blooming hyacinth. Sometimes you don't.

In the introduction I tell a story about myself as an eight-year-old child reading a story in a school book. In this story, I meet evil as deception, but my home life was warm, caring, and nurturing. How fortunate I was! I'm so grateful. But trouble and sorrow did not evade me. Suffering comes to us all.

I have suffered variously during my seven decades, and I have handled it variously. Sometimes I could speak of it. Sometimes I could not identify it enough to articulate it. Sometimes I ignored it or denied it. Or maybe I made excuses for it, abusing God-given powers of reason. At times, I probably redefined it, dressing it in attractive clothing, or if not attractive, at least to me tolerable attire. I have fussed and I have feared. Yet I've experienced periods of trusting the Lord and not worrying, leaning on Jesus and not my understanding (Prov. 3:5-7; Phi. 4:6-7).

As I review my life, I observe suffering in the forms of stress, physical injury, relational misunderstanding, personal rejection, chronic illness, and pain for the suffering of others. During and after three periods of specific afflictions, one physical and two relational, I responded in emotional paralysis. I was so paralyzed by its unfamiliar and dangerous shapes I withdrew into myself, though I carried on in the motions of life, duty by duty. And at the worst of times, I was so paralyzed I couldn't function.

Moving out of dazed paralysis back into some general normalcy of engaged processing with growing emotional, mental, and spiritual equilibrium took between one year in the one case and five years in another. A deep grief has never left me but seems to have become some kind of ballast in my depths. As increased joy in the littlest of appreciative observations grew, as my conversation with God deepened, as persistent dialogue, honest and loving with those closest to me continued, God cultivated me in Christ so that my inner person has been growing more resilient.

Of the five categories of Pedestrian Theologians (PTs) above, what category am I in? I have been in all five. Currently, I'm majorly in category three, yet I'm still broken, carrying residual, category five sadness. To tailor-write a category-six description of me, I'd take ideas from categories two, three, and five. Wording it with my own description, it might look something like this:

Category #6. Tailor-Made for Me:

Karen Olsen is a Wounded Elder-lady Pedestrian Theologian.

Karen Olsen, Wounded Elder-lady PT: I'm a busy but slow, retired woman, caring for a wonderful, retired husband and a lovely home, involved with church and in a small group, growing in my faith, relating to neighbors and family members, working on my health (diet and exercise), and writing a blog and a book. Injury and chronic health issues such as Fibromyalgia have changed my life, limited my opportunities, and impacted relationships both positively and negatively. Some wounds have healed. I've accepted that in this life some wounds may never heal properly. My call is to trust God and help others come to terms with their lives, to grow up and grow in Christ, and to comfort them with the comfort and joy God keeps giving me through my hardships and in my many blessings.

Now it's your turn. Look over the five categories of Pedestrian Theologians. Consider one or two adjectives that would best describe you and tailor-make your own #6 PT title and paragraph description.

This is not an activity we'd naturally want to do, and we must be careful with it. Yet this can be a good *tool* to help us examine ourselves and to help us grow. We do not need to share it with anyone, and no one should expect you to share it. We are describing ourselves within our context (though there is far more to us). No descriptor or category is hardened cement. By God's grace, we are growing. We are being transformed by Christ to be like Him. Amazing!

My Tailor-made #6 Category:

_____ is a _____

    Your Name   Pedestrian Theologian

Next, please write a few sentences that explain and describe why or how your #6 title describes you. Borrow any phrases or sentences from the above five categories that you want. Write your own description.

I hope you find this helpful.

* * *

Instructions for the #5 PTSD Pedestrian Theologians: Glean and Lean

I realize that if you are coming to this study mainly as a #5, a PTSD/MTSD Pedestrian Theologian, you will struggle to make this journey. I've been there and understand. I want to encourage you to keep with it as best you can. You will find it worth whatever effort you can give it. God's grace will enable you. His Word will nourish and lead you. You will be glad you kept going.

Don't worry about handling *all* of this material. I have several suggestions to help you to glean some nourishment and to lean on the Lord.

1. Ask God to strengthen and enable you. Continuously ask. Continuously trust.
2. Any step forward is a good step. Take a step. Read a sentence, a verse, a page. Pray.
3. I recommend you do this study with another person. Even if you are doing it in a group, seek a partner with whom you can share the journey. Yet doing it without a partner is better than not taking the journey. Remember, the Lord is always with you, so you truly never travel alone.
4. *You are in the gleaner's mode.* You do not *have to* read every word, answer every question, and do every activity. Pray and read what you can—pushing yourself enough to expect a bit more of yourself. Take a deep breath and do something—read some paragraphs. With colored pencils highlight words, verses, and sentences jumping out at you. Maybe you can answer some of the questions. Journaling helps some people but not others. You decide. You may prefer to jot quotes or ideas on 3 x 5 cards to place strategically as reminders of God's truth and His work in your life.
5. Avoid quitting. If you get overwhelmed, pull back some, but keep going with the study at a slow, persistent pace. Lean on the Lord. And lean a bit on the prayers, faith, and study of others (but don't become totally dependent upon others).
6. If you are in a group study, show up and listen to everyone. Even if you've done none or little of the week's study, show up. Take some notes and learn from others. Glean what you can and be fine with that for now. You will grow stronger.

7. Listen to the Scriptures read aloud to you as often as you can: in the morning, on lunch break, in the evening right before lights out. Listen from an app on your phone, from a CD, or from an internet site such as Biblegateway.com.

8. You are making this Traveler's Guide a friend to return to over and over again. As you return to it, you will glean more, study more, and gain more. You will grow stronger!

9. Wrap it all in prayer, and know that I, the author of this traveler's guide, have walked this route, and I am praying for you.

"Check out www.KarenThomasOlsen.com
for Traveler's Guide resources to support you in your journey."

TOUR 1: ADDITIONAL RESOURCES FOR PERSONAL STUDY

KEY WORKS ON SUFFERING

Carson, D. A. *How Long, O Lord?* Grand Rapids, Michigan: Baker Academic, 2006.

Case, Thomas. *A Treatise on Afflictions.* Westfield, Indiana: Digital Puritan Press, 1652, 2011.

Chay, Fred. *Suffering Successfully*. USA: Grace Line, Inc., 2014.

Kaiser, Jr., Walter C. *A Biblical Approach to Personal Suffering.* Chicago: Moody Press, 1982.

Lewis, C. S. *The Problem of Pain*. San Francisco: HarperCollins Publishers, 1940.

Morgan, Christopher W. and Robert A. Peterson, editors, *Suffering and the Goodness of God.* Wheaton, Illinois: Crossway Books, 2008.

Peterman, Gerald W. and Andrew J. Schmutzer. *Between Pain & Grace*. Chicago: Moody Press, 2016.

KEY WORKS ON JOY

Alcorn, Randy. *Happiness.* Carol Stream, Illinois: Tyndale House Publishers, 2015.

Morrice, William. *Joy in the New Testament.* Grand Rapids, Michigan: Eerdmans Pub., 1984.

Strauss, Richard L. *The Joy of Knowing God.* Neptune, New Jersey: Loizeaux Brothers, 1984.

Thigpen, Thomas Paul. *A Reason for Joy.* Colorado Springs, Colorado: NavPress, 1988.

KEY WORKS ON JOY AND SUFFERING

Fernando, Ajith. *The Call to Joy and Pain.* Wheaton, Illinois: Crossway Books, 2007.

Olsen, Karen Thomas. *A Traveler's Guide through Suffering and Joy.* Houston Texas: Silversmith Press, 2024.

SIGNIFICANT, PERSONAL WRITINGS ON SUFFERING AND JOY

Elliot, Elizabeth. *A Path through Suffering.* Ann Arbor, Michigan: Servant Publications, 1990.

_____. *Shadow of the Almighty.* San Francisco: Harper & Row, Publishers, 1958.

_____. *Suffering is Never for Nothing.* Nashville Tennessee: B&H Publishing Group, 2019.

Lewis, C. S. *A Grief Observed.* San Francisco: HarperCollins Publishers. 1961.

_____. *Surprised by Joy.* London: Collins Clear-Type Press, 1955.

Wurmbrand, Richard. *If Prison Walls Could Speak.* Bartlesville, Oklahoma: Living Sacrifice Book Company, 2000.

_____. *100 Prison Meditations.* Bartlesville, Oklahoma: Living Sacrifice Book Company, 2000.

_____. *Tortured for Christ.* Bartlesville, Oklahoma: Living Sacrifice Book Company, 1967, 1998.

RECENT WORKS ON CHRONIC ILLNESS

Means, Casey with Calley Means. *Good Energy.* New York: Avery/Penguin Random House, 2024. caseymeans.com.

Norton, Sally K. *Toxic Superfoods.* New York: Rodale, 2022. Sallyknorton.com.

Trevor, Daniel. *Unholy Trinity*. Orlando, Florida, 2024. DanielTrevor.com.

SOURCES OF SONGS AND SONG STORIES

Morgan, Robert J. *Then Sings My Soul*, Volumes 1 &2. Nashville, TN: Thomas Nelson, 2003.

The Hymnal for Worship & Celebration. Waco, Texas: Word Music, 1986.

Online: https://hymnary.org/; http://www.hymntime.com/tch/.

TrinityPsalter Hymnal. Willow Grove, PA: Trinity Psalter Hymnal Joint Venture, 2018.

A DEVOTIONAL AND PERSONAL STUDY PATH

I have a three to four-pronged, spiritual anchor to my soul. My anchor is my Bible—God's Word and my authority: I use multiple, good translations and study Bibles. Next, I access resources that increase my biblical understanding: Bible dictionaries, good commentaries, and/or good, expository books on the theme or Bible book that I'm exploring. Books by reliable Christian leaders, such as Elisabeth Elliot's classic, *A Path Through Suffering* (or maybe another book such as these listed) will enhance my study, meditation, prayers, and application. Finally, I include a hymnbook or a book of hymn stories in which to learn backstories and to explore rich, worshipful poetry and song.

TOUR 2: ADDITIONAL RESOURCES FOR EXTENDED STUDY[1]

Adams, Jay E. *How to Handle Trouble.* Phillipsburg, NJ: P & R Publishers, 1982.

Alcorn, Randy. *If God is Good.* Colorado Springs, Colorado: Multnomah Books, 2009.

———. *Happiness.* Carol Stream, Illinois: Tyndale House Publishers, 2015.

Berg, Jim. *Changed into His Image.* Greenville, S. Carolina: BJU Press, 1999.

Beyond Suffering Bible. Tyndale House Publishers, Inc., Carol Stream, Illinois, 2016.

Boa, Kenneth. *Conformed to His Image.* Grand Rapids, Michigan: Zondervan Academics, 2001 or 2020.

Brand, Paul and Philip Yancey. *In His Image.* Grand Rapids, Michigan: Zondervan Publishing House, 1984.

Carson, D. A. *How Long, O Lord?* Grand Rapids, Michigan: Baker Academic, 2006.

Case, Thomas. *A Treatise on Afflictions.* Westfield, Indiana: Digital Puritan Press, 1652, 2011.

Chapian, Marie. *Of Whom the World Was Not Worthy.* Minneapolis, Minnesota: Bethany Fellowship Inc., 1978.

Chao, Colleen, *In the Hands of a Fiercely Tender God,* Chicago: Moody Publishers, 2022.

---

1. This bibliography contains more sources than referenced in the book, but I want to direct your reading and studying travels toward some other good tours.

Chay, Fred. *Suffering Successfully*. USA: Grace Line, Inc., 2014.

Dreher, Rod. *Live Not by Lies.* New York City: Sentinel, 2020.

Elliot, Elizabeth. *A Path through Suffering*. Ann Arbor, Michigan: Servant Publications, 1990.

_____. *Shadow of the Almighty*. San Francisco: Harper & Row, Publishers, 1958.

_____. *Suffering is Never for Nothing*. Nashville Tennessee: B&H Publishing Group, 2019.

Enns, Paul. *The Moody Handbook of Theology*. Chicago: Moody Publishers, 2008.

Fernando, Ajith. *The Call to Joy and Pain*. Wheaton, Illinois: Crossway Books, 2007.

Fitzpatrick, Elyse and Laura Hendrickson, *Will Medicine Stop the Pain?* Chicago: Moody Press, 2006.

Foxe, George. *Fox's Book of Martyrs*. Ed. W. Grinton Berry. Grand Rapids, Michigan: Baker Book House Company, 2002.

Gangel, Kenneth O. & James C. Wilhoit. *The Christian Educator's Handbook of Spiritual Formation*. Grand Rapids, Michigan: Baker Books, 1994.

Grudem, Wayne. *Systematic Theology*. Leicester, England: IVP and Grand Rapids, Michigan: Zondervan, 1994.

Hearts of Fire. Bartlesville, OK: The Voice of the Martyrs (VOM), 2015.

Helm, Paul. *The Providence of God*. Downers Grove, Illinois: InterVarsity Press, 1993.

Hodge, Charles. *Systematic Theology*. Volumes I, II, and III. Peabody, Maine: Hendrickson Publishers, 2003.

Holland, Linda. *Alabaster Doves*. Chicago: Moody Press, 1995.

Kaiser, Jr., Walter C. *A Biblical Approach to Personal Suffering*. Chicago: Moody Press, 1982.

_____. *Ecclesiastes Total Life*. Chicago: Moody Press, 1979.

_____. "Suffering and the Goodness of God in the Old Testament." *Suffering and the Goodness of God*, ed. Christopher W. Morgan and Robert A. Peterson (Wheaton, Illinois: Crossway Books, 2008), 47-78.

Lawrence, John W. *Down to Earth: The Laws of Harvest*. Sisters, Oregon: Multnomah Press, 1975.

Lewis, C.S. *A Grief Observed*. San Francisco: HarperCollins Publishers. 1961.

_____. *God in the Dock*. Grand Rapids, Michigan: Wm. B. Eerdmans Publishing, Co., 2014.

_____. *Mere Christianity and The Screwtape Letters*, New York: HarperCollins Publishers, 2003.

_____. *The Problem of Pain*. San Francisco: HarperCollins Publishers, 1940.

_____. *Surprised by Joy*. London: Collins Clear-Type Press, 1955.

Luther, Martin. *Don't Tell Me That!* Translated and Adapted by Paul Strawn. Minneapolis: Lutheran Press, 2004.

Lutzer, Erwin W. *Cries from the Cross*. Chicago: Moody Press, 2002.

MacArthur, John. *The Keys to Spiritual Growth*. Wheaton, Illinois: Crossway, 1991.

MacDonald, William. *Believer's Bible Commentary*. Nashville, TN: Thomas Nelson Publishers, 1995.

Mack, Wayne A. & Wayne Erick Johnston. *A Christian Growth and Discipleship Manual*. MN: Focus Publishing.

Morgan, Christopher W., and Robert A. Peterson. *Suffering and the Goodness of God*. Wheaton, Illinois: Crossway Books, 2008.

Morgan, Robert J. *Then Sings My Soul*, Volumes 1 &2. Nashville, TN: Thomas Nelson, 2003.

Morrice, William. *Joy in the New Testament*. Grand Rapids, Michigan: Eerdmans Pub., 1984.

Mouw, Richard J. and Douglas A. Sweeney. *The Suffering and Victorious Christ*. Grand Rapids, Michigan: Baker Academic, 2013.

Peterman, Gerald W. Peterman and Andrew J Schmutzer. *Between Pain & Grace*. Chicago: Moody Publishers, 2016.

Petersen, William J. *Johann Sebastian Bach Had a Wife*. Wheaton, Illinois: Tyndale House Publishers Inc., 1987.

Piper, John and Justin Taylor, Eds. *Suffering and the Sovereignty of God*. Wheaton, Illinois: Crossway Books, 2006.

Piper, John. *The Hidden Smile of God*. Wheaton, Illinois: Crossway Books, 2001.

Rutherford, Samuel. *Letters of Samuel Rutherford*. London: The Banner of Truth Trust, 1664, 1973.

Sanders, J. Oswald. *The Incomparable Christ*. Chicago: Moody Press, 1952, 1971.

Skoglund, Elizabeth. *Found Faithful.* USA: Discovery House Publishers, 2003.

Spurbeck, David K. Sr. *The Christian "In Christ."* Forest Grove, Oregon: Know to Grow Publications, 1999.

Spurgeon, Charles. "Grieving the Holy Spirit." A Sermon. Number 276. The Spurgeon Archives. www.spurgeon.org/sermons/0278.htm.

Storms, Sam. *Pleasures Forevermore.* Colorado Springs, Colorado: NavPress, 2000.

Strauss, Richard L. *The Joy of Knowing God.* Neptune, New Jersey: Loizeaux Brothers, 1984.

Tada, Joni Eareckson. *Glorious Intruder.* Portland, Oregon: Multnomah, 1989.

Tennent, Timothy C. *Theology in the Context of World Christianity*. Grand Rapids, Michigan: Zondervan, 2007.

Thigpen, Thomas Paul. *A Reason for Joy.* Colorado Springs, Colorado: NavPress, 1988.

Josef Ton. Suffering, *Martyrdom, and Rewards in Heaven.* Wheaton, Illinois: The Romanian Missionary Society, 1997.

Tozer, A.W. *The Pursuit of God*. Camp Hill, PA: Wing Spread Publishers, 1982.

Tripp, Paul David. *Instruments in the Redeemer's Hands.* Phillipsburg, NJ: P&R Publishing, 2002.

Tripp, Tedd. *Shepherding a Child's Heart*, Wapwallopen PA: Shepherd Press, 1995.

Tucker, Ruth A. *From Jerusalem to Irian Jaya.* Grand Rapids, Michigan: Academic Books, Zondervan Publishing House, 1983.

Tyndale Bible Dictionary. Logos Bible Software.

Vanhoozer, Kevin, Editor. *Nothing Greater Nothing Better.* Grand Rapids, Michigan: Eerdmans Publishing Company, 2001.

Veith, Gene Edward, Jr. *God at Work.* Wheaton, Illinois: Crossway Books, 2002.

Viars, Stephen. *Putting Your Past in Its Place.* Eugene, Oregon: Harvest House Publishers, 2011.

Vins, Georgi. *Let the Waters Roar.* Grand Rapids, Michigan: Baker Book House, 1989.

_____. *The Gospel in Bonds.* Elkart, Indiana: Russian Gospel Ministries, 1995.

Willard, Dallas. *The Divine Conspiracy.* San Francisco, California: Harper Collins, 1998.

_____. *The Spirit of the Disciplines.* San Francisco, California: Harper Collins, 1988.

Wurmbrand, Richard. *If Prison Walls Could Speak.* Bartlesville, Oklahoma: Living Sacrifice Book Company, 2000.

_____. *100 Prison Meditations*. Bartlesville, Oklahoma: Living Sacrifice Book Company, 2000.

_____. *Tortured for Christ*. Bartlesville, Oklahoma: Living Sacrifice Book Company, 1967, 1998.

Zacharias, Ravi and Vince Vitale. *Why Suffering?* Nashville: Faith Words, 2014.

Zeoli, Anthony. *Why Do Christians Suffer?* Wyncote, Pa: Evangelist Anthony Zeoli, 1943.

Zodhiates, Spiros. *The Complete Word Study Dictionary*. Chattanooga, TN: AMG Publishers, 1992.

Zvi, *The Best of Zvi.* Bellmawr, NJ: The Friends of Israel Gospel Ministry, Inc., 1998.

BIOGRAPHIES AS ILLUSTRATIONS OF PASCHAROLOGICAL THEMES

Endless examples of the biblical categories and principles of pascharology are found within biographies. Some biographies are listed in the above bibliography. Any biography, about a Christian or non-Christian, offers illustrations. Biographies of Christians offer more than illustrations: they offer models, warnings, and inspiration (Phil. 4:9). Biographies about the following Christians will provide you with a good core resource selection. Add others to this list. Also check out the online sources listed below.

Gladys Aylward	C.S. Lewis	Helen Roseveare	Georgi Vins
Deitrich Bonhoeffer	Eric Lindell	Darlene Deibler Rose	Susanna Wesley
John Bunyan	Catherine & Peter Marshall	Edith Schaeffer	Charles & John Wesley
David Brainerd	George Muller	Mary Slessor	William Wilberforce
Amy Carmichael	John Newton	Charles Spurgeon	Richard & Sabina Wurmbrand
Elisabeth & Jim Elliott		Joni Eareckson Tada	
		Hudson Taylor	
		Corrie Ten Boom	
		Josef Tson (or Ton)	
		William Tyndale	

The following websites list many excellent biographies:

https://www.onlinechristiancolleges.com/50-best-christian-biographies/

https://onethingalone.com/christian-biographies/

Check out www.KarenThomasOlsen.com
for Traveler's Guide resources to support you in your journey.

My SoJournal

My SoJournal